LANGUAGE OF FICTION

DISCARDED

LANGUAGE
OF
FICTION

Essays in Criticism and Verbal Analysis
of the English Novel

DAVID LODGE

NEW YORK: COLUMBIA UNIVERSITY PRESS

To Park and Jeannette

Contents

Contents

Preface

THE novelist's medium is language: whatever he does, *qua* novelist, he does in and through language. That, to me, is an axiom, and will, I believe, be generally acceptable as such. But the implications of this axiom for literary criticism are not so easily determined or agreed upon. Criticism of the novel which bases its arguments on detailed reference to the language novelists use (such as the essays on English fiction of the nineteenth and twentieth centuries presented in the second part of this book) still needs to justify itself on theoretical grounds; and the process of justification involves many interesting and important issues concerning the nature of literature and the principles of criticism. The first part of this book is devoted to an extended discussion of such issues.

In Section I of this essay, I begin by attempting to trace the sources of uncertainty in modern criticism about the function of language in prose fiction, and proceed to engage with some representative arguments which have sought to limit or deny the significance of the novelist's use of language. I state my reasons for taking the opposite view. In Section II, I discuss the usefulness and limitations, as I see them, of certain critical and analytical methods which have been applied to the language of the novel, chiefly in the field of stylistics. In Section III, I draw some tentative conclusions, and explain the guiding principles of my own criticism.

Although the purpose of this essay is partly introductory, I have deliberately extended its range beyond that of an Introduction. I have not confined myself to making promises which are kept in the studies of particular texts in Part Two, but have pursued certain lines of theoretical inquiry as far as I felt able to follow them. Most of the ideas I put forward and discuss are not new, but I have not seen them all considered together before. To have brought them together will, I hope, be considered a useful enterprise, whether my own position meets with agreement or disagreement.

I hope that the allusions and references in both Parts of this book sufficiently indicate my awareness of the valuable work that has been done on the language of the novel and the development of critical methods for dealing with it. But I should like to acknowledge a special indebtedness to the following authors: Wayne Booth, John Holloway, Mark Schorer, Dorothy Van Ghent, Ian Watt, and W. K. Wimsatt.

Wayne Booth's *The Rhetoric of Fiction* (Chicago, 1961) is primarily concerned to classify the categories of narrative method in terms of 'point of view', and in particular to challenge the post-Jamesian assumption that 'impersonal' narration, mediated through the consciousness of a created character, is necessarily superior to traditional omniscient methods. Although Booth's neo-Aristotelian principles differ from my own and lead him away from verbal analysis, his general argument that the novelist's art, whatever narrative method used, is essentially rhetorical, is very close to my own view; and I have found his book a source of encouragement and guidance in many ways. John Holloway's *The Victorian Sage* (1953)* first suggested to me how criticism might carry its study of the language of extended prose works beyond the limits of stylistic description. In approaching the novel in this way I am conscious of the influence, direct and indirect, of Mark Schorer's articles, 'Technique as Discovery' (*Hudson Review*, I (1948) pp. 67–87) and 'Fiction and the Analogical Matrix,' (*Kenyon Review*, XI (1949) pp. 539–60). Dorothy Van Ghent's *The English Novel: Form and Function* (New York, 1953) is a dazzling and perpetually challenging achievement in explicatory novel-criticism. Ian Watt's *The Rise of the Novel* (1957), although primarily a work of literary history, offers many invaluable insights

---

* The place of publication of all books cited is London, unless otherwise indicated.

into the formal characteristics of the novel; while his article on 'The First Paragraph of *The Ambassadors*' (*Essays in Criticism*, X (1960), pp. 250–74), is a model of close analysis applied to narrative prose, and includes a succinct and penetrating account of the present state of criticism in this field. Among the many works of critical theory which have concerned themselves with the nature of literary language, I have found W. K. Wimsatt's *The Verbal Icon* (Lexington, Ky., 1954), which includes two important essays written in collaboration with Monroe C. Beardsley, the most helpful.

Tribute should be paid, also, to Vernon Lee's rather neglected pioneering book, *The Handling of Words and Other Studies in Literary Psychology* (1923), which considering its date, is a remarkable achievement, full of useful insights and suggestions, and which includes what are probably the first examples in English criticism of close, methodical analysis applied to narrative prose.* Vernon Lee's work has had some influence on the criticism associated with the name of Leavis, which is itself obviously relevant to my undertaking in this book; but I postpone the consideration of this criticism to a later stage. Finally, I should like to acknowledge here my gratitude for the very useful bibliography of criticism, compiled by Harold C. Martin and Richard M. Ohmann, in *Style in Prose Fiction*, English Institute Essays 1958, ed. Harold C. Martin (New York, 1959).

In trying to elucidate critical problems, both general and specific, I have found it useful to cite and debate the opinions of other critics, including some of those listed above. I apologize in advance to anyone who feels himself or herself to have been misrepresented or invidiously distinguished in this way.

This book owes a great deal to the exchange of ideas, about novels and The Novel, with many people—teachers, colleagues, and students—over an extended period of time. I should like to thank particularly Malcolm Bradbury, Elsie Duncan-Jones, Ian Gregor, Park Honan, Richard Hoggart, and Terence Spencer, who have read part or all of this book in one form or another, and who have given generous assistance and valuable advice (which, I should add in fairness to them, I have not always followed).

* Vernon Lee's analysis of an extract from *Tess of the D'Urbervilles* is discussed in some detail in Part II, Chapter 4.

Preface

I am grateful to Professor J. M. Cameron for permission to quote extensively from his essay 'Poetry and Dialectic'; to the editors of *Nineteenth Century Fiction* and the *Critical Quarterly* for permission to use material which first appeared in those journals; and to the University of Birmingham Library for its services in obtaining research materials. Grateful acknowledgement is also made to the holders of copyright material from which extracts have been quoted in this book: the Executors of the Wells Estate for passages from H. G. Wells's *Tono Bungay;* The Bodley Head Ltd. for a passage from Vernon Lee's *The Handling of Words and Other Studies in Literary Psychology*; Eyre and Spottiswoode (Publishers) Ltd. and the Houghton Mifflin Co. for a passage from John Braine's *Room at the Top*; John Farquharson Ltd. and Charles Scribner's Sons for passages from Henry James's *The Ambassadors*; Victor Gollancz Ltd. and Kingsley Amis for permission to quote passages from *Take a Girl Like You*, *That Uncertain Feeling* and *I Like It Here*; Victor Gollancz Ltd. and Doubleday & Co. Inc. for passages from *Lucky Jim* by the same author; and Macmillan & Co. Ltd. and the Trustees of the Hardy Estate for passages from Thomas Hardy's *Tess of the d'Urbervilles*. Finally, I thank my wife, Mary, for her help in the checking of references, for her valuable criticism, and for her unfailing patience and encouragement.

I

INTRODUCTORY

Literary theory and criticism concerned with the novel are much
inferior in both quantity and quality to theory and criticism of
poetry.*

IN the modern period, as far as English studies are concerned,
critical theory and practice have been dominated by what may be
called the New Criticism, in the widest sense of that term—that
is, the critical effort extending from T. S. Eliot and I. A. Richards
to, say, W. K. Wimsatt, characterized by the belief that a poem
acquires its meaning and unique identity by virtue of its verbal
organization, and that good critical practice depends above all on
close and sensitive reading. We might say, therefore, that if what
Wellek and Warren alleged in 1949 was true, it was because the
New.Criticism had not shown its principles and procedures to be
as effective when applied to prose fiction as when applied to
poetry. At that time, however, there was some disagreement
about whether (to borrow Chesterton's epigram on Christianity)
the application had been tried and found wanting, or simply not
tried. Mark Schorer, writing in 1948, was of the latter opinion.
Summarizing the principles of modern criticism, founded on the
'exacting scrutiny of literary texts', and leading to a view of form
(or 'technique') and content as inseparable, he says:

* R. Wellek and A. Warren, *Theory of Literature* (New York, 1949),
p. 219.

3

We are no longer able to regard as seriously intended criticism of poetry which does not assume these generalisations; but the case for fiction has not yet been established. The novel is still read as though its content has some value in itself, as though the subject matter of fiction has greater or lesser value in itself, and as though technique were not a primary but a supplementary element, capable perhaps of not unattractive embellishments upon the surface of the subject, but hardly of its essence. Or technique is thought of in blunter terms than those which one associates with poetry, as such relatively obvious matters as the arrangement of events to create plot; or, within plot, of suspense and climax; or as the means of revealing character motivation, relationship and development, or as the use of point of view. . . . As for the resources of language, these, somehow, we almost never think of as part of the technique of fiction—language as used to create a certain texture and tone which in themselves state and define themes and meanings; or language, the counters of our ordinary speech, as forced, through conscious manipulation, into all those larger meanings which our ordinary speech almost never intends.[1]

Philip Rahv, however, while he agrees that criticism of the novel is in an unsatisfactory state—

20th Century criticism has as yet failed to evolve a theory and a set of practical procedures dealing with the prose-medium that are as satisfactory in their exactness, subtlety and variety as the theory and procedures worked out in the past few decades by the critics of poetry[2]

—argues that what has caused the trouble is the very application of neo-critical theories and procedures for which Schorer pleads:

the commanding position assumed by poetic analysis has led to the indiscriminate importation of its characteristic assumptions and approaches into a field [i.e. prose fiction] which requires generic critical terms and criteria of value that are unmistakably its own.[3]

Rahv gives three examples of this pernicious influence: an obsession with tracing allegories, symbols, and mythic patterns in novels; the suggestion that style is the essential activity of imaginative prose; and the attempt to reduce a novel to the sum of its techniques. This sounds like a direct counterblast to Schorer, but is in fact part of a debate with J. C. Ransom, who had said:

Let it be proposed to Mr Rahv, therefore, that we should not approve any fictionist who does not possess a prose style. Running over in our minds some memorable fiction, I believe we are likely to identify it with certain instances, or at least with certain remembered kinds, of complexes, or concentrations, which consist in linguistic manoeuvres in the first place (i.e. on the surface) and of feeling-tones or affects in the second place (when it comes to our responses); and not with gross or overall effects such as plots or ideologies. We do not make this discovery any more truly about a play by Shakespeare. And if we are challenged to defend our judgment of the work we do not take up the book in order to refresh ourselves on the plot or moral, but in order to find specific passages, the right passages, for our peculiar evidence. Can we not say that fiction, in being literature, will have style for its essential activity?[4]

Some of the characteristic postures of the debate about literary criticism and the language of prose fiction here come into focus. We see that it is a new version of the venerable form-content argument. The protagonists are agreed that form and content are inseparable in poetry, but they differ with regard to prose fiction. Rahv warns us against 'confusing the intensive speech proper to poetry with the more openly communicative, functional and extensive language proper to prose'.[5] 'All that we can legitimately ask of a novelist in the matter of language,' he says, 'is that it be appropriate to the matter in hand. What is said must not stand in a contradictory relation to the way it is said, for that would be to dispel the illusion of life, and with it the credibility of fiction.'[6] From this point of view it would appear that life, not language, is the novelist's medium: that it is the way he manipulates and organizes and evaluates the life or, more precisely, the imitation-life of his fictions, that constitutes his literary activity; that his language is merely a transparent window through which the reader regards this life—the writer's responsibility being merely to keep the glass clean. The function of the critic then becomes that of discerning and assessing the quality of life in a given novel —the plausibility and interest of its characters and their actions, and the nature of its moral discriminations and values.

Since the late '40s and early '50s, when the views quoted above were first expressed, there has been a sufficiently striking shift in criticism to make one question whether the assertion of Wellek and Warren can stand unqualified. Of a growth in the quantity of novel-criticism there can be no doubt, and much of it has been of high quality. Several critics (such as those mentioned in my Preface) have made valuable contributions to the critical study of language in fiction. But it would be hard to say that we are any nearer to a resolution of the debate outlined above.

Most attempts to apply neo-critical techniques to prose fiction have taken the form of studying patterns of imagery and symbolism in novels. But too often one feels that the listing of images has not been controlled by an active engagement with the text and the wider critical challenges it presents. Such work brings the verbal analysis of fiction into disrepute, as Philip Rahv's protest indicates; and the good examples of such criticism are generally lacking in a sound theoretical defence of the method. On the whole, the tide seems to be turning against the orthodoxies of the New Criticism, and such enterprises as Northrop Frye's systematic theory of myths and genres, or Leslie Fiedler's essays in bold cultural and psychological interpretation of fiction, have been welcomed in the name of a reaction against the narrow and myopic procedures associated with those orthodoxies.[7]

It is my own opinion that we are in danger of jettisoning the principles of the New Criticism before we have fully exploited their possibilities. The temptation to do so, however, is strong, particularly in the case of the novel, where, it still seems to me as it seemed to Mark Schorer, modern criticism has never approached the general level of achievement in the close and subtle analysis of language which it attained in the case of poetry. Indeed, in some ways, it has actually inhibited the useful analysis of the function of language in fiction. It is worth inquiring why this should be so; and I believe we may obtain a partial answer by reference to two characteristic assumptions implicit or explicit in the mainstream of modern criticism: that the lyric poem is the literary norm, or the proper basis for generalizing about literature; and that there are two quite different kinds of language, the literary and the non-literary.

MODERN CRITICISM AND LITERARY LANGUAGE

M. H. Abrams and Frank Kermode have shown clearly and perceptively (in *The Mirror and the Lamp* and *Romantic Image* respectively[1]) how the idea of the lyric poem as the literary norm evolved out of the theory and practice of the English Romantic poets and, later, of the French Symbolist poets, contributing to the modern critical doctrine that a poem is autotelic, non-para-phrasable, non-translatable, a verbal object in which every part is organically related to every other part and to the whole, some-thing which 'should not mean but be'. Closely associated with this doctrine are a number of theories about the difference between literary and non-literary language. These theories also go back to the Romantics, and even earlier, but for modern criticism I. A. Richards's formulation has probably been the most influential:

> A statement may be used for the sake of the reference, true or false, which it causes. This is the *scientific* use of language. But it may also be used for the sake of the effects in emotion and attitude produced by the reference it occasions. This is the *emotive* use of language.[2]

Richards's formulation is coloured by his own psychological and affective theory of literary value, which is not universally shared. But the notion of two basic types of discourse is pervasive in modern criticism. Northrop Frye, for example, despite his de-clared dissatisfaction with the concepts of modern criticism, is making basically the same distinction in talking of 'inward-' and 'outward-pointing structures':

> Whenever we read anything, we find our attention moving in two directions at once. One direction is outward or centrifugal, in which we keep going outside our reading, from the individual words to the things they mean, or in practice to our memory of the conventional associations between them. The other direction is inward, or centripetal, in which we try to develop from the words a sense of the larger verbal pattern they make. . . . In all literary structures the final direction of meaning is inward.[3]

Examples of other critics formulating similar views could be multiplied. Empson's 'ambiguity', Blackmur's 'gesture', Ransom's 'texture', Brooks's 'irony', are essentially concepts offered to define the peculiar qualities of literary language, and to distin-guish it from other kinds of language.[4]

Now, none of these critics is concerned to deny prose fiction the status of literature, but its claims to be so considered can appear somewhat tenuous in the light of their poetics. Richards's distinction is valid in so far as it states that we may use language for different purposes, i.e. to assert different orders of truth. But there is a temptation, to which many critics have yielded, to look for reflections of linguistic purpose in linguistic form. Because of the dominance of the lyric in post-Romantic poetics, we then get a concentration of attention on a particular kind of verbal intensity, on paradox, irony, ambiguity, and metaphorical density. Literature which does not manifest these qualities to any striking extent tends to be subjected either to disparagement (as in the notorious case of Milton) or to a critical approach which does not concern itself closely with language (as in the case of the novel).

In Richards's scheme, 'the supreme form of emotive language is poetry',[5] while referential language is typified by scientific description. The novel, however, comes nearer to the latter than to the former in the formal character of its language, which is prose; and this has been a source of much confusion about the genre's literary identity. It will be useful, therefore, to glance briefly at literary thinking about poetry and prose from the Romantic period to modern times.

POETRY AND PROSE

'The difference between verse and prose is self-evident, but it is a sheer waste of time to look for a definition of the difference between poetry and prose.'[1] Auden's advice is sound, but unlikely to discourage discussion of a problem which has perennial fascination.

To the Romantics, 'poetry' was a qualitative and not merely a descriptive term. It referred to a special way of perceiving things, as well as to a special way of saying things. 'Poetry' was the rallying-cry of a campaign against the claims of scientific materialism to the sole title of knowledge. Thus Wordsworth suggests two new antitheses in place of the conventional one of *poetry*: *prose*, namely, *poetry*: *science* (a distinction much like Richards's) and *metrical composition*: *prose* (two formally differentiated kinds of 'poetry').[2] But he does not show much real interest in the properties of imaginative prose; in fact his anxiety to establish a united front for all imaginative writing, and his special concern to break away from 'poetic diction', lead him to minimize the differences between metrical composition and prose, and he explains his own choice of the former, rather lamely, on the grounds that it provides an added 'charm' and helps to temper the distress that can be caused by painful subject matter.[3]

Shelley, in his *Defence of Poetry*, also seeks to make 'poetry' a term which will include everything of literary interest and value. The prose-writers whom he dignifies with the title of 'poet', however, tend to be discursive writers of an idealistic or revolutionary cast. The novel would appear to be, in Shelley's aesthetic, an example of prose discourse which does not deserve the title of poetry:

> A poem is the very image of life expressed in its eternal truth.
> There is this difference between a story and a poem, that a story is
> a catalogue of detached facts, which have no other connexion than
> time, place, circumstance, cause and effect; the other is the creation
> of actions according to the unchangeable forms of human nature,
> as existing in the mind of the Creator, which is itself the image of
> all other minds.[4]

Coleridge grapples with the same problem, as one would expect, more subtly and more obscurely. He proposes a distinction between 'poem' and 'poetry'. A poem is defined functionally: it is 'that species of composition, which is opposed to works of science, by proposing for its *immediate* object, pleasure, not truth; and from all other species (having *this* object in common with it) [e.g. novels] it is discriminated by proposing to itself such delight from the *whole* as is compatible with a distinct gratification from each component *part*.'[5] It is the special property of metre that it calls attention to each component part, and thus requires that the latter supply the appropriate gratification. This formulation is complicated, however, by the introduction of the qualitative concept, 'poetry', which Coleridge goes on to define in terms of his well-known theory of Imagination. He acknowledges that 'poetry' is to be found in the work of prose-writers such as Plato, Bishop Taylor, Burnet, and Isaiah, of whom it can hardly be said that their immediate object was pleasure, not truth.

> In short, whatever *specific* import we attach to the word, poetry,
> there will be found involved in it, as a necessary consequence, that
> a poem of any length neither can be, nor ought to be all poetry.
> Yet if an harmonious whole is to be produced, the remaining parts
> must be preserved *in keeping* with the poetry; and this can be no
> otherwise affected than by such a studied selection and artificial
> arrangement, as will partake of *one*, though not a *peculiar* property

of poetry. And this again can be no other than the property of exciting a more continuous and equal attention than the language of prose aims at, whether colloquial or written.[6]

This is a puzzling passage, for several reasons, but principally because 'prose' has to stand as the antithesis of both 'poem' and 'poetry'. Taken out of context, it might appear to be concerned with the 'long poem'; but in fact it follows on from the discussion of prose-writers. If 'the studied selection and artificial arrangement' is not peculiar to poetry, but not to be found in prose, where else is it to be found? The answer seems to be: in long works which may or may not conform to the formal definition of 'poem', but which contain some 'poetry'. Novels might come into this category, for they gather themselves up into periodic surges of 'poetic' intensity, buttressed by passages of less intense but still 'studied' and 'artificial' language. There is no indication, however, that Coleridge would have allowed this. Though a sensitive descriptive critic of fiction, he placed narrative literature fairly low in his aesthetic, as is implied in another interesting observation on the subject of poetry and prose:

> The definition of good prose is—proper words in their proper places; of good verse—the most proper words in their proper places. The propriety is in either case relative. The words in prose ought to express the intended meaning, and no more; if they attract attention to themselves, it is, in general, a fault. . . . But in verse you must do more: there the words, the *media* must be beautiful, and ought to attract your notice—yet not so much and so perpetually as to destroy the unity which ought to result from the whole poem. This is the general rule, but, of course, subject to some modifications, according to the different kinds of prose or verse. Some prose may approach towards verse, as oratory, and therefore a more studied exhibition of the *media* may be proper; and some verse may border on mere narrative, and there the style should be simpler.[7]

The use of the term *verse* makes this passage much clearer than the one previously quoted. And Coleridge's reference to oratory shows that his distinction is a flexible one. This cannot be said of later exponents of the Romantic–Symbolist aesthetic, such as Paul Valéry, who has asserted the discontinuity of prose and verse in terms of an analogy with walking and dancing:

Walking, like prose, always has a definite object. It is an act directed *towards* some object that we aim to reach. The actual circumstances—the nature of the object, my need, the impulse of my desire, the state of my body and of the ground—regulate the rhythm of walking, prescribe its direction, speed and termination. . . .

Dancing is quite different. It is, of course, a system of acts, but acts whose end is in themselves. It goes nowhere. Or if it pursues anything it is only an ideal object, a state, a delight, the phantom of a flower, or some transport out of oneself, an extreme of life, a summit, a supreme form of being. . . .[8]

Poetry, of course, is like dancing.

Thus understood, poetry is radically different from all prose: in particular, it is clearly opposed to the description and narration of events that tend to give the illusion of reality, that is to the novel and the tale when their aim is to give the force of truth to stories, portraits, scenes, and other representations of real life.[9]

Valéry's theories are usefully discussed by Laurence Lerner in his book *The Truest Poetry*, where he notes that for those holding theories 'of pure poetry, of emotive language, of literature as tending towards the condition of music or the dance':

The language of the novel, trying to do so many things at once, is hardly literary language at all: the cognitive interferes with the expressive, the dramatic with the lyrical, the human with the perfection of the aesthetic. The most perfect poetry is for them a spell. But this mixture of functions which they dislike is also the characteristic of man's archetypal creative act, the most basic and far-reaching, the act of speech.[10]

In another passage, Lerner justifiably says, 'Perhaps we should question the very idea of classifying language into two kinds, rather than describing it as a continuum, between—say—the poles of mathematics and dream.'[11]

Another critic who has cogently questioned the critical *apartheid* which some theorists have sought to impose upon poetry and prose, is Allen Tate:

We say today that there is poetry in prose fiction and, wherever you have narrative, fiction in poetry. But it ought to be easy to see that the murk enveloping the question when we try to carry it further than this arises from a certain kind of fallacy of abstraction.

We are thinking in terms of substance, or essence. Those who believe that poetry and prose fiction differ in some fundamental sense assume that poetry is a distinct essence; whether prose has an essence is irrelevant, since it could not have the essence of poetry; and therefore, prose fiction being a kind of prose, it is essentially different from poetry.[12]

Even if we avoid thinking of poetry as an essence, however, it is possible to argue that the formal differences between poetry and prose are considerable enough to suggest that they have essentially different functions. I wish now to consider two critics who have adopted this position, and applied it to the question of the literary identity of the novel: F. W. Bateson and Christopher Caudwell.

F. W. BATESON: IDEAS AND LOGIC

In his introduction to *English Poetry and the English Language* (1934),* Mr Bateson states what is now the modern critical orthodoxy: that poetry is an essentially verbal activity, and that 'it is only by observing the words that the reader can become aware of the poem's structure'.[1] What is interesting about his argument is that he follows through its implications for the criticism of prose, including prose fiction. After citing the first part of the passage last quoted from Coleridge, Mr Bateson notes:

> The question that Coleridge's definition immediately raises is this: If words are the *media* of poetry, what are the *media* of prose? And the answer would seem to be, Ideas.[2]

Prose uses only the denotations of words; poetry exploits their connotations as well. Prose is essentially logical; poetry creates non-logical patterns by means of metre, rhythm, alliteration, etc. Prose is essentially progressive; poetry 'stands still':

> The structure of prose is, in the widest sense of the word, *logical*; its statements are always ultimately reducible to a syllogistic form.

* It should be emphasized that Mr Bateson may not still hold the views expressed in this book. As co-editor of *Essays in Criticism* he has encouraged discussion of the language of prose fiction and has made a valuable contribution of his own which is discussed below (see p. 43). I have thought it useful to engage with his earlier opinion as I believe it represents one still widely held.

A passage of prose, *any* passage, not even excluding so called 'poetic' prose, resolves itself under analysis into a series of explanations, definitions, and conclusions. It is by these means that the book progresses.[3]

Bateson illustrates this argument by quoting and commenting on a passage from *Persuasion*:

> Captain Wentworth had no fortune. He had been lucky in his profession, but spending freely what had come freely had realized nothing. But he was confident that he should soon be rich; full of life and ardour he knew that he should soon have a ship and soon be on a station that would lead to everything he wanted. He had always been lucky; he knew that he should be so still. Such confidence, powerful in its own warmth and bewitching in the wit which often expressed it, must have been enough for Anne; but Lady Russell saw it very differently. His sanguine temper and fearlessness of mind operated very differently on her. She saw in it but an aggravation of the evil. It only added a dangerous character to himself. He was brilliant, he was headstrong; Lady Russell had little taste for wit and of anything approaching to imprudence a horror. She deprecated the connection in every light.[4]

Bateson comments:

> The statement that Captain Wentworth had no fortune is followed by a *definition* of 'no fortune'. He had had money but had spent it. The *explanation* of his having had money was that he had been lucky; and it was *because* he had been lucky that he expected his luck to continue. His self-confidence was the *reason* that made Anne agree and Lady Russell disagree with him. The latter *concluded* that the connection was undesirable.[5]

Bateson states his case very clearly, and there is much good sense in it. That the language of poetry calls attention to itself by virtue of its non-logical elements is a useful notion which has been further developed by other critics, notably W. K. Wimsatt.[6] One can accept this point, however, without admitting that prose is purely logical discourse in which the words have no intrinsic interest—though this is what Bateson seems to suggest: 'In prose . . . the words tend to be submerged in the ideas or things they represent. One synonym is as good as another.'[7]

The concept of synonymy is a complicated one. It is tenable only if we think of utterances as having several different levels of meaning—'mere sense, sense and implications, feeling, the speaker's attitude to whatever it is, to his audience, the speaker's confidence and other things', as I. A. Richards has put it.[8] Only on the first level can synonymy exist. But does the language of the novel operate solely on the level of 'mere sense'? Bateson's commentary certainly gives us the mere sense of the paragraph from *Persuasion*. But is it an adequate critical account?

Take for example the phrase *must have been enough for Anne*. On the level of mere sense, *was* would be an acceptable synonym for *must have been*. *Was enough for Anne* would, however, create a slight but not unimportant difference of effect. It would suggest that Anne was submitting blindly and unresistingly to the charm of Captain Wentworth. *Must have been* suggests the idea of a strong, instinctive emotional response, but since *must* is a word associated with moral obligation, and since it is used by an authorial voice which speaks with authority here and throughout the novel, we sense a qualified approval or, perhaps more precisely, a lack of disapproval, of Anne's disposition towards Wentworth. This use of *must* in the past tense has rather dropped out of modern English; but it is a form which Jane Austen uses extensively in all her novels, for it enables her to convey a moral judgment of her characters without appearing to violate their independent life.

What gives the whole passage its logical character is, in the first place, its grammar, which organizes the material in antitheses, distinctions, and qualifications. The diction or 'lexis' lends support by being largely nominal and abstract. But the words of logical argument italicized in Bateson's commentary do not themselves appear in the passage. The grammar does their job, allowing the lexis to describe a wide range of attitudes, which are, however, all evoked by the same thing. The passage presents the character of Captain Wentworth from four points of view in succession: (1) the narrator's, (2) Wentworth's own, (3) Anne's, (4) Lady Russell's.

(1) The first two sentences. These seem neutral and simply informational. However, the words *fortune* and *realized* have a discreet ironic effect, which helps to place Wentworth. A *lucky* man without *fortune* is a paradoxical kind of creature; and much of the action of the novel turns on Wentworth's failure to *realize* certain things.

(2) The third and fourth sentences. Wentworth's slightly facile optimism about his prospects. The fourth sentence is free indirect speech—we seem to hear him speaking to Anne, or to himself.*

(3) The fifth sentence as far as 'Anne'. This gives us Anne's favourable response to Wentworth: *confidence, powerful, warmth, bewitching, wit.*

(4) The whole passage turns on the second half of the fifth sentence: 'but Lady Russell saw it very differently'. In the rest of the passage the same characteristics of Wentworth are rehearsed, but differently named and differently evaluated; particularly by words of severe disapprobation such as *aggravation, evil, dangerous, headstrong, imprudence*, and *horror* (this last given a special emphasis by the syntactical inversion which places it last in the sentence).

What we have in this passage is order imposed with assurance and tact upon the flux of human emotion and irrationality. The general effect is pervasive in Jane Austen: an ironic detachment combined with a carefully discriminating sympathy and understanding. It is indeed a logical passage; but such logic applied to human experience in fiction is not normative. It constitutes the special quality of Jane Austen's vision of experience, and is communicated to us through a special kind of language, language which is more than the transparent container of Ideas.

CHRISTOPHER CAUDWELL: THE CURRENT OF MOCK REALITY

Caudwell's argument in *Illusion and Reality* (1937) overlaps Bateson's at several points, and it is interesting to find a Marxist freelance and a professional academic critic propounding such similar theories of poetry. Caudwell's description of how novels work is, however, sufficiently distinct from Bateson's to merit separate treatment. His position is neatly summarized in this sentence: 'The poem and the story both use sounds which awake images of outer reality and affective reverberations; but in poetry the

---

* This is not obvious, but is, I think, indicated by the word *knew*. If the narrator's voice were speaking with full authority here, some more guarded word like *thought, supposed, believed*, would have been used. Free indirect speech is a deviation from strict grammar and strict logic, and thus perhaps comparable to the more obvious non-logical linguistic features of poetry. It is a device that has been extensively used by modern novelists from Flaubert onwards, and usefully studied in the field of stylistics. Cf. Stephen Ullmann, *Style in the French Novel* (Cambridge, 1957), Chapter II.

affective reverberations are organized by the structure of the language, while in the novel they are organized by the structure of the outer reality portrayed.'[1] But this statement is probably too cryptic without some notion of the preceding argument:

> [P]oetry in its use of language continually distorts and denies the structure of reality to exalt the structure of the self. By means of rhyme, assonance or alliteration it couples together words which have no rational connection, that is, no nexus through the world of external reality. It breaks the words up into lines of arbitrary length, cutting across their logical construction. It breaks down their associations, derived from the world of external reality, by means of inversion and every variety of artificial stressing and counterpoint.
>
> Thus the world of external reality recedes and the world of instinct, the affective emotional linkage behind the words, becomes the world of reality. . . .
>
> In the novel, too, the subjective elements are valued for themselves, and rise to view, but in a different way. The novel blots out external reality by substituting a more or less consistent mock reality which has sufficient 'stuff' to stand between the reader and reality. This means that in the novel the emotional associations attach not to words but to the moving current of mock reality symbolised by the words. This is why rhythm, 'preciousness', and style are alien to the novel; why the novel translates so well; why novels are not composed of words. They are composed of scenes, actions, *stuff*, people, just as plays are.[2]

It will be noted that in the first of these two quotations, the word 'story' stands in the same relation to 'poetry' as 'novel' does in the second. This is because Caudwell subscribes to the idea of the lyric as the poetic norm. Thus he is able to discuss the distinctive qualities of poetry in terms of the differences between the lyric and the narrative or dramatic modes.

> By poetry we mean modern poetry, because not only have we a special and intimate understanding of the poetry of our own age and time, but we look at the poetry of all ages through the mist of our own. Modern poetry is poetry which is already separate from story. . . .[3]

There are two ways of challenging Caudwell's position. The first is to say that we are entitled to ask of any general poetics that it take account of all the available data, and that there is a good deal of traditional poetry, not to mention drama and fiction, which does not fit neatly into Caudwell's categories. The second is to say that no kind of discourse can be so detached from 'external reality' as to constitute a special and self-contained system of language—which is what Caudwell, like Valéry, implies. Wimsatt and Beardsley have argued very persuasively against this position in their essay 'The Affective Fallacy', reaching the conclusion that 'a poetry of pure emotion is an illusion. . . . Poetry is characteristically a discourse about both emotions and objects, or about the emotive quality of objects.'[4]

The importance of these two objections is that, if accepted, they encourage us, in Laurence Lerner's words, 'to question the very idea of classifying language into two kinds, rather than describing it as a continuum'.[5] For it is the notion of a radical discontinuity between the language of poetry and the language of other kinds of discourse which has inhibited the study of the language of the novel. Once we conceive of language as a continuum in which the proportion of 'emotive' to 'referential' varies, but in which neither element is ever entirely absent, we may begin to see the novelist's medium as language rather than life.

Caudwell's argument has a certain pragmatic appeal which must be recognized. We *are* usually less conscious of a novelist's use of language than of a poet's. We *do* tend to experience and recall a novel, not as a system of words, images, symbols, and sounds, but as a system of actions, situations, settings, and we continue to find the terms 'plot' and 'character' indispensable. The fact remains that these latter concepts are abstractions formed from accumulated messages conveyed through language. R. A. Sayce has stated well the teasing nature of the problem: 'We are conscious of literary experiences which appear to transcend language: plot, character, personality, form in a wider sense, landscape, the sea and the stars, indeed everything that exists. Yet all these experiences are communicated by linguistic means. This is the paradox with which we are confronted.'[6]

Caudwell does not acknowledge this paradox, and does not avoid confusion. Asserting that 'in the novel, the emotional associations attach not to the words but to the moving current of mock reality symbolized by the words', he makes an artificial distinction: the 'reality' of fiction has no existence independent of the words—that is why it is 'mock' reality—and our emotional responses are directed by the words. As Caudwell himself says, 'language [i.e. all language, not just poetic language] communicates not simply a dead image of outer reality but also and simultaneously an attitude towards it'.[7] If this is true—and it surely is—then reality is structured by the novelist not only in the particular characters, events, and objects in which he represents it, but initially in the words and arrangements of words with which he creates these characters, events, and objects. In this case a novel is made of words just as much as a poem is made of words.

Here, I think, we approach the philosophical heart of the matter: the relation of literary language to reality. But before proceeding any further I wish to consider two empirical arguments frequently used to suggest that the novelist's use of language differs radically from the poet's, and in such a way as not to merit the kind of attention we give to the poet's. I call them the argument from translation and the argument from bad writing.

THE ARGUMENT FROM TRANSLATION

That poetry is untranslatable is a basic tenet of modern criticism and appears to follow logically from any critical theory which holds that form and content are inseparable, and which accounts for the literary effects of a given work principally or exclusively in terms of its verbal organization. Like most of the ideas we have been considering, it starts with the Romantics. Shelley, for instance, talks of the 'vanity of translation':

> [I]t were as wise to cast a violet into a crucible that you might discover the formal principle of its colour and odour, as seek to transfuse from one language into another the creations of a poet. The plant must spring again from its seed, or it will bear no flower, —and this is the burthen of the curse of Babel.[1]

Novels, on the other hand, are apparently translatable, in the sense that we all read translated novels with some confidence in our judgment of them and their authors. Hence, it is argued, the identity of a novel cannot be determined by the words of which it is composed—as a poem is so determined—because this identity is not changed when the novel is translated into other, different words.

This argument is found in the texts by Bateson and Caudwell discussed above. It is also used by Arnold Kettle, who takes it over from Caudwell.[2] Robert Liddell states it most emphatically:

> If 'the way in which words are used' is the only and final criterion, then English readers who do not know Russian have no right to praise the novels of Tolstoy or Dostievsky, but only to praise the minds of Louise and Aylmer Maude or of Constance Garnett.[3]

Liddell professes to be attacking Mrs Leavis here, but in fact in *Fiction and the Reading Public* (1932) she took up a position not very far removed from his own. (Indeed the significance attached to the novelist's use of language by Mrs Leavis and by the whole Leavis–*Scrutiny* school is somewhat equivocal, as I shall try to show later.)

> [W]hile *Faust* and *Le Cimetière Marin* cannot be apprehended as works of art in English, we can get something comparable to the original experience and so make a rough guess at the value of *Anna Karenina* or *The Possessed* or *A la Recherche du Temps Perdu* in another language than that in which it was written.[4]

This Mrs Leavis sees as an 'advantage' of the novel form, but one which adds to the problems of the novel-critic, since it is one of the factors which puts the novel outside the range of I. A. Richards's poetics, which otherwise she finds satisfactory.[5]

To use the argument from translation as Mr Liddell uses it is essentially unfair, because there is a much more reliable basis on which to settle the issue—the issue being whether or not the words of a novel can be changed without altering the meaning— and that is, paraphrase. Translation from one tongue to another is altogether too complicated and mysterious a process to provide clear-cut conclusions about the novelist's art, but I believe it can be convincingly argued that novels are non-paraphrasable. I describe such an argument below (see p. 36). But I propose to consider further the argument from translation because of its pragmatic plausibility, and because it raises interesting questions about literature and language.

Let me lay my hand on my heart and aver that although I have read many foreign novels in translation with great pleasure and benefit, and have passed judgment on them, I have never felt that I 'possessed' any of them in the sense in which I possess the

English novels I read and admire. I invite the reader to ask himself if this is not his own experience, and if it is not accountable in the end only in terms of the insecurity felt in the process of reading: the accumulative effect of innumerable, minute uncertainties, awkwardnesses, anomalies, and ambiguities in the language. That this sense of insecurity does not entirely inhibit our critical faculties can be explained. It is virtually impossible for an educated and sensitive reader to read a translated novel without realizing that it *is* translated, even if for some reason he overlooks the title-page and relies on internal evidence alone. Thus the reader makes a 'contract' with a translated novel which is different from the one he makes with a novel in his own language. He approaches it with a recognition of cultural differences which obstruct communication; he expects to feel insecure in the verbal world of a translated novel, just as he expects to feel insecure in a foreign country in whose language he is not fluent.

The question of translation bristles with problems, particularly of verification. To test the closeness of any translation to its original, one would have to be not only bi-lingual but—to coin a rather ugly phrase—bicultural, i.e. possessed of the whole complex of emotions, associations, and ideas which intricately relate a nation's language to its life and tradition, but possessed not only of one such complex—as we all are to some extent—but of two. Writers like Conrad or Beckett might qualify for such an undertaking, but most of us must rely on the comparatively clumsy method of comparative analysis, carried out in the recognition of our unequal competence in the two things compared. I propose to do a little exercise of this kind with a view to showing the kinds of changes which may occur in translations of prose fiction. I shall compare a sentence from Proust with its translation by Scott Moncrieff, usually acknowledged to be a fine translator.

PROUST AND SCOTT MONCRIEFF COMPARED

The sentence comes from the first section or 'Overture' of *Du Côté de Chez Swann*, where the narrator says that his only consolation when, as a child, he went to bed, was when his mother came upstairs to kiss him good night. He continues:

> Mais ce bonsoir durait si peu de temps, elle redescendait si vite, que le moment où je l'entendais monter, puis où passait dans le

couloir à double porte le bruit léger de sa robe de jardin en mousseline bleue, à laquelle pendaient de petits cordons de paille tressée, était pour moi un moment douloureux.[1]

Scott Moncrieff translates:

But this goodnight lasted for so short a time: she went down again so soon that the moment in which I heard her climb the stairs, and then caught the sound of her garden dress of blue muslin, from which hung little tassels of plaited straw, rustling along the double-doored corridor, was for me a moment of the keenest sorrow.[2]

The narrator, here, is describing, or, more precisely, remembering, a particular action of his mother's, and his own emotional response to it. It is a complex response. Though triggered off by the sense of hearing, it is also clearly visual—i.e. the child in bed reconstructs the appearance of his mother from the evidence of his hearing, assisted by his visual memory. The sentence thus exemplifies in microcosm the synaesthesia which informs the whole novel's treatment of memory. Then, although the passage communicates a sense of joy, in the loving description of the mother's person, it asserts that the moment was one of sorrow, because, although the mother's movements presaged the long-desired kiss, they also implied that the kiss would soon be over, and that there would be nothing left to look forward to for the rest of the night. We encounter another central theme of the novel—time: its elusiveness, its inexorable movement forward, careless of the emotional content of this or that moment for any individual.

If this is a valid account of the meaning of the sentence, we will find, I think, that this meaning is vitally connected with the linguistic form of the sentence; and it may be interesting to see how much of this has been carried over in translation. For convenience of reference, Proust's sentence may be broken down into clauses as follows:

(1) Mais ce bonsoir durait si peu de temps,
(2) elle redescendait si vite,
(3) que le moment. . . .
(4) où je l'entendais monter,
(5) puis où passait dans le couloir à double porte le bruit léger de sa robe de jardin en mousseline bleue,

(6) à laquelle pendaient de petits cordons de paille tressée,
(3) . . . était pour moi un moment douloureux.

The most obvious syntactical feature of the sentence is the long delayed predicate of clause 3, which is separated from its subject by three subordinate clauses (4, 5, and 6) so extended that the word *moment* has to be repeated (not, of course, that this is the only reason for the repetition). This separation and delay expresses the most important tensions and paradoxes of the narrator's emotion. For, when we come at last to the statement that the moment announced several lines before was one of sorrow, it is, notwithstanding the logical explanations provided by clauses 1 and 2, with a faint shock of surprise, because the description of what was happening in that moment suggested love and affection and joy.

This delaying of the predicate is available to the English translator, and, as we see, he has used it. But the effect of this delay is supported and amplified by two inversions in clauses 5 and 6, only the second and less important of which Scott Moncrieff has managed to accommodate. The delay of the predicate *était pour moi un moment douloureux* expresses an irony that works against the narrator, which might be crudely expressed as 'all good things come to an end'. But the delay of the subjects in clauses 5 and 6 indicates the narrator's resistance to this fact. The verbs *passait* and *pendaient* are followed by nouns which are lengthily and elaborately qualified, suggesting (to me at least) that against the inexorable passing of time the boy is desperately pitting his keen sensuous responsiveness to his mother's person, expressed in the nouns and adjectives. It is as if, by extending and concentrating on the catalogue of concrete details, he can arrest time; but the hopelessness of this effort is indicated by the return to the predicate of clause 3, which will not be held off any longer.

The principles of English prose enable Scott Moncrieff to retain the second inversion—*from which hung*—but not the first: *when passed* would be awkward and jarring.* He is obliged to transfer the verb from the mother (or, more exactly, from the sound of her dress) to the narrator, and this involves other changes. He has to specify the sound of the dress as a *rustle*.

---

* One might also note that English lacks an exact equivalent to the French imperfect tense.

Proust does not specify, but merely suggests a sound in the sibilants of *passait, mousseline* and *tressée*. The transfer of the verb from the sound to the narrator means that *the double-doored corridor* has to be shifted to the end of the subordinate clauses. In Proust's sentence, the order of words and phrases follows the pattern of the narrator's thought, which tends towards finer and finer, more and more anguished concentration on smaller and smaller details of his beloved mother's appearance. The clause which immediately precedes the explicit declaration of sorrow is the description, in affectionate detail, of the little tassels of plaited straw. In Moncrieff, however, this crucial position is occupied by the relatively unimportant double-doored corridor. The translation also produces (to my ear, at least) an unfortunate treble-rhyme: *straw . . . double-doored corridor.*

In the above comparison I have confined myself to what can be studied objectively in language: word-order, tense, clause structure, and the more obviously mimetic use of sound. I have not attempted to penetrate into the mystery of tongues, to consider, for instance, whether *of the keenest sorrow* can convey to an English reader exactly what *douloureux* conveys to a French reader. So far as it goes, the experiment suggests that Scott Moncrieff has succeeded in conveying a good deal of the meaning of the original (in so far as that original meaning is discernible by myself) but that he has also lost a good deal. The loss is felt not on the level of 'mere sense' but in the higher categories of Richards's levels of meaning, or in what is sometimes called, in modern linguistics, 'delicacy'. The degree of loss is not, in my opinion, entirely trivial. And while it is true that not all novelists pose the same kind of problems to a translator as Proust does, it may be that his very virtuosity alerts us to the possibility of aesthetic loss, which we may overlook in the case of writing which is superficially innocent of verbal cunning.*

TRANSLATION: POETRY AND PROSE

The reason why poetry is on the whole more difficult to translate than prose, including prose fiction, is very simple. Language has

---

* One naturally tends to assume that the changes involved in translation result in a 'loss'. But there are cases—Baudelaire's translations of Poe, for example—where it seems to have resulted in aesthetic gain.

been defined as 'a structured system of arbitrary sounds and sound sequences which is used in communication and which is a fairly complete catalogue of the things, events and processes in a given environment.'[1] This is a modern linguist's definition, and modern linguists place great stress on the arbitrariness of the sound-structures of language, pouring scorn on the notion of 'sound symbolism' (i.e. that there is some connection between the sounds of words and their meanings).[2] It is, however, possible to hold that sound is an element in language which may be exploited by writers for expressive and mimetic purposes, without falling into the cruder kind of fallacies about sound and meaning.

Poetry and prose can only be usefully distinguished, as Auden suggests, if by 'poetry' we mean 'verse'. The difference is then the presence of metre, with or without rhyme, in poetry. And the essential function of metre and rhyme is to make patterns out of the arbitrary sound-systems of language—patterns which have literary, though rarely logical, significance.* The essential difference between any two tongues is the difference of sound-structure, or phonology. It follows, therefore, that poetry, which is committed by virtue of its metre to the exploitation of sound, will usually be more difficult to translate than prose, which is not so committed. That sound is at the heart of the translation problem has been recognized by most of those who have seriously considered the subject. Shelley makes the point just before the passage quoted above:

> Sounds as well as thoughts have relations both between each other and towards that which they represent, and a perception of the order of those relations has always been found connected with a perception of the order of the relations of thought. Hence the language of poets has ever affected a certain uniform and harmonious recurrence of sound, without which it were not poetry, and which is scarcely less indispensable to the communication of its influence, than the words themselves, without reference to that peculiar order.[3]

It is worth recalling, however, that Shelley includes some prose writers in the category of 'poets'; and it is certainly untrue to say that prose writers do not exploit the sound-value of words. The

* This has been ably demonstrated by Wimsatt in several essays in *The Verbal Icon*, particularly 'One Relation of Rhyme to Reason'. (*Op. cit.*, pp. 153–66.)

pun is an obvious example of a sound-meaning device which occurs in prose as well as in poetry, and always causes trouble for a translator. Joyce's fondness for puns, and his generally elaborate exploitation of the phonological level of language, probably make *Ulysses* a more formidable task for the translator than the *Odyssey*.

The high degree of phonological activity in poetry is not, in other words, a valid reason for regarding its language as essentially different from that of prose. It can encourage such a view, however, if the lyric, particularly the modern lyric, is taken as the poetic norm. Here, the phonological element plays a crucial role in organizing our responses to a semantic content which is often too complicated and ambivalent to submit to the logical organization of grammar. It is the phonology of words which most encourages us to think of them as in some way 'solid', as shapes in the mouth, as concrete embodiments of abstract meaning. But it is dangerous to restrict the literary use of language to that which gives us this sense of the solidity of language in its most heightened form. According to such a view, the truest poetry would be a poetry of pure sound. But a poetry of pure sound is as impossible as a poetry of pure emotion. Poetry, like all human speech, cannot exist without meanings derived from the common perceptual world.

Auden makes this point very well, when discussing the futility of trying to define the difference between poetry and prose:

> Frost's definition of poetry as the untranslatable element in language looks plausible at first sight but, on closer examination, will not quite do. In the first place, even in the most rarified poetry, there are some elements which are translatable. The sound of the words, their rhythmical relations, and all meanings and association of meanings which depend upon sound, like rhymes and puns, are, of course, untranslatable, but poetry is not, like music, pure sound. Any elements in a poem which are not based on verbal experience are, to some degree, translatable into another tongue, for example, images, similes and metaphors which are drawn from sensory experience. Moreover, because one characteristic that all men, whatever their culture, have in common is uniqueness— every man is a member of a class of one—the unique perspective on the world which every genuine poet has survives translation.[4]

It may seem that I have been inconsistent in attacking the argument from translation at each end: first, by suggesting that novels are not completely translatable, and secondly by suggesting that poems are not completely *un*translatable. But these two arguments do not cancel each other out: they point to a view of language as a continuum, rather than two sharply divided modes. We can place works of literature in this continuum according to the way they use language, determined by certain tests, e.g. the degree to which their meaning is determined by phonological organization. But such placing will not always coincide with conventional genre classifications, nor will it correspond to an order of literary value, nor will it demonstrate that the language of one literary text is more or less integral to its meaning than that of another, widely separated from it in the continuum. The argument from translation does not prove that the words of a novel may be changed with impunity as long as their denotations are not affected, for in translation, particularly of prose, change is largely a matter of exchange, which cannot be compared to what happens when we paraphrase a text using different words in the same tongue. In terms of literary meaning and effect, *chat* is closer to *cat* than *feline quadruped*.

THE ARGUMENT FROM BAD WRITING

That major novelists may write badly without forfeiting our esteem is a view often brought forward to diminish the importance of language in the art of the novel; and as such it is often associated with the argument from translation. Marvin Mudrick, for example, writes:

> In prose fiction the unit is not, as in poetry, the word, but the event—a fact that helps to explain why prose fiction so remarkably survives the sea-change of language even in bad translations. . . . Yet great fiction can survive, not only translation, but a measurable amount of bad or dull writing in the original. . . .[1]

A similar view has been expressed by Ian Watt (though it has not prevented him from writing with uncommon perceptiveness about the language of the novel):

> It would appear, then, that the function of language is much more largely referential in the novel than in other literary forms. . . . This fact would no doubt explain both why the novel is the most translatable of the genres; [and] why many undoubtedly

great novelists, from Richardson and Balzac to Hardy and Dostoevsky, often write gracelessly, and sometimes with downright vulgarity; . . .[2]

The argument from bad writing will detain us more briefly than the argument from translation because, as is evident from the above quotations, it always boils down to the questions: 'What do you mean by bad writing?' and 'How much bad writing are you willing to accept?'

Novels are long and ambitious structures, particularly those by the authors Watt cites; it is not surprising if even the greatest novelists should occasionally falter, and such local flaws will not disturb our final estimate of their work. The same is true of long poems, such as epics, as Mudrick admits. He makes only a distinction of degree: thus, the argument from bad writing cannot be used to establish a dichotomy between the language of verse and the language of prose fiction.

When bad writing becomes frequent or affects crucial parts of a particular work, whether in prose or verse, it seems to me that we must modify our estimate accordingly, and that in practice all responsible critics, including the two cited above, do so. No critic, I suppose, has ever claimed major status for a novel which he concedes is badly written from start to finish. But there are certain cases—the criticism of Hardy and Lawrence comes to mind—where concessions of this kind accumulate to the point where they are difficult to reconcile with the assessment finally offered. One feels that either the assessment is too high, or that expressive writing has been inaccurately described as 'bad' through the application of inadequate criteria of 'good' writing. Thus it seems necessary to assert that the badly-written great, or even good, novel is a contradiction in terms. A work of art cannot be successfully achieved if its medium is misused.

Joseph Conrad demonstrated the point very neatly in a letter to Garnett, in which he commented on a review of *The Outcast of the Islands* by H. G. Wells. Wells had praised the novel very warmly, but concluded by saying: 'he writes despicably. He writes so as to mask and dishonour the greatness that is in him.' Conrad defended himself thus: 'Something brings the impression off—makes its effect. What? It can be nothing but the expression—the arrangement of words, the style—Ergo: the style is not dishonourable.'[3] Of course it can be argued that Wells was right about the style of the book. But in that case he was wrong in his general assessment of it—unless we regard good 'style' as something which may or may not be present in a literary text, something which will add grace by its presence, but which may be absent without irreparable damage. This notion of style, which has largely disappeared from the discussion of poetry, still clings tenaciously to criticism of prose—which is one reason why I have avoided using the word (see Section II of this essay).

THE MODERN MOVEMENT IN FICTION: A DIGRESSION

As I have had occasion to cite Proust and Conrad above, this seems an appropriate point at which to acknowledge the problems of illustrating an argument of this kind.

In the course of this essay I have suggested that debate about the function of language in prose fiction has its roots in modern poetics, which itself grew out of the poetical revolutions of Romanticism and Symbolism. A parallel revolution can be observed in prose fiction over roughly the same period and with roughly the same kind of geographical movement: i.e. starting in Europe in the mid-nineteenth century, and later conveyed to the world of English letters through cosmopolitan agents, Irish, American, and European. In the fictional revolution, novelists like Flaubert, Maupassant, Turgenev, James, Conrad, Ford, and Joyce, occupy very similar positions to those of Baudelaire, Mallarmé, Valéry, Pound, Eliot, and Yeats in the poetic revolution.

In seeking to establish their revolution, the novelists I have mentioned traversed much of the ground considered above. We find George Sand, for instance, using the Argument from Bad Writing against Flaubert:

> You seek for nothing more than the well-made sentence, it is something, but only something—it isn't the whole of art, it isn't even the half of it, it's a quarter at most, and when the other three quarters are beautiful, people will overlook the one that isn't[1]

and Flaubert replying to another correspondent:

> You say that I pay too much attention to form. Alas! it is like body and soul: form and content to me are one; I don't know what either is without the other. The finer the idea, be sure, the finer-sounding the sentence. The exactness of the thought makes for (and is itself) that of the word.[2]

We find James formulating with fine discrimination the mystery of translation in discussing Turgenev:

> We touch here upon the remarkable side, to our vision, of the writer's fortune—the anomaly of his having constrained to intimacy even those who are shut out from the enjoyment of his medium, for whom that question is positively prevented from existing. Putting aside extrinsic intimations, it is impossible to read him without the conviction of his being, in the vividness of his own tongue, of the strong type of those made to bring home to us the happy truth of the unity, in a generous talent, of material and form—of their being inevitable faces of the same medal; the type of those, in a word, whose example deals death to the perpetual clumsy assumption that subject and style are—aesthetically speaking, or in the living work—different and separable things. We are conscious, reading him in a language not his own, of not being reached by his personal tone, his individual accent.[3]

We find Conrad, in his artistic *credo*, laying this kind of emphasis on the writer's traffic with language:

> ... it is only through complete, unswerving devotion to the perfect blending of form and substance; it is only through an unremitting care for the shape and ring of sentences that an approach can be made to plasticity, to colour, and that the light of magic suggestiveness may be brought to play for an evanescent instant over the commonplace surface of words: of the old, old words, worn thin, defaced by ages of constant usage.[4]

That form and content are inseparable, that style is not a decorative embellishment upon subject matter, but the very medium in which the subject is turned into art—these and similar principles are exemplified abundantly in the theory and practice of the novelists I have named. It is tempting, therefore, for the critic concerned to assert the importance of the novelist's use of language, to look primarily or exclusively to these novelists for support and illustration. But it is a temptation to be resisted if criticism is to improve its capacity to deal with the language of *all* novels.

The 'modern' novel, the novel of Flaubert, James, Joyce, and their like, is clearly under the magnetic attraction of symbolist aesthetics, and thus very largely amenable to modern poetics: it delights in irony and ambiguity, it is rich in figurative devices, it exploits the phonological level of language extensively (and is thus difficult to translate), it probes deep into the private subjective world of vision and dream, and its climaxes are 'epiphanies', moments of piercing insight analogous to the images and symbols of the modern poet. Modern criticism has therefore naturally and rightly approached such fiction with tools sharpened on modern poetry. That Joyce's medium was language, that his language demands our central attention as critics, is a proposition that no one is likely to challenge. But in so far as the study of the novelist's language is limited to those who most obviously invite it, because their use of language answers immediately to our view of how literary language works, we risk implying that the language of other, earlier novelists is less integrally related to their achievements, or we encourage a crudely evolutionary view of the novel according to which it gets better and better, or we encourage invidious comparisons between novelists. We do not want a normative concept of the language of prose fiction which will predictably give the first prize to Flaubert and the wooden spoon to George Eliot,* though this was the tendency of some early attempts to apply the principles of New Criticism to the novel. If the criticism of the novelist as a verbal artist is to command authority, it must show its relevance to all the available material, and not to one section of it merely. I hope this determination is reflected in the range of illustration in this essay, and in the selection of texts for detailed study in Part II.

SUMMARY OF ARGUMENTS

I think I can best draw together the arguments against considering the novelist as a verbal artist in the sense in which a poet is generally acknowledged to be a verbal artist, by distilling from those considered above and from others which I have not had space to discuss, their essential and most persuasive drift. Let us

---

* Neither, of course, does one want to see the order reversed, as Dr Leavis would seem to wish. Since George Eliot has been mentioned, I should like to note here that her work has recently attracted two excellent critical studies which are notable for their attention to language: Barbara Hardy's *The Novels of George Eliot* (1959) and W. J. Harvey's *The Art of George Eliot* (1961).

imagine a kind of 'familiar compound ghost' of a critic, putting forward the following view.

'All examples of human discourse can be placed on a scale according to the extent to which each example *draws attention to the way it is manipulating language.* A metaphysical lyric—say, Donne's "Valediction Forbidding Mourning", is an example which does so to a very striking extent. Ordinary casual conversation, on the other hand, provides countless examples of discourse which scarcely calls any attention to the way it is manipulating language, for it is concerned to call attention to something specific outside itself—an object, a situation, an emotion. John Robinson, for instance, says to a woman: "I've got to go away for a while, darling, but don't be upset. I'll soon be back, and I'll be thinking of you all the time."

Our response to any particular item of discourse, and the kind of comment we feel ready to make on it, are determined by its place on the above-mentioned scale. If asked to comment on "A Valediction", we should naturally and properly indicate the way the poet gives interest and particularity to a conventional and generalized idea—parting, with its attendant sadness and consolations—by manipulating language: by selecting, using, and discarding a series of analogies until he settles on one which gathers to itself and reconciles the tensions in the poem, the conduct of this argument-by-analogy being supported by a cunning exploitation of sound and rhythm. Such questions as, "Does the poem refer to an actual situation? if so, what was the identity of the woman? was Donne sincere?"—these questions have a certain interest, but they are not the first considerations for an educated reader, and their relevance to the poem *qua* poem is doubtful.

Of John Robinson's parting words, however, the reverse is true. If asked to comment on them (in a context in which such a request would seem natural—i.e. ordinary social intercourse) it would matter very much whether John Robinson was addressing his wife or his mistress, and one would be concerned chiefly with how far his words reflected his real feelings, whether the consolation offered was effective, what light the utterance threw upon the relationship between the two people, and so on. To comment in detail upon the diction and grammar would not be appropriate, or useful.

The novel covers a fairly wide portion of the scale between Donne's poem and John Robinson's utterance, but it leans, on the whole, towards the latter. The novelist creates a fictional likeness of the real world, in which the behaviour and utterances of people arouse the kind of interests, pose the kind of questions, that belong to John Robinson's discourse rather than to John Donne's. The difference between John Robinson's utterance and the utterance of a character in a novel is, of course, that in the real world we comment on such utterances by referring to our empirical knowledge of the context—what we know or suspect or have observed about the people involved. We apply the same kind of knowledge to an utterance in the fictional world, but such knowledge derives from the novelist—it is he who has given us the information we need to satisfy the questions raised by any individual utterance. In recognizing this we are able to make a *literary* judgment of a novel even though the kind of interests aroused by a novel are essentially the same as those aroused by events in life. We assess a novelist according to the success with which he constructs a fictional world in which every action or utterance contributes to our understanding of any other. Since this is a created world we look for a logic, consistency, and design in the whole which eludes us in the real world. In both worlds the same kinds of questions are raised, the same kinds of thought-processes are set in motion, but in the fictional world we have stronger expectations of finding answers and reaching conclusions. In the ordered, selective world of the novelist we gain insights which enrich our understanding of the real world, though such insights can never totally encompass its endless flux. In so far as the activity of the novelist relates to human behaviour, we talk of his *characterization*. In so far as it relates to cause and effect, we talk of his handling of *plot*. Such terms are properly central in formal criticism of the novel because they recognize that the fictional world runs parallel to the experiential world, while being at the same time more ordered and more patterned—in other words, a "made thing". Language is the point of departure and the terminus of the criticism of poetry, but only the point of departure of novel-criticism.'

I have tried to put this case as persuasively as possible, and there is much in it with which one must agree. It is true that the language of poetry calls attention to itself and thus invites critical attention, whereas the language of prose fiction approximates more to casual speech, and arouses the interests of ordinary life. X's argument is in fact more plausible as an account of the methodology of novel criticism, than as an account of what might be called the epistemology of novel-criticism—i.e. the means by which we come to know what we criticize. I would argue that these means are linguistic in a sense which obliges us to find a method appropriate for dealing with them.

At the end of my discussion of Christopher Caudwell's theories, I suggested that at the heart of the whole debate was a philosophical problem concerning the relationship of literary language to reality. To carry the argument further, I must lean heavily on a contemporary philosopher who is also distinguished by his knowledge and understanding of literature.

J. M. CAMERON: THESE WORDS IN THIS ORDER

In his inaugural lecture as Professor of Philosophy at Leeds University, entitled 'Poetry and Dialectic', J. M. Cameron addressed himself to the question which has most haunted writers and critics since the Romantic period, namely, whether 'there are grounds for thinking that truth is applicable to poetic discourse and for putting that value upon it which belongs to those types of discourse in which we make plain to each other and to ourselves the character of human life and of its predicaments'.[1] In examining this problem, and in coming to an affirmative conclusion, Professor Cameron makes several points which are highly relevant to the present discussion.

By 'poetry' Professor Cameron means all literary discourse, including prose fiction. His argument can sustain this definition because he distinguishes poetic from non-poetic discourse not in terms of the *way* it uses language, but in terms of the *purpose* with which it uses language, that purpose being 'the making of fictions'. Attempts to define poetry, when 'poetry' is used in the wide generic sense, according to the way or ways it uses language nearly always come to grief because there is no linguistic device which is *peculiar* to poetry, in the sense that we could not use it in other types of discourse. This is why linguistic *form* (as distinct from function) should be seen as a continuum, rather than as sharply divided into two kinds.

Still, our instinct is that, since the poet's medium is language, there must be something peculiar about his use of it. This instinct is right, and the definition of poetry as 'the making of fictions' will not account for this peculiarity unless it is followed up in a particular way.

The definition of poetry as 'the making of fictions' is, as

Cameron acknowledges, essentially Aristotle's notion of *mimesis*. What dissatisfies us about Aristotle's and some neo-Aristotelian criticism is that it presents imitation as a process of means to end, in which the verbal means are relegated to an inferior position.* Modern, post-Romantic criticism has corrected this tendency by asserting that in poetry what is said is not distinguishable from the way it is said. But it has not been able, or has not wished to assert this for poetry in the wide generic sense that would include novels, considered as wholes.

The basis of this assertion was well stated by Coleridge, who seems to have derived it from his excellent schoolmaster, the Rev. James Bowyer:[2]

> whatever lines can be translated into other words of the same language, without diminution of their significance, either in sense, or association, or in any worthy feeling, are so far vicious in their diction.[3]

This is the familiar commonplace of modern criticism, that poetry is distinguished from other kinds of discourse by being non-paraphrasable. (A parallel and, as I have suggested, less easily verifiable formula is that poetry is untranslatable.) Now, in so far as this argument depends upon practical demonstration, it is most convincing when tested on poems, and particularly lyric poems, where the verbal, syntactical and phonological organization is highly complex, concentrated and 'artificial'; and the effect of any small change or omission can be easily appreciated. Few modern critics trouble to prove that poetry is non-paraphrasable, but their justification of every minute part of a good poem on aesthetic grounds implies this. Novels, however, do not, on the whole, invite this kind of analysis, for various reasons: because they are so long, because it is impossible to hold all their words in the mind at once, because their language has the feel of casual

---

* Wimsatt conveniently illustrates the point in discussing the Chicago school of neo-Aristotelian critics: 'Olson and, echoing him recently, the Chicago sympathiser Hoyt Trowbridge say that if a critic begins with the words of a poem, it is just as if he were to say that "the shape and function of a saw are determined by the steel of which it is made".' Wimsatt's reply seems unanswerable: 'But why wouldn't modern criticism of verbal meaning be more like saying that the goodness of a saw, its capacity to cut, is determined by the steel *fashioned in a certain shape*?' (*The Verbal Icon*, pp. 62–3.)

speech, and so on. Paraphrase, in the sense of summary, is as in-dispensable to the novel-critic as close analysis is to the critic of lyric poetry. The natural deduction is that novels are para-phrasable whereas poems are not. But this is a false deduction because close analysis is itself a disguised form of paraphrase, differing from the paraphrase of conventional novel-criticism only in that it tends towards expansion rather than compression. It is the inevitable irony of our position as critics that we are obliged, whatever kind of imaginative work we examine, to paraphrase the unparaphrasable. Whenever we try to express our understanding and appreciation of a literary text, we are obliged to state its meanings in different words; and it is in the *distance* between the original words and our own words, when the latter are brought to their maximum of sensitive and articulate re-sponsiveness, that we feel the uniqueness of the writer's achieve-ment.*

To return to Cameron: he cuts through this confusion by providing a *logical* proof of the non-paraphrasability of literary discourse. First, he considers the general question of 'how words and expressions and sentences of various logical types get the sense they have', and in particular the traditional notion, very characteristic of eighteenth-century thought, and still vigorous, that 'a thought is one thing and the way it is expressed another'.[4] He concludes that it is allowable to talk about a sentence and the thought it expresses, because the same thought can be expressed in different words of the same language, or in different languages; but that it does not follow that we can think of 'two objects, as it were, the sentence and the thought' because 'the notion that there can be thought quite apart from a vehicle of thought is a superstition, so far, at least, as human thinking is concerned'.[5] He then considers the effects of this superstition on traditional poetics, and how it has been corrected by the Romantics, and by modern critics specializing in close analysis. He then considers the objection that, since this criticism has concerned itself almost exclusively with material that is self-evidently difficult to para-phrase, and since it has been conceded that some discourse can be paraphrased, we cannot be sure that poetry in the wide generic sense is always non-paraphrasable.

Cameron takes his stand on the proposition that 'some of the

* Cf. the quotation from Walter J. Ong below, p. 72.

entailments that belong to other kinds of discourse are, in poetic discourse, cut'.[6] By this he means that

> it is characteristic of a fiction that certain questions cannot appropriately be asked about it. We cannot ask how many children Lady Macbeth had; or what courses Hamlet pursued at the University of Wittenberg; or what kind of caterpillar caused the sickness of the rose in Blake's poem; or whether Mr Jingle's talking, in the year 1827, about the 1830 Revolution, is or is not a case of extrasensory perception.[7]

There is no need to linger over this argument: it is another of the commonplaces of modern criticism. But the logical implications seen in it by Professor Cameron have not, I think, been seen before. Briefly, they are that the distinction we are able to make in ordinary discourse between what is said and the way it is said is a condition of the entailments that are cut in fictional discourse. 'When we for example describe the world, how we describe it has much to do with the *force* of our description, very little—provided we make no syntactical blunders—to do with its accuracy.' He instances some descriptive uses of language, and concludes:

> what all these instances have in common, and what makes such uses susceptible of paraphrase, is that in each case the adequacy of what is said is governed by some state of affairs, prior to and independent of what is said. . . . Now, the adequacy of what is said in the form of poetic fiction is not, in any straight-forward sense, governed by any state of affairs prior to and independent of what is said. Fictitious descriptions are neither true nor false in the way real descriptions are true or false and this follows from their being fictions. . . . It follows from this that I could not give an *alternative* poetic description, for there could be no criterion (as there would be in the case of a real description) for deciding whether or not the alternative description had succeeded. The poetic description has the form of a description; but it exists only as *this* description, these words in this order. What is said and how it is said are thus not distinguishable in the way they are in other forms of discourse.[8]

This is roughly the half-way stage of Cameron's essay. What he has to say in the latter part is no less interesting. Briefly, his conclusion is that we rightly value poetry because, in its unique combination of universality and rich particularity, it compensates for the inadequacy we find in 'concepts drawn from the common stock'[9] to the uniqueness of our own experience as individuals, though without that common stock of concepts we should not be conscious of experience at all. Thus, I cannot identify in myself a sensation like 'pain', or a state of emotion like 'being in love', without knowing what those words mean in the public language.

> Nevertheless, because each of us is himself and not another, unique in his history and in his relations to others, a characterization of our individual feelings through concepts drawn from the common stock leaves us with a feeling of injustice; for the feelings are rendered, not in their particularity, but in respect of their likeness to the feelings of others. . . . The consolation of the poetic representation of human love is that it reveals to us that condition of feeling we share with others—it gives us 'the image of man and nature'—but not, or not wholly, as articulated in the common run of concepts, but as articulated in a particular concrete representation that speaks to us and for us in our individual situation, and only *through* this to and for our common humanity. It belongs to the poetic representation that it is wholly individual, these words in this order, and that no paraphrase can be given; so that although we know that this poem that speaks to us and for us speaks also to and for others, it is still as though it speaks to us alone.[10]

Cameron's conclusions do not differ widely from those of other modern literary theorists and aestheticians. What is interesting is the route by which he reaches these conclusions, which enables him to formulate them in a particularly persuasive and precise way. To make one comparison: his description has much in common with Richards's distinction between 'emotive' and 'referential' language, but it accounts much more satisfactorily for the fact that, on the one hand, emotive language is frequently used in non-poetic discourse, and on the other hand, that the language of a good deal of literature has the appearance of being referential. Similarly, Cameron's vindication of the truth and value of poetic discourse is more satisfying than Richards's psychological theory of literary value as the integration and appeasement of appetencies, because more directly related to the writer's special skills in the medium of language.

It should be emphasized that Cameron's definition of poetic discourse, by reference to the purpose with which it uses language, does not mean that other types of discourse are utterly distinct. Discourse which ostensibly sets out to describe actuality may also use language with a poetic purpose; and this accounts for the fact that many works of an apparently descriptive nature, particularly philosophical treatises, survive the demonstration of their descriptive falsity, and retain a power to affect and interest us, so that we ascribe to them a quasi-literary value. Professor Cameron himself, in another essay, cites Hobbes's *Leviathan* and Pascal's political writings as cases of this kind:

> On particular questions Hobbes and Pascal were right or wrong, what they said was true or false. But the enduring charm of what they said about political man is more to be grasped through the analogy of the poetic whole than through the analogy of Newton's *Principia*. This may go some way to explain what at first sight seems puzzling, and puzzling not only in connection with the thinkers I have named: the co-presence of logical incoherence and a felt power to illuminate political relations.[11]

For my purposes, the most important element in Cameron's essay is his demonstration that all poetic fictions exist only as certain words in a certain order. Clearly, for the purposes of actual criticism, this principle must be modified according to the material under consideration. In the case of drama, for instance, we must allow for the non-verbal and variable elements of theatrical production—movement, spectacle, music, etc. And in discussing orally-transmitted literature we must take into account the constant process of modification and accretion which occurs in any 'one' work. But such questions scarcely affect the novel, which of all the literary genres is the one most firmly fixed in the Gutenberg galaxy. It is the characteristic literary product of the printing press. In the eighteenth and nineteenth centuries, of course, novels were often read aloud to an assembled audience—but they were *read*, not recited: the words were fixed on the printed page in the order determined by the novelist. The novelist might subsequently change the words—in which case his revisions were fixed on another printed page, and we have a slightly different novel to deal with. Apart from the possibility of textual corruption having occurred in the process of printing (where the critic must rely upon the assistance of textual scholarship), we may, in citing a reliable text and sticking to it, be confident that we are dealing with an artistic whole.

LANGUAGE AND FICTIONAL ILLUSION

When considering the novel in the light of Cameron's general description of the nature of poetic discourse, we might suggest that this genre tends to disguise the fact that in it 'the normal entailments' are cut. He notes that we are tempted to ask the kind of questions that are inappropriate to poetic fictions (like, 'How many children had Lady Macbeth') because 'poetic discourse moves in the mode of possibility; so that nothing can be said poetically that would not be appropriate in discourse of another kind'.[1] But in metrical discourse the mere presence of metre acts as a signal to all but the most unsophisticated reader or auditor that the discourse concerns things imagined and not real. The prose medium, approximating more closely to casual speech and discursive writing, encourages us to ask questions which are obviously inappropriate to poems; and to some extent the undertaking of the novelist makes them appropriate. If the anachronism in *The Pickwick Papers* noted by Professor Cameron were not an isolated instance, but paralleled many times, our response to the novel would be disturbed. We rightly ask, 'How many children had Moll Flanders?' and are rightly dissatisfied when we cannot answer the question with any confidence.*

A recent article by Roy Pascal[2] described the thesis of a contemporary German critic, Dr Käte Hamburger, that *tense* in the novel has certain peculiar features which denote the fictional nature of the novelistic world. This is obviously relevant to the question of how far the formal properties of the novel indicate its 'poetic' purpose. Dr Hamburger argues that the past tense of most narrative fiction, or 'epic preterite', has an essentially different function from the past tense of historical description, a difference indicated by the fact that the epic preterite can be used with 'deictic' adverbs (like *now, yesterday, tomorrow*) which in conventional grammar can modify only verbs in the present and future tenses; and that we habitually convert the past tense of novels into the present when summarizing their action. She concludes that the epic preterite denotes neither an identifiable present, nor an identifiable past, but a fictive universe outside

---

* I am not of the party that sees Moll's vagueness about the number and fortunes of her children as a brilliant stroke of characterization on Defoe's part.

real time and place. 'Thus, "Mr X was in America when the war broke out" can be a plain historical statement, which implies a particular time and place for Mr X and for the author of the statement. But if we have: "Mr X was in America. Tomorrow his plane was leaving", we are in the realm of fiction; the author has obliterated his separate identity, and we experience the statement as being neither in the past nor in the present.'[3]

There is clearly a useful insight here, but, as Pascal's perceptive discussion shows, the attempt to classify works of literature on the basis of tense raises more problems than it solves. Dr Hamburger's thesis leads her to propose a radical distinction between the first-person novel and the third-person novel, grouping the former with the lyric poem as genres which are not truly fictional; to deny the artistic significance of many novelists' efforts to establish the action of their novels in a particular historical context; and to maintain that the use of the present tense in fiction is a pointless device since it operates within a timeless universe. Our experience of actual novels, however, contradicts these propositions; and Pascal is right to point out that Dr Hamburger's thesis oversimplifies the infinite gradations and varieties of illusion possible in the novel, where tense derives its expressive significance from its particular context.[4] Dr Hamburger usefully reminds us that the fictional world is a verbally created world, not to be confused with the real world. (As Pascal observes, we acknowledge this by summarizing novels in the present tense, thus indicating that the events of a novel 'recur' whenever we read it.)[5] But we cannot ignore the fact that the novel as a genre is rooted in the convention of realism. 'Mr X was in America when the war broke out' is not *necessarily* a historical statement: it could easily be a fictional statement.

Cameron notes that we do not ascribe truth to poetic fictions on the grounds that we have been tricked into mistaking the representation for the thing represented, just as we do not regard *trompe l'œil* painting as serious art.[6] However, the earliest English novelists, Defoe and Richardson, came near to perpetrating such deceptions on their readers, and the means by which they did so are not altogether separable from the means by which their novels succeed with readers who recognize them as fictions. Defoe's presentation of *Robinson Crusoe* as the memoirs of a historical person would not hold up without the minutely circumstantial character of the narrative; but this same minutely circumstantial quality makes for the success of the book as 'poetic fiction', as 'myth'.[7]

It would seem that the 'concrete particularity' which Cameron sees as an essential source of the truth and value we find in literature is, as regards the novel, in the first place a particularity of circumstance. Novels are, more than other narrative forms, full of facts—dates, times, place-names, and proper names—which are consistent with each other; the characters perform their actions in a world which can be described spatially and temporally in the same way as the world we inhabit. Richardson's worry during the composition of *Clarissa*—'the fixing of dates has been a task to me. I am afraid I make the writers do too much in the time'[8]—reflects a kind of technical problem that is peculiar to the novelist. And not only to the novelist seeking an effect of literal authenticity: Fielding makes no attempt to disguise the fact that his novels are fictions—he conducts his narrative with a deliberate display of artifice, and mocks in *Joseph Andrews* at Richardson's abundance of circumstantial detail;* nevertheless, it appears that the action of *Tom Jones* was worked out with the aid of an almanac, so that events are chronologically consistent with each other and with public events in the year 1745.[9] At a much later stage of the novel's development, we find Joyce writing to his aunt, Mrs William Murray, in Dublin, when working on the last stages of *Ulysses* in Paris:

> Is it possible for an ordinary person to climb over the area railings of no. 7 Eccles St., either from the path or the steps, lower himself down from the lowest part of the railings till his feet are within 2 feet or 3 of the ground and drop unhurt? I saw it done myself but by a man of rather athletic build. I require this information in detail in order to determine the wording of a paragraph.[10]

Obviously this kind of circumstantial matching of fiction with fact has no great literary value in itself; it is rather the necessary context within which the novelist achieves his more complicated and profound effects. It is in a sense more important to the novelist than to the reader. And it is a convention, though it seems to be the reverse of what we normally understand by a

---

* E.g. 'He accordingly ate either a rabbit or a fowl, I never could with any tolerable certainty discover which.' *Joseph Andrews*, I, 15.

convention (i.e. an agreement between writer and audience to change or omit some of the normal contingencies of experience in the interests of aesthetic effect). It is a convention for two reasons.

(1) Because, no matter how many circumstantial details the novelist supplies, no matter how carefully he matches his fictional events with the accidents of historical time and place, he can never reproduce the multiplicity, 'givenness' and 'open-endedness' of actual experience. He cannot avoid selection and emphasis, and the aesthetic effects which follow. He must limit the reader's expectations of documentary provenance for the events described. In so far as he seeks to escape these conditions, his structure disintegrates, and he is led further and further from what he originally set out to describe—as Sterne so brilliantly demonstrates in *Tristram Shandy*.

(2) Because, however many 'true facts' there may be in a novel, what the novel states as a whole cannot be verified. It may have taken x days for a man to travel from Upton to London in 1745, but nothing can prove that a man called Tom Jones did so. It may be possible for a man to drop down from the area railings of No. 7 Eccles St, but nothing can prove that a man called Leopold Bloom did so on the night of 16 June 1904. If we felt impelled to attempt such verification, *Tom Jones* and *Ulysses* would be, as fictions, failures.

The circumstantial particularity of the novel is thus a kind of anti-convention. It attempts to disguise the fact that a novel is discontinuous with real life. It suggests that the life of a novel is a bit of real life which we happen not to have heard about before, but which somewhere is or was going on. The novelist peoples the world of verifiable data (Dublin, a seaport, capital of Ireland, contains a street called Eccles St) with fictitious characters and events (Leopold Bloom, Jew, advertising salesman, married, one daughter living, one son dead, is cuckolded, befriends a young man). The novelist moves cautiously from the real to the fictional world, and takes pains to conceal the movement. Fictional characters are therefore provided with a context of particularity much like that with which we define ourselves and others in the real world: they have names, parents, possessions, occupations, etc., ordered in such a way as not to violate our sense of probability derived from the empirical world. This is what X means by saying that the novelist creates a fictional likeness of the real world. The question remains: are the linguistic means by which all this information is imparted of critical interest?

F. W. BATESON AND B. SHAKEVITCH: PARTICULARITY

This question has been interestingly discussed by F. W. Bateson and B. Shakevitch in an article, 'Katherine Mansfield's *The Fly*: a Critical Exercise'[1] and by several contributors to a debate which followed in *Essays in Criticism*.[2] Bateson and Shakevitch take 'particularity' to be the staple of prose fiction:

> The concrete details in a proverb are all functional. Nobody wants to know what kind of stone it is that gathers no moss, or that is thrown by the inhabitants of glasshouses. The exact size, colour, weight and shape of the respective stones are irrelevant, because a proverb demands immediate implicit conceptualization. . . . But in a realistic short story the particularity is a large part of the meaning. Suppress Mr Woodifield's name, the colour of the arm-chair, the day of the week allotted to his City visits, and the convention collapses. They are indispensable signals from author to reader; they also assume a common interest and confidence in the concrete detail of a phenomenal world.[3]

The writers proceed to note certain linguistic features in *The Fly* which play an important part in determining its meaning, particularly Katherine Mansfield's use of free indirect speech, and her refusal to disclose the name of the 'boss', a word which she spells with a miniscule, as if it were a common noun. They argue that

> the point at which a linguistic device, either of vocabulary (the boss) or syntax (the indirect speech) becomes a rhetorical figure should not be detectable in realistic fiction. The reader has suspended his disbelief on condition that the naturalistic particularities are maintained, as they certainly are in *The Fly*. . . . But in some of the devices here analysed language has unquestionably become rhetoric. The repetition of *any* phrase or construction will give it if repeated often enough a new semantic dimension.[4]

The article produced a lively response from other critics, most of whom were concerned to challenge the particular interpretation of *The Fly* put forward by Bateson and Shakevitch, with which I am not concerned here. But the discussion also went into more general questions. E. B. Greenwood, for instance, argued that 'realism is not just "a trick" whereby descriptive trivia are incorporated in a story to break down the reader's disbelief in the actuality of the events narrated'. Description of such things as furniture in *The Fly* functioned as a form of metonomy or synecdoche. Realism was one way of getting at the 'concrete universal'.[5] Defending himself and his collaborator and making his aims more explicit, Bateson replied:

> The initial premise was that a short story's technical organization is likely to be much the same as a poem's.* Both poem and story are statements about human nature, 'criticisms of life'; they are both intended to survive the immediate context of their origins; both therefore distort normal speech in one way or another so as to achieve such a degree of memorability. The poet uses metre, poetic diction, figures of speech, topoi, etc., the short story writer does not seem to, or only to a limited extent. What then *are* realistic prose fiction's equivalents of metre, etc? . . . [largely] I still insist, the plethora of concrete detail (the convention of phenomenal particularity). . . .[6]

The line dividing Bateson from Greenwood is a fine but important one. If, as Bateson suggests, the particularity of realistic prose fiction is functional only *en masse* as a means of obtaining suspension of disbelief, its constituent details being arbitrarily selected, one detail being as good as another, then it will be difficult to discuss this aspect of the novelist's craft in terms of 'form' or language. If Greenwood's idea of descriptive detail as a form of metonomy or synecdoche is acceptable, then the meaning of a work of prose fiction is determined at every point by the language the writer uses. The nature of the issue is conveniently illustrated by a comment of Bateson's:

> The boss's armchair is no doubt . . . a functional consequence of the plot and characterisation; it is the addition of greenness to the chair, a non-functional detail, that is the mark of the realistic convention.[7]

It is doubtful whether such a question can ever be resolved by critical analysis. Our tools are insufficiently precise to determine conclusively whether the greenness of the armchair is functional,

---

* This is a significant modification of the views expressed earlier by the same writer in *English Poetry and the English Language*.

or whether it would have made no difference if it had been red. Nor, as Professor Cameron would remind us, have we any prior knowledge of the armchair with which we could compare Katherine Mansfield's description of it. What we can say, however, is that the phenomenal particularity of the novel can never be, in the absolute sense, arbitrary.

Proper names will illustrate the point. In life, our surnames are determined by chance, our Christian names by our parents: in both cases we have no control over the names. (On those occasions when we do have control over our names, as when we change them for professional reasons, quasi-literary considerations govern the choice.) Thus we do not expect to find any correspondence between a person's name and a person's character, and if some such correspondence does strike us we feel that in some freakish way art has trespassed into life. In the fictional world, however, characters rise up before the mind of the artist and, like Adam, he has to name them. Novelists respond to this task in different ways: some delight in the possibilities of symbolic names, while others seek an unobtrusive ordinariness in their names. But even in the latter case a process of selection has taken place, one out of innumerable possibilities has been chosen, and the only possible motive for the ultimate choice is an aesthetic one. Ian Watt has pointed out that the earliest English novelists, Defoe and Richardson, broke with previous literary tradition in giving their characters ordinary, non-symbolic names, but notes that this was not incompatible with a certain discreet appropriateness in the names.[8] The point is quickly made if we try to imagine Moll Flanders and Clarissa Harlowe with their names exchanged. I have a colleague and good friend whose name is Brewer. Not until the moment of writing have I been conscious of the associations of this name with the various contexts of the word *brew*. But it seems to me impossible that a sensitive novelist should choose such a name, or a sensitive reader encounter it, without bringing some of these associations into play.

The novelist, then, can never reproduce the neutrality, the 'givenness' of names in the real world. And the same conclusion applies to the whole apparatus of phenomenal particularity. Nothing in the novel can be wholly neutral. As Greenwood says, 'the details [of descriptive particularity in fiction] are surrogates . . . for the mass of observed detail which would have been there in actuality.'[9] The selection and ordering of these surrogates must have an aesthetic motive and an aesthetic effect, though both writer and reader may be to some extent unconscious of the processes involved. Criticism, of course, is only competent to deal with what we can be made conscious of. But we must utilize our resources to their extreme limits.

According to Bateson and Shakevitch, the functional or linguistically significant elements in a work of realistic prose fiction—those which determine our understanding and evaluation of the characters and actions involved—emerge out of a ruck of non-functional, descriptive particularity and the points at which they emerge 'should not be detectable'. (This last cannot be literally true, since the writers detect them in *The Fly*. However, what is really meant—and it is a valid point—is that the novelist characteristically takes pains to disguise the fact that he is manipulating language to aesthetic ends.) But if critical analysis can go thus far, may it not go further, sustained by the *a priori* conviction that nothing in a novel can be totally arbitrary, totally neutral? May it not reveal some pattern, some order of significance, in the ruck of apparently random specificity? It seems to me that Bateson and Shakevitch have themselves given a useful lead in this direction: 'The repetition of any phrase or construction will give it, if repeated often enough, a new semantic dimension'. We may apply this principle of repetition on a wider scale than they suggest. But this is a topic I must postpone till a later part of this essay.

CONCLUSIONS TO SECTION I

To return to our compound critic, X, we are now in a position to appreciate the significance of his concession that while 'in the real world we comment on utterances by referring to our empirical knowledge of the context . . . in the fictional world . . . such knowledge derives from the novelist.' Cameron, as we have seen, uses this distinction to demonstrate the non-paraphrasability of all poetic fictions, including novels. The fictional world of a novel is a verbal world, determined at every point by the words in which it is represented. Therefore, there can be no essential difference between the criticism of poetry and the criticism of prose fiction, such as X postulates in his final sentence. To say

46

this is not to deny X's formulation of the nature of the interests aroused by prose fiction, or to prohibit the conceptualization of certain verbal complexes as 'characters' or 'plots'.

X's argument gains plausibility by taking 'utterance' as its basic term, and by using a lyric poem and a conversational remark as illustrations. It is in dialogue, above all, that the novelist has most opportunity, if he so wishes, to suggest continuity between his fictional world and the real world, and to allow his own activity as 'verbal maker' to recede from sight. There is no line of dialogue from a novel that could not easily be imagined proceeding from the mouth of an actual person. John Robinson's banal and colourless remark could exist in a good novel. Modern realistic fiction, however, concerned to imitate a world in which the public language is imaginatively impoverished, will tend to compensate by loading its indirect representation of consciousness with a more sensitive and complicated verbalization of experience, as we see in novelists as different as Henry James and Kingsley Amis.

'There can be no pretence, of course, that how language works can be fully explained.'[1] I. A. Richards's observation should be a motto for all investigators into the subject. I am far from thinking that all the questions raised in the preceding pages have been satisfactorily settled. But I think the unanswered, or unanswerable questions apply equally to all kinds of literary discourse, and can be traced back to an awkward but undeniable fact with which every writer and critic grapples in the exercise of his craft or discipline. That is, that the writer's medium differs from the media of most other arts—pigment, stone, musical notes, etc.— in that it is never virgin: words come to the writer already violated by other men, impressed with meanings derived from the world of common experience. Thus, there is always a natural temptation to regard the writer as a man who tells us something, rather than as a man who tells us something by making something. The formal properties of literary language weaken this temptation in the case of poetry, but strengthen it in the case of prose fiction. What I hope to have shown is that, if we are right to regard the art of poetry as essentially an art of language, then so is the art of the novel; and that the critic of the novel has no special dispensation from that close and sensitive engagement with language which we naturally expect from the critic of poetry, though the former will have to adopt different techniques of description, analysis, and evaluation. Addressing a conference on 'Style and Language', René Wellek had this to say:

> There is poetry like that of Gerard Manley Hopkins which forces us to pay attention to the surface of words, to their sounds, to what Hopkins himself called quaintly their 'inscape'; and, on the other end of the scale, there are writers in whom language becomes almost diaphanous, where we hardly seem to notice the verbal surface. Many novels seem not to require any close attention to style. But even a novel by Dreiser is either written well or badly, and unobtrusively the verbal surface will influence our feelings and finally our judgment. This is the place for the style of an individual work, the 'work style'.[2]

This quotation leads naturally enough to the next section of this essay. Assuming that the novelist's medium is language, in the critically significant sense I ascribe to that statement, what methods are available for dealing with that language? Most of the methods proposed or practised have been based on a concept of 'style'.

II

CONCEPTS OF STYLE

> There is no branch of criticism in which learning as well as good sense, is more required than to the forming an accurate judgment of style, though there is none, I believe, in which every trifling reader is more ready to give his decision.[1]

HENRY FIELDING'S cautionary words deserve to be borne in mind by everyone who attempts to discuss the concept of 'style', surely one of the most vexed terms in the vocabulary of literary criticism, and of aesthetics generally. Several modern critics have, however, attempted to sort out the various meanings attached to the word. Let us begin with Middleton Murry, who discriminates between 'Style, as personal idiosyncrasy; Style, as technique of exposition; Style, as the highest achievement of literature'.[2]

The most familiar formulation of the first of these concepts is, of course, Buffon's 'the style is the man'. As Abrams shows in *The Mirror and the Lamp*,[3] it was extensively canvassed in the eighteenth century as a means of accounting for and legitimizing those differences between one writer and another which were perceived within a poetics which placed emphasis on agreement, tradition, imitation, generalization, and impersonality. The Romantic Movement, with its expressive poetics and cult of personality, encouraged and extended the idea, and the nineteenth century is notable for a flowering of many diverse and idiosyncractic styles.

49

The idea that every writer displays his own unique 'signature' in the way he uses language, something which all his works, however diverse, have in common, and which distinguishes them from the work of any other writer, is one which recommends itself at once to any experienced reader, and which has recently had a certain amount of scientific verification. It has been valuable (though not always accurate beyond dispute) in settling problems of authorship. Modern linguists have applied the concept universally, and ascribe to every individual speaker an 'idiolect' or way of using language which is unique. Obviously, the concept of style as the man is a useful and legitimate one in literary criticism, but only in so far as it is applied in a critical procedure that works from stylistic features to the individual work which manifests them, and from this work to other works by the same author, and regards this body of work as the literary articulation of the man. In so far as we move directly from the style to the man, ignoring the particular artefacts in which we encounter this style, we move from the domain of literary criticism to that of psychological or biographical speculation.

Murry's second category, Style as a technique of exposition, should perhaps have been placed first, since it is older. It derives from classical and neo-classical theories of rhetoric. It therefore has an orientation towards discursive and persuasive prose, and tends to be expressed prescriptively, i.e. in terms of rules for 'good writing'. Though the norms on which such prescriptive theories of style are necessarily based have been under heavy fire from modern literary critics and linguists, the tradition doggedly survives in manuals and school grammars, and is discernible in a good deal of sophisticated criticism.* However, the rhetorical tradition itself is a noble one. To it we owe most of our terminology for describing the various devices of verbal expression —metaphor, simile, paradox, oxymoron, etc., and no one has yet devised a more satisfactory terminology which has acquired general currency. The most damaging aspect of this concept of style is perhaps that it nourishes what Cameron describes as the

* E.g. 'It is best to call a spade a spade unless there are good reasons for doing otherwise', from a book written by an academic critic and teacher as a general account of modern critical principles and procedures. The implication that one does not need a reason for calling a spade a spade is revealing.

'superstition' that we can think of a thought and the way it is expressed as two independent entities.

Murry's third category, 'Style as the highest achievement of literature' is a little vague, but is clarified elsewhere in the book, and by a more precise definition, *viz*., 'the complete realization of a universal significance in a personal and particular expression'.[4] It is an all-inclusive concept of style, in the sense that it takes in everything that we value in literary works of art. It assumes that such works make their effects through language, and that in so far as we account for these effects we are talking about style. It is, however, precisely at this point that the word 'style' usually drops out of modern literary criticism. 'The complete realization of a universal significance in a personal and particular expression' is a characteristic criterion of modern criticism of lyric poetry; yet the word 'style' rarely occurs in such criticism—indeed it is rarely applied, today, to any poet, with the exception of Milton, where it is hallowed by the epithet 'grand'.

Murry's third concept of style, then, implies the whole of modern poetics; but the word 'style' is most likely to be invoked in modern criticism when the texts under consideration do not seem amenable to this poetics, i.e. prose works such as essays, satires, and other kinds of polemical or discursive writing. Northrop Frye notes that 'Style . . . is the chief literary term applied to works of prose generally classified as non-literary'.[5] A scrutiny of the examination papers in most of the English schools of our universities would show that questions on style are invariably set on such authors as Bacon, Browne, Swift, Addison, Hazlitt, De Quincey, Carlyle, etc. The novel has a characteristically ambivalent status in this respect: 'style' is not as important a term in the discussion of fiction as in the discussion of discursive prose, but it is much more in evidence in the former than in the discussion of poetry.

I conclude that 'style' still denotes, in ordinary usage, the first and second of Murry's categories—style as the man and style as normative rhetoric—and not his third. It is difficult, therefore, to use the term 'style' in novel criticism without appearing to be talking about less than the whole work. For this reason I have abstained as far as possible from using the term 'style' in the second part of this book. This is a purely personal decision and does not, of course, exclude the possibility of a useful approach being made to the novelist's use of language with the aid of a concept of style. The obvious place to look for approaches of this kind is in the field of stylistics.

STYLISTICS

Modern stylistics has addressed itself to several interrelated tasks: to clarify the concept of style, to establish for 'style' a central place in the study of literature, and to develop more precise, inclusive, and objective methods of describing style than the impressionistic generalizations of traditional criticism. The first thing that must be said about modern stylistics is that it is largely a Continental phenomenon. Stylistics as such scarcely exists as an influential force in Anglo-American criticism of literature in English. We have no Spitzer, no Auerbach, no Ullmann. We have no body of work comparable to that revealed by a glance through Hatzfeld's *Critical Bibliography of the New Stylistics Applied to the Romance Languages* (1953). There is in this respect a chasm between Anglo-American studies and modern language studies which is rarely bridged. The loss has, I think, been mutual. Anglo-American criticism has ignored valuable developments in methods of accounting for the literary use of language flexible enough to take in both poetry and prose. English criticism, in particular, has maintained a somewhat provincial mistrust of formal grammatical analysis and description from which its own characteristically intuitive and empirical approach could benefit.* Continental stylistics, on the other hand, generally yields up thinner results, in terms of interpretation and evaluation of individual texts, than the best Anglo-American criticism. It has not really asked itself the fundamental questions about the nature of literary discourse discussed in the first section of this essay, which are the commonplaces of literary theorizing in England and America. It remains blandly convinced of a success which is not altogether apparent to an outsider.

* Characteristic of this attitude is the following remark, taken from the book quoted above in connection with calling spades 'spades': 'real literary analysis has no affinities with grammatical sentence analysis. Its accuracy is not that of classification. It is that of a delicate discernment and assessment of the experience, of the "felt life" (Henry James's phrase) in and behind the words that are being examined.'

Both the virtues and the limitations of Continental stylistics can be traced in its origins. It developed rapidly after the First World War, to fill a vacuum existing in the humanities in Europe between, on the one hand, a dryly academic philology preoccupied with the formulation of laws to explain phonological and semantic change, and on the other a peculiarly barren form of literary history which was interested in every question about a work except 'what does it mean?' Leo Spitzer has graphically described this situation, and his own response to it as a young post-graduate, in his essay, 'Linguistics and Literary History'.[1] His solution to the problem was stylistics: 'Stylistics, I thought, might bridge the gap between linguistics and literary history.'[2]

Spitzer is usually considered to have been the father of 'the New Stylistics'. His achievement was twofold. Firstly, he asserted and demonstrated that in causally relating a particular literary effect to a particular ordering of language, criticism takes a significant step forward from impressionistic appreciation—goes perhaps as far as it can go in 'explaining' the effectiveness of a literary text. Winifred Nowottny cites a particularly forceful example of this in her book, *The Language Poets Use*:

> many people have observed the sublime effect of the passage (Genesis 1. 3.) 'And God said, let there be light: and there was light', but it was left to Spitzer to trace the sublime effect to its cause—in the fact that the syntax in which the fulfilment of God's command is described is as close as possible to the syntax of the command itself. (In the original Hebrew, as Spitzer points out, the parallelism of command and fulfilment is even closer: *jehi aur vajehi aur*.)[3]

Spitzer's second main achievement was his development of a method for dealing with the style of long and complex structures, such as novels. It has been described as the 'linguistic' or 'philological circle'.[4] Here is Spitzer's own description of the genesis of the method:

> In my reading of modern French novels, I had acquired the habit of underlining expressions which struck me as aberrant from general usage, and it often happened that the underlined passages, taken together, seemed to offer a certain consistency. I wondered if it would not be possible to establish a common denominator for all or most of these deviations; could not the common spiritual etymon, the psychological root, of several individual 'traits of

style' in a writer be found, just as we have found an etymon common to various fanciful word formations?[5]

In reading a novel of the Parisian underworld, *Bubu de Montparnasse* (1905) by Charles Louis-Philippe, Spitzer is struck by a particular use of ' "*à cause de*", suggesting causality, where the average person would see only coincidence'.[6] Further examination reveals a similarly individual use of '*parce que*' and '*car*'.

> Now I submit the hypothesis that all these expansions of causal usages in Philippe cannot be due to chance: there must be 'something the matter' with his conception of causality. And now we must pass from Philippe's style to the psychological etymon, to the radix in his soul. I have called the phenomenon in question 'pseudo-objective motivation': Philippe, when presenting causality as binding for his characters, seems to recognize a rather objective cogency in their sometimes awkward, sometimes platitudinous, sometimes semipoetic reasonings; his attitude shows a fatalistic, half-critical, half-understanding, humorous sympathy with the necessary errors and thwarted strivings of these underworld beings dwarfed by inexorable social forces. The pseudo-objective motivation, manifest in his style, is the clue to Philippe's *Weltanschauung*; he sees, as has also been observed by literary critics, without revolt but with deep grief and a Christian spirit of contemplativity, the world functioning wrongly with an appearance of rightness, of objective logic. The different word-usages, grouped together . . . lead towards the psychological etymon, which is at the bottom of the linguistic as well as of the literary inspiration of Philippe.[7]

I am not competent to assess the validity of this interpretation, and quote it merely to illustrate the nature of Spitzer's method. As a method it is perhaps vulnerable, and I want to make quite clear what to me seems valuable, and what questionable, in it. In the general idea of a movement of critical response from particular example to a hypothetical general interpretation, and back again to further examples which confirm or modify the hypothesis, Spitzer provides a sound model for critical procedure, its novelty inhering mainly in its application to linguistic usage. What is unsatisfactory about Spitzer's method—to an English critic, at least —is its orientation to psychological explanation and interpretation of the artist, and to the formulation of those grand schematic theories about cultural change and the history of ideas so dear to the Germanic scholarly mind. Not that either kind of speculation is invalid, but they can obscure the unique interest and value of the particular text with which the critic starts. The linguistic circle, in other words, will be most useful if it works with a hypothesis about the text considered as a whole, and not, except by inference, with a hypothesis about the psyche of the author or about his age.

Spitzer's method has been criticized for being insufficiently objective and scientific. But a true 'science' of stylistics is a chimera, as I shall argue later. Few men have borne more persuasive witness than Spitzer to the necessary part played by intuition in literary criticism. Criticism can be more objective, more 'scientific' if you wish, than it often is; but in the last resort we rely on 'talent, experience, and faith'.[8]

There is, however, in Spitzer's method a certain bias which it is important to recognize. This is, very naturally, a philological bias. The linguistic features which interest Spitzer are those which deviate from the norm: 'I had acquired the habit of underlining expressions which struck me as aberrant from general usage.' And this explains why Spitzer's interest is in connecting—not linguistics and literary *criticism*—but linguistics and literary *history*: 'The individual stylistic deviation from the general norm must represent a historical step taken by the author, I argued: it must reveal a shift of the soul of the epoch, a shift of which the writer has become conscious and which he would translate into a necessarily new linguistic form'.[9] This may be true, but it by no means follows that what strikes the philologically-trained reader as an important deviation from normal linguistic usage is equally important in determining the literary identity of a given text; still less that deviation thus conceived is the sole area of stylistic activity. As René Wellek has pointed out: 'often the most commonplace, the most normal linguistic elements are the constituents of literary structure.'[10]

This built-in philological bias, and its contingent emphasis on 'deviation' is characteristic of the 'Continental' school of stylistics (or 'New Stylistics' as it is sometimes called).* Consider, for

* It explains, too, why the New Stylistics and Anglo-American New Criticism have diverged so greatly though they were both revolutionary movements designed to solve a similar crisis in the humanities, i.e. the inadequacy of traditional philology and traditional literary criticism. The stylistics revolution was led by men like Spitzer, whose essential bent was

instance, Professor Stephen Ullmann's study *Style in the French Novel* (1957). Ullmann belongs to a later generation than Spitzer's and offers a more sophisticated theoretical apparatus, and one more congenial to the English critic. He recognizes, for instance, that 'the same device of style may give rise to a variety of effects',[11] and that 'To study the integration of a stylistic device into the structure of a novel, one must examine it at the level of the entire work of art.'[12] But the interests, the principles behind the book, are essentially philological. Ullmann isolates certain stylistic devices, such as free indirect speech, and inversion, and examines with great subtlety and perception their functioning in the work of certain French novelists. But he starts with a philological rather than a critical response: the devices are selected for close examination, it would appear, not because they relate crucially to his reading of particular texts, but because they interest him as deviations from normal usage. And in exploring the function of such devices, Ullmann relies heavily on the consensus of existing critical opinion about his authors, on which his findings constitute a kind of philological gloss.

'The tasks of stylistics are . . . primarily descriptive,' says Ullmann.[13] This follows logically from the philological principles of stylistics of this type; but it suggests that stylistics can never become a fully comprehensive method of literary criticism. The difference may be stated in this way: for both stylistician and critic, the interest and meaning of any linguistic element is determined by its context; but for the latter the context is, in the first place, the individual text considered as a whole, while for the former it is the language considered as a whole. There is a further and more important distinction: the stylistician seems obliged to rely upon an implied or accepted scale of value, or to put aside questions of value altogether; whereas the literary critic undertakes to combine analysis with evaluation.

STYLE AND MODERN LINGUISTICS

The embarrassment caused to stylistics by questions of value is even clearer in discussions of style in the context of modern

---

philological; the neo-critical revolution by men like Eliot and Richards, whose bent was literary, philosophical and psychological, and who were often creative writers themselves.

linguistics as practised in Britain and America (usually termed 'structural linguistics'). Modern linguists claim to be in the process of evolving a theoretical and descriptive apparatus which will provide us with a more satisfactory means of accounting for the nature and function of language than has hitherto been available. It seems certain that this claim will be made good, and that literary criticism will benefit enormously from the new and much more accurate terminology of linguistic analysis and description. It will take some time, however, to bring this about: not only must linguists reach more agreement among themselves than they enjoy at present, but the new methods and terms will have to enter fully into general currency, and become the natural and familiar way of thinking and talking about language. In the present uneasy and difficult period of transition the literary critic has no alternative, in my view, but to manage as best he can with the categories of traditional grammar.

This said, one still feels obliged to assert that the discipline of linguistics will never *replace* literary criticism, or radically change the bases of its claims to be a useful and meaningful form of human inquiry. It is the essential characteristic of modern linguistics that it claims to be a science. It is the essential characteristic of literature that it concerns values. And values are not amenable to scientific method.* Most linguists would recognize that literary criticism has its own province in which conclusions are not scientifically verifiable, even if at the same time they rather look down upon it; but there are recurrent attempts to import the 'scientific' methods of linguistics into literary criticism *via* stylistics. Michael Riffaterre's article, 'Criteria for Style Analysis' (*Word*, XV, 1959, pp. 154–74), is a convenient example to consider.

* The consequences of not recognizing this fundamental distinction are well illustrated by *Style in Language* Ed. Thomas E. Sebeok (Cambridge, Mass., 1960), the record of a conference in which linguists, psychologists and literary critics were brought together in 1958 'to explore the possibility of finding a common basis for discussing, and hopefully, understanding . . . the characteristics of style in language.' (Editor's Foreword, p. v.) Though such an exchange cannot be without value, the conference was, as regards its aim, a total failure. Most of the participants seem to have acknowledged this; and any remaining doubts should have been dispelled by Gordon Messing's long and mordant review of the volume in *Language*, XXXVII, 1961, pp. 256–66.

M. RIFFATERRE: SCIENTIFIC STYLISTICS

Riffaterre begins his article with a characteristic invocation of 'science':

> Subjective impressionism, normative rhetoric and premature aesthetic evaluation have long interfered with the development of stylistics as a science, especially as a science of literary styles.[1]

He says that what is required is a set of criteria to separate the 'stylistic' elements from the 'neutral' elements in any given text, so that we may subject the former to linguistic analysis. Style is understood as 'an emphasis (expressive, affective, or aesthetic) added to the information conveyed by the linguistic structure, without alteration of meaning'.[2] (I shall waive at this point the question whether there can be neutral elements in a literary structure, or whether meaning in literature can survive different stylistic emphases unchanged.) Style is the means by which the writer, or in linguistic jargon 'encoder', ensures that his 'message' is 'decoded' in such a way that the reader not only understands the information conveyed, but shares the writer's attitude towards it. In speech, communication is 'elliptical': many signals can be ignored by the receiver, who is assisted by context, situation, and predictability. The writer aims to avoid this erratic, elliptical communication by 'encoding', at the points he deems important along the written chain, features that will be inescapable, no matter how perfunctory the reception. And since predictability is what makes elliptical decoding sufficient for the reader, *inescapable elements will have to be unpredictable*'.[3] The analyst of style is therefore concerned with 'the elements which limit freedom of perception in the process of decoding'. (This, of course, runs counter to much literary theorizing of the Empsonian kind.) Riffaterre then makes the important point that the author's *encoding* is permanent, but the process of decoding changes as the language changes in the course of time. '[S]tylistics should encompass this simultaneity of permanence and change.'[4] (He does not tell us how, and indeed it is difficult to see how it could be encompassed 'scientifically'. The paradoxical relationship between the formally fixed artefact and the necessarily variable human responses to it is one of the grounds for asserting that literary criticism can never be a science.)

The simplest way of identifying stylistic devices (or 'SDs') as defined would be, Riffaterre suggests, to compare the author's intentions with his realization of them. But he recognizes the intentional fallacy. So he turns to the reader's response.

> Our problem is to transform a fundamentally subjective reaction to style into an objective analytic tool, to find the constant (encoded potentialities) beneath the variety of judgments, in short to transform value judgments into judgments of existence. The way to do it is, I believe, simply to disregard totally the content of the value judgment and to treat the judgment *as a signal only*.[5]

Accordingly, he proposes that the style analyst should record the responses of a sample of readers to a literary text, categorizing every linguistic feature commented on by the readers as an SD, whether the readers considered that it represented artistic success or failure. The results of this sample are then consolidated as the Average Reader (AR) criterion for distinguishing stylistic devices.

Acknowledging some of the shortcomings of the AR criterion, Riffaterre proposes an objective characteristic of SDs which will control the AR experiment, and indicate when the AR has mistaken a neutral element for a stylistic element. This is the concept of deviation in a more sophisticated form: stylistic devices deviate—not from an external linguistic norm (the existence of which is doubtful, in any case)—but from the linguistic norm set up in its immediate context. Thus a Verb–Subject order will be a stylistic device if the context establishes Subject–Verb as the norm, and *vice versa*. This concept is buttressed by the notion of 'convergence', where several stylistic devices which, taken independently, would be expressive in their own right, together 'converge into one especially striking emphasis'.[6] Riffaterre illustrates this with a good commentary on a sentence from *Moby Dick*.

It is interesting to trace the logical stages of Riffaterre's pursuit of a science of literary styles. They may be set out as follows:

	(1)	Style is the means by which a writer obtains certain effects in communication.
So	(2)	One way of studying style would be to relate the writer's intentions to the verbal forms he uses.
But	(3)	Intentions are not recoverable.
So	(4)	We study the responses of readers.

But	(5) Readers' responses are distorted by subjective value judgments.
So	(6) We consider the readers' responses as mere indications of the presence of stylistic devices.
But	(7) Readers' responses may be unreliable merely as indications of the presence of stylistic devices.
So	(8) We shall control the evidence of readers' responses by the structural criteria of deviation from contextual norms.

Then . . .

Then what? The style analyst has his *data*, a catalogue of all the stylistic devices in a given text,* but he is still confronted with the task of deciding whether (*a*) any particular SD has worked, and (*b*) how it has worked in relation to all the other SDs in the text. Is there any objective, 'scientific' way of answering such questions? I think not. The basic contradiction in Riffaterre's argument is that, while he holds that style is the means by which a writer ensures that his 'message' is 'decoded' according to his intentions, he regards any particular decoding as inherently unreliable evidence of stylistic effect. This amounts to saying that style is rarely, if ever, successful.

The assumption behind Riffaterre's argument, that a 'scientific' description of style must precede any discussion of its literary function and value, so far from assisting such discussion, actually impedes it. His method will burden the literary critic with a mass of indiscriminate data without advancing him one inch towards the completion of his critical task. This is not to say that some of the linguistic concepts used by Riffaterre are not useful. His own commentary on the Melville passage gains from the precision of his terminology. But there is no evidence that this commentary was produced by the application of his own laborious method. Rather, it seems as though, like any literary critic, he was struck by the literary interest and value of the sentence and of the whole novel of which it is part, and was moved to analyse the objective means by which this subjective response was evoked.

J. WARBURG: APPROPRIATE CHOICE

Jeremy Warburg's article, 'Some Aspects of Style' (*The Teaching of English*, Studies in Communication 3, ed. Randolph Quirk and

* Supposing, that is, that the method is practicable, which seems doubtful.

A. H. Smith (1959), pp. 47–75), does not employ the specialized terminology of modern linguistics, but it is entirely characteristic of the latter in substituting a theory of efficiency for a theory of value. The theory or theories of value which it rejects, are those of the old-fashioned normative rhetoric (e.g. 'Fowler's injunction to "prefer the Saxon word to the Romance" '[1]). Such ideas are properly exposed as fallacies by Warburg. It is doubtful, however, whether his own concept of style as appropriate choice is very helpful to the literary critic. He begins by attacking the notion of 'treating form and content as though they were separate entities, as though we knew the meaning of an utterance by any other way than by the way it had been said'.[2] But his own concept of style seems to demand that we make such suppositions.

Warburg begins by postulating that the province of style is the connotative and not the denotative:

> The good use of a *language*, then, consists in choosing the appropriate symbolisation of the experience you wish to convey, from among all the possible words and arrangements of words (by saying, for example, *dog* rather than *cat*). Good *style*, it seems to me, consists in choosing the appropriate symbolisation of the experience you wish to convey, from among a number of words *whose meaning-area is roughly, but only roughly, the same* (by saying *cat*, for example, rather than *pussy*). That is to say, matters of style are necessarily linguistic matters: linguistic matters are not necessarily —it is a common but misleading view—matters of style.[3]

Now, I would argue that, if style is to be a comprehensive term for the activity of the literary artist, then in art (as distinct from life) linguistic matters are necessarily matters of style. Since the imaginative writer does not use language to describe an existing set of circumstances, his 'denotative' use of words is of aesthetic significance. It is significant that Mr T. S. Eliot uses the word *dog* (instead of the *wolf* of Webster's original lines) in,

> Oh keep the Dog far hence, that's friend to men
> Or with his nails he'll dig it up again![4]

Turning to Warburg's criteria for good style, one is bound to ask: who is to measure the appropriateness of the symbolization? The way Warburg expresses himself suggests that the speaker or writer will be in the best position to do so. But this will be of little assistance to the critic. It seems that the critic must identify the experience which the writer is trying to express and then assess the appropriateness of the symbolization. If he looks for this 'experience' outside the utterance, however, he falls into the intentional fallacy, and Warburg, who quotes Wimsatt extensively, can scarcely mean that. But if the critic has knowledge of the experience only in the text or utterance itself, is he not back where he started, with the 'style' he set out to assess?

Warburg would presumably reply—No, because the language of the utterance is not all 'style'. He would have to argue, I think, that the denotative level of the text conveys to us what the experience 'is', and that we recognize varying degrees of appropriateness in the connotative symbolization. Some such idea seems to underlie his comment on *Finnegans Wake*: 'in cases of this kind—like Joyce's, it may be hard—certainly at first—to make an assessment of the style, to decide whether or not it is conveying the experience it is intended to convey in the most efficient way; simply because we cannot be sure that we have understood the experience'.[5] But, as I have just argued, we cannot assume in *poetics* that there is a denotative level of language at which meaning is embodied prior to the expressive activity of the writer.

It seems to me that Warburg is circling round a profound paradox at the heart of literary language, without ever quite recognizing it. The paradox—inherent in Cameron's argument—is that the imaginative writer creates what he describes. It follows from this that every imaginative utterance is an 'appropriate' symbolization of the experience it conveys, since there is no possible alternative symbolization of 'the same' experience.

The confusion in Warburg's argument can be traced back to his initial proposition that we know the meaning of an utterance by no other way than by the way it is said. This proposition is true as applied to *literary* utterances, but not as applied to non-literary utterances. (We may be assisted in understanding an utterance like 'It's raining' by physical evidence of rain.) It is, however, *non*-literary utterance which Warburg takes as the model for his investigation of style. For it is only in relation to non-literary discourse that we can legitimately think of an experience as existing independently of some more or less appropriate symbolization of it.

Yet it is easy to see how we slip into the habit of thinking about literary discourse in the same way. The words used by the writer are meaningful only in so far as we connect them with the 'real' world of experience from which they acquire their meaning. We have all, as readers, experienced the 'thrill of recognition'. If, in assessing literary texts, we are not assessing the appropriateness of symbolization to experience, what *are* we assessing?

I think we can only answer that question by saying that we are measuring *realization*, by which I mean, the art which exploits the resources of language in such a way that words 'become' what in non-literary discourse they merely represent. A number of critics have formulated this idea in different ways. A. N. Whitehead said that 'The art of literature, vocal or written, is to adjust the language so that it embodies what it indicates.'[6] W. K. Wimsatt uses the analogy of the icon: the devices of literary language '*present* the things which language is otherwise occupied in designating'.[7] Winifred Nowottny has put it this way:

> The great and amazing peculiarity of poetic language is its power to bridge or seem to bridge the gap between what has meaning but no particularity (that is, ordinary language) and what has particularity but no meaning (that is, the reality language is 'about').[8]

Since, as Cameron points out, literary discourse has the appearance of description though it is not true description, we naturally tend to think of the writer's use of language in terms of appropriate choice. But we must recognize the limited scope of this concept. Clearly, the writer's practice of his art can be described as a process of choosing certain verbal formulations in preference to others. But whereas in non-literary description, choice is limited by what is there to be described, the writer's choice is strictly speaking, unlimited.* If I wish to describe an actual person, Mr Brown, I might be able to choose between calling him *tall* or *big*, *dark* or *swarthy*, and this would be stylistic choice in Warburg's sense. But I could never 'choose' between calling him *tall* or *short*, *dark* or *fair*. If he is a character in a novel,

---

* A linguist might object, here, that it is only in *lexis* that the writer's choice is unlimited, since grammar is a system of closed choices (e.g. in respect of number we can only choose between singular and plural). In talking about literary language, however, we are necessarily talking about units of particularized meaning, and hence about combinations of lexis *and* grammar. One cannot conceive of a literary work that was all grammar and no lexis.

however, I can choose to describe him as tall and fair, or short and dark, or short and fair, or tall and dark. I can also call him Mr Green or Mr Grey or by any other name. I could conceivably call him all these things for a special literary effect: *Mr Brown, or Green as he was sometimes called, was short, but tall with it. His fair-complexioned face was swarthy. As one of his friends remarked, 'Grey is a difficult man to pin down.'*

This freedom of choice makes the writer's task not less but more difficult than that of ordinary descriptive writing. Everything becomes choice, and nothing determines his choice but his sense of the aesthetic logic and aesthetic possibilities of his literary structure. As Richard M. Ohmann puts it:

> The stream of experience is the background against which 'choice' is a meaningful concept, in terms of which the phrase '*way of saying it*' makes sense, though 'it' is no longer a variable. Form and content are truly separate if 'content' is not bodiless ideas, but the formless world-stuff.[9]

Thus, when we say that a certain literary description is 'inappropriate' we can only mean that it fails to satisfy the expectations aroused by the literary structure of which it is a part. Similarly with choice: our sense of the 'rightness' of any particular literary description may be accompanied by our sense of other, weaker possible or actual descriptions within roughly the same area of reference. But we are not, in this case, discriminating between various descriptions of the 'same' thing, but recognizing that the thing offered is more moving, interesting, beautiful, etc., than other similar things. In critical reading we often find that a literary description is unsuccessful, and we may express this by saying that the 'wrong' choice of words has been made. But we do not feel obliged to say what the 'right' choice of words would have been. To do so would involve writing another, different text—it would be an act of creation, not of criticism.

In short, what I am suggesting is that in literary discourse, the writer discovers what he has to say in the process of saying it,*

---

* Since writing this I have come across the following remark by Mary McCarthy: 'I learn what I want to say in the course of saying it. I think this must be true of most fiction-writers.' 'Letter to a Translator about *The Group*', *Encounter* XXIII (Nov. 1964), p. 76. This 'letter' is an interesting, and rather rare case of detailed analysis of verbal effects carried out by a practising writer on her own work.

and the reader discovers what is said in responding to the way it is said. In the reading of literature, therefore, the expressive, the cognitive, and the affective are inextricably mingled. The writer expresses what he knows by affecting the reader; the reader knows what is expressed by being receptive to affects. The medium of this process is language. Language—the particular selection and arrangement of words of which a work of literature is composed—is the only objective and fixed *datum*. The expressive origin of the work, and its affective consequences, exist, but the former is irrecoverable, and the latter variable. From this I conclude that, while a literary structure has an objective existence which can be objectively (or 'scientifically') described, such a description has little value in literary criticism until it is related to a process of human communication which is not amenable to objective description. The language of the novel, therefore, will be most satisfactorily and completely studied by the methods, not of linguistics or stylistics (though these disciplines can make valuable contributions), but of literary criticism, which seeks to define the meaning and value of literary artefacts by relating subjective response to objective text, always pursuing exhaustiveness of explication and unanimity of judgment, but conscious that these goals are unattainable.

F. R. LEAVIS AND THE MORAL DIMENSION OF FICTION

I have a suspicion that many readers may feel at this point that I have reached, by a long and tortuous route, the position occupied for thirty years by Dr Leavis and the critics associated with him. And, indeed, since putting forward the idea of 'realization', above, I have been reminded that the same term has an important place in an essay, 'Education and the University (III): Literary Studies'[1] where Dr Leavis comes unusually near to stating his critical principles. That essay, however, draws its illustrations exclusively from poetry and poetic drama; and it seems to me that the critical movement associated with the name of Leavis has, despite its slogan 'The novel as dramatic poem', shared the tendency of most modern criticism to accord the language of the novel less importance than the language of poetry.

Dr Leavis has two distinct 'images' as a critic: he is the critic of close analysis, of 'the words on the page'; and he is the 'moral' critic *par excellence*, insisting on the responsibility of literature to be 'on the side of life'. These two images are not irreconcilable—and both can be traced to some extent in everything Leavis has written. But is it not true that we think principally of his work on poetry in connection with the first image, and of his work on the novel in connection with the second? Poets (Milton for instance) are assessed according to their awareness of the possibilities of language;[2] novelists according to their awareness of 'the possibilities of life'.[3] Of course, the novelists in the Great Tradition are 'all very much concerned with "form" '.[4] But their essential claim to greatness is that 'they are all distinguished by a vital capacity for experience, a kind of reverent openness before life, and a marked moral intensity'.[5] Flaubert is held up as an example of a writer whose excessive concern with form and style betrays a damning 'attitude to life'.[6]

This shift in emphasis in the criticism of Leavis from 'concreteness' and 'realisation' in poetry, to 'life' and 'moral intensity' in fiction, can be traced back to Mrs Leavis's *Fiction and the Reading Public* (1932), where she explicitly confronts the problem of how far the new methods of close verbal analysis developed in criticism of poetry are applicable to prose fiction:

> In so far as a novel, like a poem, is made of words, much of what Mr Richards says of poetry can be adapted to apply to the novel, but even so the critic does not get much help, for there is an important difference between the way a novel and a poem takes effect.[7]

She goes on to illustrate this difference by referring to what I have called the Argument from Translation and the Argument from Bad Writing.[8] Her intention is to state the nature of the problems rather than to discourage the study of the language of the novel, but her conclusion is significantly equivocal:

> The essential technique in an art that works by using words is the way in which words are used, and a method is only justified by the use that is made of it; a bad novel is ultimately seen to fail not because of its method but owing to a fatal inferiority in the author's make-up.[9]

This sentence illustrates in microcosm the shift of emphasis I have been discussing. The semi-colon marks a momentous conceptual leap, from a position where we seem to be concerned with the novel as verbal art, to one where the novel seems to be an expression of a more or less satisfactory capacity for life. On the basis of the first half of the sentence we could claim major status for Joyce; on the basis of the second half we could (as, of course, has been done) dismiss such a claim. Perhaps the real shift, however, lies concealed between the words 'used' and 'use'; 'the way words are used' invokes the idea of the work of art as autotelic, whereas 'the use that is made of it' seems to refer to the interaction of life and literature.

We are dealing here with great 'delicacy' of meaning. The issue, as I see it, is whether the critic concerns himself with the verbal structure of works of literature ('technique', 'method') and leaves his conclusions to reflect by implication upon the writer's moral awareness, quality of life, etc.; or whether he takes the method and technique as something through which he discerns the writer's moral awareness, quality of life, etc., which is taken to be the essential basis of assessment. There is only a difference of emphasis between the two approaches, but it is an important difference. It would be absurd to deny that moral values come into play in the study of literature; and they do so more readily, perhaps, in the novel than in any of the other genres. But the objection to putting terms like 'moral intensity' or 'reverent openness before life' at the very centre of critical judgment, is that they are not really *literary* concepts, but ethical ones. They become literary concepts, of course, in being applied to particular works or (more characteristically) to particular authors; and where there is general agreement about the appropriateness of such application, the critical results can be most fruitful. But when there is disagreement about valuations of this kind, debate tends to shift rapidly from art to life,* and to terminate in opposing testimonies to the nature of the good life.

Perhaps I can summarize the extent to which I dissent from the

* It is interesting, and a little ironical, that the popular commercial novelists questioned by Mrs Leavis, and quoted in her book, defended themselves by an appeal to 'life'. E.g., 'Even if many of them [best-sellers] are not works of art, they are on the whole (except the very bad ones) closer to the fundamentals of life and of romance than much of the cleverer stuff that springs mainly from the brain and so fails to reach the *heart*'; 'Technique is not one of the living qualities and the novel is primarily concerned with *life*. The core quality of the born novelist is human, not literary.' (*Op. cit.* p. 68.)

principles of this criticism by suggesting an emendation of a very characteristic statement of Dr Leavis's:

> when we examine the formal perfection of *Emma*, we find that it can be appreciated only in terms of the moral preoccupations that characterize the novelist's peculiar interest in life.[10]

I should prefer to say (it is not quite the same thing):

> when we examine the moral preoccupations that characterize Jane Austen's peculiar interest in life as manifested in *Emma*, we find that they can be appreciated only in terms of the formal perfection of the novel.

Literary artists and literary critics must, no doubt, have some kind of understanding of the moral life, and both the practice and study of literature certainly cultivate and extend such understanding. But there are many other, non-literary ways of acquiring and manifesting moral insights, while in literature they are of no account if they are not effectively communicated. In the last analysis, literary critics can claim special authority not as witnesses to the moral value of works of literature, but as explicators and judges of effective communication, of 'realization'.

This does not mean that critics can or should refrain from discussing the moral dimension of novels in the course of reaching a literary evaluation. But their criteria of moral health must be controlled and modified by the aesthetic experience. One takes the point of Dr Leavis's ironic epigraph (from Robert Graves's *Goodbye To All That*) to *The Common Pursuit*—

> At the end of my first term's work I attended the usual college board to give an account of myself. The spokesman coughed and said a little stiffly: 'I understand, Mr Graves, that the essays you write for your English tutor are, shall I say, a trifle temperamental. It appears indeed that you prefer some authors to others'

—but the fact is that our moral preferences are infinitely more elastic in literature than in life. Many readers, that is, find it possible to enjoy both Fielding *and* Richardson, both Jane Austen *and* Charlotte Brontë, though these pairs display radically conflicting moral perspectives.

According to Wayne Booth, '[T]he implied author of each novel is someone with whose beliefs on all subjects I must largely agree if I am going to enjoy his work.'[11] But by the term '*implied* author' Booth distinguishes the creating minds which speak to us in every word of, for example, *Tom Jones* and *Clarissa*, from the historic individuals Henry Fielding and Samuel Richardson. We can agree with both the former, but not with both the latter (they certainly couldn't agree with each other).

In reading *Tom Jones* or *Clarissa* or any other novel, we enter a unique linguistic universe; we learn a new language designed to carry a particular view of experience. (This explains why, in general, our reading-speed accelerates as we progress through a novel, without any adverse effect on the depth of our understanding.) If this language has its own internal logic and beauty, if it can consistently bring off the feat of realization, we adopt it, and give our assent to the beliefs of the implied author, for the duration of the reading experience.* But if this language is characterized by confusion, contradiction, internal inconsistencies and expectations unfulfilled, we will not adopt it, even temporarily, nor the view of experience it carries, however worthy and sincere the latter may be. All writers necessarily say what they say at the expense of not saying what they do not say, but only the unsatisfactory writer reminds us of this.

* By 'the reading experience' I mean the sustained effort of critical understanding focused on a particular text, which usually continues long after we have 'finished' it. Even after this process is concluded, or abandoned, a book does not, of course, cease to affect us. But its affects will mingle with and be modified by the affects of all the other books we have read and of other kinds of experience; and our assent to the beliefs of the implied author, if it survives at all, will be less complete than when we were reading him.

III

CONCLUSIONS: PRINCIPLES

No definition of 'excellent poem' has ever been achieved in a merely neutral, scientifically measurable predicate. Value is not translatable into neutrality. If value resides in the whole, then analysis must tend towards neutrality.

Nevertheless, our intuition of any complex whole will be improved by analysis.[1]

THIS quotation comes from an essay, 'Explication as Criticism' in which W. K. Wimsatt considers how far evaluation and explication are integrally related activities. In the course of it he suggests that critical vocabulary can be classified in three categories:

at one extreme the terms of most general positive and negative valuing (of which 'good poem' or 'excellent poem' may be taken as the centre and type), at the other extreme the numerous neutral or nearly neutral terms of more or less technical description (*verse, rhyme, spondee, drama, narrative*) and along with these the whole vocabulary of referential content (*love, war, life* and *death*), and then in between those extremes the numerous and varied terms of special valuation—*dreary, determined, careful, precise, strong, simple*—terms which of course assume their character of positive or negative valuing partly from the complex of more neutral terms among which they are set and partly from the flow of valuing started by more general and explicit value terms—*success, successful, genial, creative.*[2]

Wimsatt then argues that 'the effort of critical analysis and of explication is inevitably an effort to bring the two extremes of the critical scale together, the means or boosters towards this end being the intermediate terms of value. . . .'[3]

This seems to me an excellent account of the nature of critical activity. But it must be remembered that Wimsatt's own notion of explication is of a particularly austere kind, in which the literary work of art is deemed to be 'an object of public knowledge'[4] explicable without reference either to the writer (the 'intentional fallacy') or to the individual reader (the 'affective fallacy').

No critic who has not considered the arguments of Wimsatt and his collaborator, Monroe Beardsley, in their essays on these two 'fallacies' is, I think, to be trusted. But the limitations of such a view, which is characteristic of New Criticism in general, have I think been usefully suggested by Walter J. Ong S.J. in some of his essays in *The Barbarian Within*.[5] He points out that whereas New Criticism encourages us to think of works of literature as 'objects' (Eliot's 'monuments', Brooks's 'well-wrought urn', Wimsatt's 'icon') isolated and defined in space, it must be recognized that 'all verbalisation, including all literature, is radically a cry, a sound emitted from the interior of a person'[6]

> once we have granted to the work of art the kind of autonomy which the artistic situation demands, once we have decided to allow it to slough its irrelevancies, which would dissipate its own objective being in the confusion of personal issues out of which it perhaps arose, a further question presents itself: Is it not in the last analysis cruel to face a human being with merely an object as such, a being which is less than a person? As soon as contemplation enters beyond a certain stage of awareness, is not the human being going to be unsatisfied if he cannot find another, a person, a *you*, in whatever it is he is concerned with?[7]

Ong does not see the 'objective' and 'personalist' approaches to literature as irreconcilable. For literary art does strive to detach itself from its creative sources, and sets between author and reader 'barriers' such as the dramatic mask:

> All communication takes place across barriers. . . . Provided that communication is going on, the interposition of further barriers has a tantalising effect. It teases us to more vigorous attempts, sharper alertness, greater efforts at compassion or sympathy.[8]

But recognizing the 'personal utterance' aspect of literature also involves recognizing the paradoxical nature of critical activity, which inevitably does violence to that which it seeks to serve:

> The 'art object', literary or other, precisely in so far as it is an 'object', invites being treated with words. For, in spite of everything, words are more intelligible, more alive, and in this sense more real than what we perceive in space, even analogously. We use words to process, understand and assimilate spatial conceptions. We learn *from* sight, but we think *in* words, mental and vocal. We explain diagrams *in* words. The art 'object', in so far as it is an object, with at least an oblique spatial reference, and not a word, has somehow divorced itself from the flow of conversation and understanding in which human life moves. It must be returned to this flow, related somehow to the continuum of actuality, that is to say, to what concrete, existent persons are actually saying and thinking. Undertaking to talk about the art object, the critic undertakes to effect this relationship or reintegration. But in doing so, he must somehow violate the work of art in its effort to subsist alone. For by talking about it he advertises the fact that it does not really and wholly and entirely exist alone.[9]

Literary criticism will, I think, best perform its task by striking a balance between the approaches represented by Wimsatt and Ong respectively. The exact weight given to either approach will, however, be conditioned by the particular critical context. In the criticism of the novel, it seems to me, we need to compensate on the side of Wimsatt rather than of Ong. For the activity of returning the work of art to 'the continuum of actuality' is made treacherously easy in the novel, whose formal conventions themselves seek the illusion of continuity with life.

If Ong is right, the 'affective fallacy' is, strictly speaking, unavoidable; but he is far from advocating a totally subjective response to literature. The subjective, or affective, element in reading can only *become* criticism, can only become part of a meaningful dialogue between readers and writers, when it is controlled by a demonstrated relationship with the objective text —in other words, by what Wimsatt calls explication. But there are special difficulties in the explication of narrative prose.

The basic descriptive terms of novel-criticism—*plot, character, background*—are, as long as they are kept in Wimsatt's basement of descriptive neutrality, much less precise than the basic descriptive terms of, for instance, lyric poetry—*sonnet, ode, iambic, simile*, etc. 'The central character of *Mansfield Park* is Fanny Price, who is involved in a plot concerning marriage against the background of the life of the English landed gentry in the early nineteenth century' does not take us very far. In novel criticism, the usual way of making these terms more precise is to describe in more detail the character of Fanny, the nature of the events in which she is involved, etc., in other words, to summarize and paraphrase. But as soon as we do this we are likely to exchange the language of formal description for the language of moral preference: instead of the delicate mediation between neutral analysis and general evaluation recommended by Wimsatt, we get a kind of rapid escalation from the former to the latter. The nature of the difficulty has been forcefully stated by C. H. Rickword, one of the first modern critics to insist on the importance of language in the novel:

> 'character' is merely the term by which the reader alludes to the pseudo-objective image he composes of his responses to an author's verbal arrangements. Unfortunately, that image once composed, it can be criticized from many irrelevant angles—its moral, political, social, or religious significance considered, all as though it possessed actual objectivity, was a figure of the inferior realm of real life.[10]

If only the issue were as simple as that! Of course, these 'angles' are not necessarily as irrelevant as Rickword alleges. They do, however, give enormous room to irrelevancy; and the best way to avoid the latter is, in my opinion, to go deeper than the basic descriptive terms, such as 'character' and 'plot', and to examine the 'verbal arrangements' in which these are created.

Such a procedure is most likely to encounter objections on the grounds that it distorts the function of 'plot' in the novel—plot being something that transcends or is otherwise separable from language. In this connection one thinks first of the efforts of the Chicago school of critics, notably R. S. Crane, to refine and develop the concepts of Aristotle's *Poetics* into a fully comprehensive critical system in which, not surprisingly, *plot* has a primary importance. In his essay 'The Concept of Plot and the Plot of *Tom Jones*'[11] Crane offers the following definition of plot:

> [T]he plot of any novel or drama is the particular temporal synthesis effected by the writer of the elements of action, character

and thought that constitute the matter of his invention. It is impossible, therefore, to state adequately what any plot is unless we include in our formula all three of the elements or causes of which the plot is the synthesis; and it follows also that plots will differ in structure according as one or another of the three causal ingredients is employed as the synthesizing principle. There are, thus, plots of action, plots of character, and plots of thought. In the first, the synthesizing principle is a completed change, gradual or sudden, in the situation of the protagonist, determined and effected by character and thought (as in *Oedipus* and *The Brothers Karamazov*); in the second, the principle is a completed process of change in the moral character of the protagonist, precipitated or molded by action, and made manifest both in it and in thought and feeling (as in James's *The Portrait of a Lady*); in the third, the principle is a completed process of change in the thought of the protagonist and consequently in his feelings, conditioned and directed by character and action (as in Pater's *Marius the Epicurean*).[12]

This scheme is not without its attractions, but its very neatness, its mathematical symmetry, should put us on our guard. The chain of deductive reasoning—'therefore . . . it follows . . . thus . . .'—is persuasive only as long as we grant the autonomous existence of Crane's 'elements'. But there cannot be action without characters to perform it; there cannot be thought without characters to think it; and there cannot be characters who do not both act and think. In talking of plots of action, plots of character, and plots of thought, Crane is classifying novels according to the kind of human interests they derive from and evoke. This is a perfectly valid and useful procedure, but the 'synthesizing principle' of all literary structures is language: all plots are plots of language. Crane seems to acknowledge this when he says:

> [T]he positive excellence [of a good plot] depends upon the power of its peculiar synthesis of character, action and thought, *as inferable from the sequence of words*, to move our feelings powerfully and pleasurably in a certain definite way.[13] (*My italics.*)

But Crane and his associates tend to regard language or 'diction' (to use the Aristotelian term) as merely one of the elements or 'parts' of a literary work, rather than as the all-inclusive medium or synthesizing principle. They follow Aristotle in regarding the achievement of a good plot as in a sense prior to the verbal articulation of it:

[T]here can be no good tragedy without a good plot, since it is upon the plot that the tragic 'power' most completely depends; but there can be effective tragedies with relatively poor character (in Aristotle's sense of character as a part), relatively undistinguished thought and relatively mediocre diction. . . .[14]

This is the point at which the Aristotelian view most sharply challenges my own position. Does not Crane's brilliant analysis of the plot of *Tom Jones* (as a plot of action), it might be argued, point to the mere invention and arrangement of events (in an order that is logical, symmetrical, and calculated to hold our fears and hopes for the hero in agreeable suspense) as a source of aesthetic pleasure? And is not such invention and arrangement an act which precedes the actual process of composition? To which questions, Crane himself has given a good answer:

what has just been outlined as the 'plot' is obviously something from which, *if we had never read the work itself*, we could hardly predict with any assurance how Fielding's masterpiece, as composed for readers in a particularized sequence of words, paragraphs, chapters and books, would be likely to affect our opinions and feelings.[15] (*My italics.*)

Or, to put it another way, if Fielding, supposing that he worked out the scheme of events in *Tom Jones* in detail before setting pen to paper, had transmitted it to another writer who wrote a novel which faithfully followed the scheme, this would not have been the novel we know as *Tom Jones*, nor, necessarily, a good novel.

A rather different kind of critic, Marvin Mudrick, has argued, in an essay I have cited earlier, that character and event are formal properties of prose fiction which may be considered and evaluated independently of the particular words in which they are formulated. His viewpoint is clearly illustrated by his comments on Henry James's *The Portrait of a Lady*. He claims that all James's skill in the manipulation of language is not enough to repair a basic flaw in the design of the novel that is pre- or non-linguistic, namely, that James fails to present the process of Isobel Archer's disillusionment in her marriage to Gilbert Osmond, jumping from the heroine's decision to marry to her completely disillusioned state of mind years later. This hiatus in the presented action is, according to Mudrick, an evasion of the novelist's responsibility.

It is not that James has altogether forgotten his responsibility: soon after, he devotes a passage to the heroine's thoughts, in which we are offered some elaborately developed metaphors—a distant figure at an unreachable window, a serpent in a bank of flowers— to make up for the missing events. But the procedures of poetry will not necessarily work for fiction. And we are led, by this evasion of responsibility, to re-examine the characters who come to us by way of these metaphors, as well as by way of the events that preceded: a type of heroine, a type of blackguard, a type of gentle hero, a type of soiled woman—all of them unfolding their not very complicated natures, at enormous length, in conversation and conduct the high-minded subtlety of whose language often implies distinctions of a subtlety to be found nowhere in the text, and is liable to suggest an enervated triviality of human resources.[16]

Granting, for the sake of argument, that *The Portrait of a Lady* is an unsatisfactory novel, I think we may interpret the above comment as a confirmation, rather than a denial of the importance of language in the art of fiction. On the evidence of Mudrick's remarks it is clear that his dissatisfaction became distinct with his rejection of the superficially 'fine' but, as he found them, hollow and decorative metaphors with which James seeks to define Isobel's experiences in marriage: in other words, it was in the first place a response to language. And this response evidently crystallized certain doubts which had been held, as it were, in suspension, through the reading of the earlier part of the novel, doubts about the characters and events of the novel which also originated in responses to language. If the characterization and motivation of the novel are as false, through and through, as Mudrick alleges, then the inclusion of the 'missing events' in the presented action of the novel would not have rescued it from failure.

Confusion about the novelist's art is likely to persist as long as we think of his use of language (or 'style') as a skill that can be distinguished from, and on occasion weighed against, his ability to create characters and actions. Such skill can only be demonstrated and assessed when the language is 'about' something. To handle words is necessarily to handle meanings; and in the case of fiction we summarize such meanings in such concepts as 'plot' and 'character'.

Why then, it might be argued, should we not regard the process as one of meanings determining language, rather than language determining meanings—why not put the emphasis on the novelist's ability to extract meaning from experience?

It is true that the successful writing of fiction depends on the novelist's prior possession of certain 'gifts' or faculties, such as: precise visual and aural recall, ability to project hypothetical events and their consequences, perception of the representative and expressive possibilities of what is observed in human behaviour or the natural world, honest introspection, curiosity, wisdom, intelligence, a sense of humour . . . one could go on adding to the list. And though it would be false to hold that these faculties operate independently of language (since they are forms of consciousness which depend upon verbal concepts) it could be said that their operation is *up to a certain point* independent of 'art-language'—the concretely particularized, deliberately ordered language of imaginative literature. But it is only of what is produced beyond this point that we, as readers and critics, can have anything to say.

If a writer tells us about the 'great idea' he has for a novel, we can only wait hopefully for the completed work to say whether his confidence was justified. If he tells us enough to excite our own confidence, he will already have begun the process of forcing his vaguely defined *donnée* into a fully articulate form, in which process he makes its meaning and value clear not only to us but to himself. Henry James (whose notebooks provide vivid illustrations of this process) has commented acutely on the question under discussion here:

> This sense of the story being the idea, the starting-point of the novel, is the only one that I see in which it can be spoken of as something different from the organic whole; and since in proportion as the work is successful the idea permeates and penetrates it, informs and animates it, so that every word and every punctuation-point contribute directly to the expression, in that proportion do we lose our sense of the story being a blade which may be drawn more or less out of its sheath.[17]

It is natural that we should want to give credit to, for instance, Mr William Golding for conceiving the basic 'idea' of *The Lord of the Flies*; but a moment's reflection will convince us that this idea was not bound to burgeon into a successful novel. Whenever we praise a novelist for his 'idea' or 'story', or for more local manifestations of his gifts—his observation of a certain trait in human behaviour, or his contrivance of an unexpected but convincing turn of events—we are summarizing the complex satisfaction we derived from these things in their fully articulate form. All good criticism therefore is necessarily a response to the creative use of language, whether it is talking explicitly of 'plot' or 'character' or any other of the categories of narrative literature. These terms are useful—indeed essential—but the closer we get to defining the unique identity and interest of *this* plot, of *that* character, the closer we are brought to a consideration of the language in which we encounter these things.

CONCLUSIONS: METHODS

All novel-criticism is carried out in the teeth of methodological difficulties, which seem to press particularly hard on criticism concerned with the language of the novel. I refer to the fact, first explicitly formulated, perhaps, by Percy Lubbock,[1] that novels are such vast and complicated structures, and our experience of them is so extended in time, that it is impossible for the human mind to conceive of a novel as a whole without blurring or forgetting the parts through the accumulation of which this totality has been conveyed. In fact, I doubt whether this problem is *peculiar* to the novel. It must surely be true of epic poetry, and I suspect that even in the case of, for instance, a Shakespearian sonnet, we have only an *illusion* of an instantaneous comprehension of its complex functioning, an illusion which is dispelled by the very next reading in which we discover something new.

However, the possibility of this illusion does indicate a difference in the degree of difficulty which the novel-critic concerned with language must recognize. He is compelled to select more drastically than the critic of poetry, and the alternative procedures open to him are (1) to isolate, deliberately or at random, one or more passages, and submit them to close and exhaustive analysis, or (2) to trace significant threads through the language of an entire novel. One might label these approaches 'textural' and 'structural' respectively.

The textural approach is enormously valuable as a teaching exercise, and can often yield up very valuable critical insights. Its limitations are obvious: the meaning of any passage in a novel is largely determined by its immediate and total contexts. For this reason, textural criticism probably works most successfully on the beginnings of novels,* which by definition are not determined by anything which precedes them. It does not follow, however, that beginnings are not conditioned by what follows them, for many of our responses to the opening of a novel are, so to speak, held in suspension until the expectations they arouse are met in one way or another later in the work. And, in any case, the beginnings of novels pose the writer with special problems which he solves in special ways. Thus the opening of a novel can never be wholly representative of a novelist's art.

The structural approach has the obvious attraction that it tries to discuss the work as a whole, with a beginning, a middle, and an end. By tracing a linguistic thread or threads—a cluster of images, or value-words, or grammatical constructions—through a whole novel, we produce a kind of spatial diagram of the accumulative and temporally-extended reading experience. The structural approach, too, takes into account the fact that, in the novel, organic unity of form is not incompatible with great local variation of tone and verbal intensity. The danger of the structural approach is, of course, that of misrepresentation: one is not really dealing with 'the whole work', but taking a certain path through it. The value of the criticism depends entirely upon whether it is a useful path, which conforms to the overall shape of the terrain, and affords the best view of it on all sides. We must beware, in fact, of not seeing the wood for the oaks, or the larches, or the chestnuts. The obverse of Leavis's remark, 'in literature . . . nothing can be proved', is that in literature anything can be 'proved'. It is fatally easy to twist and squeeze a literary text to fit the mould of one's own 'interpretation'.

In the studies that follow, I have relied principally on the 'structural' approach; and where I have submitted a passage from a novel to close analysis I have been concerned chiefly to explicate it by reference to the linguistic character of the whole. While recognizing that some of my readings may be open to the kind of objection alluded to at the end of the preceding paragraph, I think that all criticism takes similar risks; and that if

* E.g. Ian Watt's article on 'The First Paragraph of *The Ambassadors*', *Essays in Criticism*, X (1960), pp. 250–74.

my approach is more than usually risky, it is also committed to being more than usually explicit about its evidence, so that, even if misguided, it should provide a basis for fruitful debate.

Because, however, the principal danger of the 'structural' approach is that it may misrepresent or distort the subtle and complex life of a text as experienced by a reader, it seems to me essential that it should be applied intuitively, in the reading experience. That is, one should not begin a novel with the intention of paying special attention to, for instance, patterns of imagery, because imagery may not be, in this particular case, an especially significant linguistic element, or—more probably—its significance may be best appreciated in the light of some other linguistic feature which is more important and illuminating.

Reading a novel critically is a very delicate and complicated activity. One begins it with an open mind, but one hopes to finish it with a mind which is at least provisionally closed— closed, that is, upon an articulate sense of its meaning and value. While reading one is both involved and detached: involved in the stream of 'life' presented by the novelist, yet able simultaneously to stand back from it and perceive how it acquires its solidity, concreteness, interest, power to move, from certain verbal configurations, from the way it is communicated. One seeks all the time to define what kind of novel it is, and how successful it is, and often one does so against the background of critical opinion already gathered around the text, or of one's own previous readings. Constantly one makes notes (which may be mental or written) about local detail: *this* is significant or irrelevant—*this* works or doesn't work—*this* connects with or contradicts *that*. Such notes are necessarily provisional, particularly in the early stages, for further acquaintance with the text may lead us to revise our criteria of significance and relevance. The novel unfolds in our memories like a piece of cloth woven upon a loom, and the more complicated the pattern the more difficult and protracted will be the process of perceiving it. But that is what we seek, the pattern: some significantly recurring thread which, however deeply hidden in the dense texture and brilliance of local colouring, accounts for our impression of a unique identity in the whole.

It is my own experience that the moment of perceiving the pattern is sudden and unexpected. All the time one has been making the tiny provisional notes, measuring each against one's developing awareness of the whole, storing them up in the blind hope that they will prove useful, and then suddenly one such small local observation sends a shock like an electric charge through all the discrete observations heaped up on all sides, so that with an exciting clatter and rattle they fly about and arrange themselves in a certain meaningful order. If this account seems too metaphorical, let me borrow the plainer words of René Wellek:

> In reading with a sense for continuity, for contextual coherence, for wholeness, there comes a moment when we feel that we have 'understood', that we have seized on the right interpretation, the real meaning. It is a process that . . . proceeds from attention to a detail to an anticipation of the whole and back again to an interpretation of the detail.[2]

Wellek is alluding particularly to Spitzer in this passage, and it is unnecessary to labour the parallels or recapitulate the differences between the method I have just described and Spitzer's 'philological circle', which was discussed earlier. Another critic who has described a not dissimilar method is Kenneth Burke. In his *The Philosophy of Literary Form* he recommends following 'leads' and 'cues' and watching for 'critical points' in order to formulate the 'equational structure' of a literary work.[3]

> By inspection of the work, you propose your description of this equational structure. Your propositions are open to discussion, as you offer your evidence for them and show how much of the plot's development your description would account for. 'Closer approximations' are possible, accounting for more. The method, in brief, can be built upon, in contrast with essentializing strategies of motivation that all begin anew.
> The general approach to the poem might be called 'pragmatic' in this sense: It assumes that a poem's structure is to be described most accurately by thinking always of the poem's function. It assumes that the poem is designed to 'do something' for the poet and his readers, and that we can make the most relevant observations about its design by considering the poem as the embodiment of this act.[4]

Abstract discussions of methodology will take us only so far. Ultimately, critical methods are characterized and justified by their practical application; and the diversity of the practical criticism of Wellek, Spitzer, and Burke sufficiently illustrates that the method I have described is neither inflexible nor predictable in its results.

REPETITION

It will be clear from the preceding pages that, in my own view, the perception of repetition is the first step towards offering an account of the way language works in extended literary texts, such as novels. The use of such evidence in literary criticism is, however, open to certain objections which I should like to try and anticipate by the following propositions.

Firstly, the significance of repetition in a given text is not conditional on its being a deliberate and conscious device on the author's part.

It is not quite sufficient to defend this proposition by a simple gesture towards the intentional fallacy. While acknowledging that criticism deals only with intentions discoverable in the work itself, we must also recognize that, on the linguistic level, some works declare their intentions more overtly than others, and that this must affect the nature of the work and our response to it. The key-words of Joseph Conrad's novels and stories, for instance—*darkness* in *Heart of Darkness*, *youth* in *Youth*, *silver* and *material interests* in *Nostromo*, for example—are kept reverberating in our ears by conscious contrivance. Conrad has in fact given us a clue to his method through the fictitious narrator of *Under Western Eyes*:

> The task is not in truth the writing in the narrative form a précis of a strange human document, but the rendering—I perceive it now clearly—of the moral conditions ruling over a large portion of the earth's surface;* conditions not easily to be understood, much less discovered in the limits of a story, till some key-word is found; a word that could stand at the back of all the words covering the pages, a word which, if not truth itself, may perchance hold truth enough to help the moral discovery which should be the object of every tale.†[1]

But with another kind of writer—Charlotte Brontë for example, one suspects that the reiteration of certain symbols or motifs was

* I.e. Russia.
† In *Under Western Eyes* the key-word is *cynicism*—a somewhat surprising one, which no doubt explains why Conrad calls attention to it so explicitly.

an intuitive or compulsive process driven by the emotional pressures behind the writing. This is not to suggest that Charlotte Brontë poured out her work in a kind of inspired trance. Mrs Gaskell tells us that

> One set of words was the truthful mirror of her thoughts; no others, however apparently identical in meaning, would do. . . . She would wait patiently, searching for the right term, until it presented itself to her. It might be provincial, it might be derived from the Latin; so that it accurately represented her idea, she did not mind whence it came. . . . She never wrote down a sentence until she deeply understood what she wanted to say, had deliberately chosen the words, and had arranged them in their right order.[2]

But Charlotte Brontë herself, on one occasion, gave an account of the creative process which has a different emphasis from Mrs Gaskell's, an emphasis which is more in accord with the quality of her writing as we experience it:

> When authors write best, or, at least, when they write most fluently, an influence wakens in them, which becomes their master —which will have its own way—putting out of view all behests but its own, dictating certain words, and insisting on their being used, whether vehement or measured in their nature . . .[3]

We might speculate that while each individual reference to, say, *fire*, in *Jane Eyre*, was formulated in a way determined by conscious artistic effort, Charlotte Brontë's persistent *return* to this word and associated words, which contributes significantly to its unity and identity, was not a consciously executed manoeuvre in the manner of Conrad. My point is merely that in perceiving and pointing out significant patterns of repetition, we do not need to be encouraged by the approving nods of the author over our shoulders.

Secondly, the significance of repetition in a given text is not conditional on its being consciously and spontaneously recognized by a majority of intelligent readers.

A failure to appreciate this point accounts, I believe, for a good deal of the resistance offered to the kind of criticism I have been recommending. Confronted with the demonstration of a certain pattern of repetition, which they have not themselves noticed, in a familiar text, many readers feel that their own reading, or way of reading, is being radically challenged. This is not necessarily the case. If both demonstration and reading are sound, the former will consolidate and enrich the latter. Criticism of the kind I propose is an analytic procedure applied to a synthetic process—the total, accumulative effect of a work of art. Most 'lay readers', and many literary critics, choose to articulate their response to a literary text by an impressionistic description of this synthesis—a valid but chancy procedure. But any significant pattern of repetition will have contributed to this synthesis.*

* I recently encountered an interesting illustration of this in Lord David Cecil's chapter on Charlotte Brontë in *Early Victorian Novelists*. I show, in Part Two Chapter II below, the prominence of references, literal and metaphorical, to *fire* in *Jane Eyre*. Lord David approaches Charlotte Brontë's work in a very different way, and I disagree with many of his judgments, but I was struck by the fact that, without explicit quotation or allusion to the text, he persistently uses fire-imagery to convey his impressions. E.g.:

'For they [the characters] come to us through the transfiguring medium of Charlotte Brontë's volcanic imagination. Lit by its lurid glare, these prosaic schools and parsonages stand out huge, secret, momentous. These commonplace drawing-rooms glow with a strange brightness, these plain corridors are sinister with stirring shadows.' (Penguin edn. (1948) p. 103.)
'Their loves and hates and ambitions are alike fiery and insatiable.' (*Ibid.*, p. 104.)
'Childish naiveté, rigid Puritanism, fiery passion. . . . (*Ibid.*, p. 105.)
'her ingenuousness . . . disinfects her imagination; blows away the smoke and sulphur which its ardent heat might be expected to generate, so that its flame blows pure and clear.' (*Ibid.*, p. 105.)
'the fire of her personality. . . .' (*Ibid.*, p. 110.)
'at every turn of its furious course Charlotte Brontë's imagination throws off some such glinting spark of phrase. And now and again the sparks blaze up into a sustained passage of De Quinceyish prose poetry.' (*Ibid.*, p. 111.)
'their strange flame [i.e. writers like Charlotte Brontë], lit as it is at the central white hot fire of creative inspiration, will in every age find them followers.' (*Ibid.*, p. 114.)

Virginia Woolf, another impressionistic critic, also invokes 'fire' in her short essay on *Jane Eyre*:

' "I could never rest in communication with strong, discreet and refined minds," she [Charlotte] writes, as any leader-writer in a provincial journal might have written; but gathering fire and speed goes on in her own authentic voice, "till I had passed the outworks of conventional reserve and won a place by their hearts' very hearthstone." It is there that she takes her seat; it is the red and fitful glow of the heart's fire which illumines her page.' (*The Common Reader*, Penguin edn. (1938), p. 157.)

Thirdly, the significance of repetition is not to be determined statistically.

The most frequently recurring word in a given text is not necessarily the most significant word. If it were, computers could perform the initial critical task for us. Only the critical intelligence can make the continual reference between part and whole which permits discrimination between degrees of significance in the recurring linguistic elements of a literary text.

Once, however, a particular iterative feature of the text has been isolated as being especially useful to the critical under-standing of the whole, its merely numerical frequency of occur-rence will have a certain interest and relevance.*

Fourthly, repetition of any kind does not, in itself, confer value on literary texts.

To use *dark* and *darkness* and associated words as often as Conrad uses them in *Heart of Darkness* is not a formula for writing a great work of literature. Yet the insistent recurrence of this verbal cluster has much to do with the power of Conrad's story. The effectiveness of the story subsists in the relationships between the overall structural scheme and the rich textural particularity of local detail. In following the structural theme of *darkness* through the texture of the story, observing each occur-rence in its context, criticism can offer some account of that sense of unity in multiplicity which works like *Heart of Darkness* impart to their readers.[4]

To take a different kind of case: Professor David Daiches has called attention to the function of certain recurrent verbal features of Virginia Woolf's novels. (1) Her use of the third person pronoun, *one* ('it was not her one hated, but the idea of her'), as a way of indicating a certain agreement on the part of the writer with a character's thoughts.[5] (2) Her use of *for* to link different stages of association in a character's stream of conscious-ness ('To dance, to ride, she had adored all that. [New para.] For they might be parted for hundreds of years, she and Peter'), *for* being 'a word which does not indicate a strict logical sequence . . .

---

* Here a computer would be useful. But I have been obliged to use clumsier and more laborious methods, for which I do not claim 100% accuracy. Any errors, however, will not in general have assisted my argu-ments: I may have missed some occurrences of a particular linguistic element in a particular text, but I have not invented any.

but does suggest a relationship which is at least half-logical'.[6]
(3) Her persistent use of present participles of action ('Such fools, we are, she thought, crossing Victoria Street') 'to allow the author to remind the reader of the character's position, without interrupting the thought stream'.[7]

There is no doubt that these are significant expressive features of Virginia Woolf's work, or that they have the effects described by Daiches. But one could go further and make the following points: (1) The use of the pronoun *one* is a characteristic upper-middle-class speech habit which, while it appears to withdraw modestly from crude assertion, slyly invokes authority from some undefined community of feeling and prejudice, into which it seeks to draw the auditor. Has Virginia Woolf entirely resolved her own attitude to characters like Mrs Dalloway, and is she entirely open about the degree of indulgence she expects the reader to extend to them? (2) The use of *for* to suggest logical connection where none exists might reveal a certain timidity in exploring the flow of consciousness and a disposition to simplify its workings. (3) The verb-participle construction establishes a divorce between cerebration and physical action which is not as normative as Virginia Woolf's fiction implies. We do not always think of eternity while serving potatoes; sometimes we just think of serving potatoes. Virginia Woolf's characters never do.

In other words, the devices brought forward by Daiches to illustrate Virginia Woolf's expressive use of language, while they certainly help to explain how her presentation of experience gets its special character, might be used as evidence for alleging certain important limitations in her art. In this event, the very frequency of occurrence which makes these devices significant would be seen as damaging, contributing to an overall effect of monotonous sameness in the presentation of consciousnesses whose unique constitutions should be reflected in the language (as for instance in the comparable fiction of Joyce). This would be a possible line of argument,* and serves to show that the same set of linguistic facts can be used to reach quite opposite critical conclusions.

Iterative patterns are thus never in themselves, explanations of meaning or value. They may, or may not, offer useful and illuminating ways of accounting for meaning and value in literary

---

* I have stated it all provisionally because it is not to my present purpose to sustain it in detail.

texts. Whether they do so, and how they do so, will depend entirely upon the critical use that is made of them.

'Aesthetics,' William Righter has observed, 'is a reason giving activity'; and he cites Wittgenstein's observation that 'reasons in aesthetics are of the nature of further descriptions'.[8] In the last analysis, criticism claims our attention, not as sets of data nor as sets of conclusions, but as human discourse.

Part Two

INTRODUCTORY

CHAPTERS I–VI below are arranged in the chronological order of the novels with which they are principally concerned, but no treatment of the historical development of the language of prose fiction has been attempted. Nor have I made very much reference to other works by the same authors. These chapters are essentially self-contained studies of particular texts; and where I have made comparisons between them it has been with the aim of discriminating between different kinds of artistic undertaking rather than between different levels of achievement.

The novels discussed are not necessarily the 'best' or most representative work of their respective authors, but they all offer interesting and important critical problems of interpretation and evaluation. The only other principle of selection has been that mentioned in Part One ('The Modern Movement in Fiction'), namely, a felt obligation to test the proposition, 'The novelist's medium is language', mainly on novelists who do not self-evidently subscribe to it, or whose use of language does not neatly coincide with the most common assumptions about the nature of literary language.

The inclusion of the final chapter (VII) on Mr Kingsley Amis, is justified on these grounds; but it is wider in scope, and less 'academic' in manner, than the preceding chapters. It shows, I hope, that critical attention to the language novelists use is not a method of reading appropriate only to well-known texts of classic status, but one that may help criticism to perform other tasks, such as literary-historical generalization, the assessment of new writing, and the definition of an author's literary identity as manifested in a succession of books.

I make no excuse for citing other critics fairly extensively, because it is my intention to show that the study of the language of prose fiction is not an approach which runs remotely parallel to the concerns of 'literary' criticism of the novel, but one which must justify itself by engaging usefully with those concerns. In trying to find such a *via media* between methodical linguistic or stylistic analysis and the freer, more widely-ranging procedures of discursive criticism, I have veered nearer one side or the other according to the kind of problems posed by a particular text. I would ask, therefore, that the usefulness of the attempt be judged on the evidence of the following chapters considered together.

Quotations from the novels principally discussed are given chapter-references, in Roman numerals, and are taken from the following editions (date of first publication in book form is given in square brackets):

I. Jane Austen, *Mansfield Park* [1814]: *The Novels of Jane Austen,* ed. R. W. Chapman, Vol. III, 2nd edn. (Oxford, 1926). This edition preserves the original three-volume division of chapters; my references are to the continuous sequence of most modern editions, which corresponds to the original order as follows:

I–XVIII	Vol. I, i–xviii
XIX–XXXI	Vol. II, i–xiii
XXXII–XLVIII	Vol. III, i–xvii

II. Charlotte Brontë, *Jane Eyre* [1847]: the 2nd edn., in three volumes (1848). My references are to the continuous sequence of chapters of most modern editions, which corresponds to the original order as follows:

I–XV	Vol. I, i–xviii
XVI–XXVI	Vol. II, i–xi
XXVII–XXXVIII	Vol. III, i–xii

III. Charles Dickens, *Hard Times* [1854]: The New Oxford Illustrated Dickens edn. (1955).

IV. Thomas, Hardy, *Tess of the D'Urbervilles* [1891]: Wessex edn. of *The Works of Thomas Hardy*, Vol. I, 3rd impression (1920).

V. Henry James, *The Ambassadors* [1903]: Norton Critical Edition, ed. S. P. Rosenbaum (New York, 1964). I am most grateful for the opportune appearance of this definitive edition, a splendid achievement of textual scholarship. As is notorious, all editions of the novel before the Everyman edition of 1959, except the English first edition published by Methuen (1903), reverse the proper order of the chapters beginning, 'He went late that evening to the Boulevard Malesherbes . . .' and 'One of the features of the restless afternoon . . .' (chapters i and ii of Book XI in the Norton edition). Apart from this, the Norton edn. follows the text of the New York edn. (1909), which was revised by James, but records significant variations from James's earlier versions. It should be pointed out that the Everyman edn. of 1959 follows the Methuen edn. of 1903 in locating the chapter beginning, 'He went late that evening to the Boulevard Malesherbes . . .' as chapter iv of Book X, whereas the Norton edn. locates it as chapter i of Book XI. Readers using the Everyman text (which is not, incidentally, wholly reliable) will have to transpose my chapter references as follows:

Norton	*Everyman*
XI, i	X, iv
XI, ii	XI, i
XI, iii	XI, ii
XI, iv	XI, iii

No other references are affected.

VI. H. G. Wells, *Tono-Bungay* [1909]: 1st edn. (1909).

VII. Kingsley Amis, *Lucky Jim* [1954]: 22nd impression (1961).
That Uncertain Feeling [1955]: 1st edn. (1955).
I Like It Here [1958]: 4th impression (1962).
Take a Girl Like You [1960]: Penguin edn. (1962).

I

The Vocabulary of 'Mansfield Park'

I N all her novels Jane Austen is concerned with the analysis and
evaluation of character and conduct, carried out with a subtlety
and penetration which continually exercise and extend our understanding of human nature. But *Mansfield Park* stands apart from
the other novels by testing character and conduct in a way
calculated to confound at every point our instinctive moral
preferences and expectations. As Lionel Trilling has observed,
'For those who admire her it is likely to make an occasion of
embarrassment. By the same token it is the novel which the
depreciators of Jane Austen may cite most tellingly in justification
of their antagonism.'[1]

Trilling constructs a brilliant defence of *Mansfield Park*, based
on the proposition that it 'is a great novel, its greatness being
commensurate with its power to offend'.[2] What I have to say
below runs parallel at many points with Trilling's essay, but I
am not so much concerned to defend *Mansfield Park* as to explicate
it. For I believe that in most readers both embarrassment and
antagonism are overwhelmed by a sense of baffled admiration:
how, we ask ourselves, have we been persuaded to endorse a
system of values with which we have no real sympathy at all? 'I
recognise that its heroine is a little prig and its hero a pompous
ass, but I do not care,' says Mr Somerset Maugham. 'And we do
not care either,' adds Miss G. B. Stern, 'for we have been con-
tentedly spell-bound; though still at a loss to understand *why* it
has become of such passionate moment for Mr Rushworth to go

quickly and fetch the key of the iron gate over the ha-ha? Or to know which of Miss Crawford's two gold necklaces Fanny will choose to wear with William's amber cross at the ball?* Or whether Maria or Julia is to play "Agatha" in "Lovers' Vows"? Or why we wait in an agony lest Henry Crawford should accept the invitation of Fanny's father to eat his mutton with the Price family, and gasp with relief to hear him politely refuse?'[3]

Such responses may seem to reflect somewhat frivolous reading, but *Mansfield Park* is likely to puzzle more austere and academic readers in a similar way. It is difficult, for instance, to see how the novel can be fitted into a tradition characterized by being 'on the side of life'. It is surely the Prices of Portsmouth who 'have all the life'† in this novel. Yet for the heroine their existence is a kind of hell. Re-united with her family after an absence of many years, she is dismayed by the noise, dirt, muddle, physical and emotional violence of the household.

> Fanny was almost stunned. The smallness of the house, and thinness of the walls, brought everything so close to her, that, added to the fatigue of her journey, and all her recent agitation, she hardly knew how to bear it. (XXXVIII)

These first impressions harden into a firm condemnation of her home:

> William was gone;—and the home he had left her in was—Fanny could not conceal it from herself—in almost every respect the reverse of what she could have wished. It was the abode of noise, disorder, and impropriety. Nobody was in their right place, nothing was done as it ought to be. She could not respect her parents, as she had hoped. On her father, her confidence had not been sanguine, but he was more negligent of his family, his habits were worse, and his manners coarser, than she had been prepared for. . . .
> She might scruple to use the words, but she must and did feel

* There seems to be some confusion here. As Miss Crawford invites Fanny to choose from 'several' necklaces, I presume Miss Stern is referring to Fanny's later (and more interesting) choice between the necklace she accepts from Miss Crawford and the necklace given her by Edmund. (See Chapters XXVI–XXVII.)

† The phrase is of course Dr Leavis's, applied to Swift's Yahoos. (*The Common Pursuit*, Penguin edn. 1962, p. 84.) The fourth Book of *Gulliver's Travels* and *Mansfield Park* challenge the reader—particularly the modern reader—in much the same way.

that her mother was a partial, ill-judging parent, a dawdle, a slattern, who neither taught nor restrained her children. . . . (XXXIX)

According to what standards are these harsh verdicts reached? According to the standards of Mansfield. On her very first evening at Portsmouth, Fanny cannot avoid considering the manner of her reception in the light of her adopted home:

> A day or two might shew the difference. *She* only was to blame. Yet she thought it would not have been so at Mansfield. No, in her uncle's house there would have been a consideration of times and seasons, a regulation of subject, a propriety, an attention towards everybody which there was not here. (XXXVIII)

Her considered opinion is the same:

> Such was the home which was to put Mansfield out of her head, and teach her to think of her cousin Edmund with moderated feelings. On the contrary, she could think of nothing but Mansfield, its beloved inmates, its happy ways. Everything where she now was was in full contrast to it. The elegance, propriety, regularity, harmony—and perhaps, above all, the peace and tranquillity of Mansfield, were brought to her remembrance every hour of the day, by the prevalence of everything opposite to them *here*. (XXXIX)

Yet the actual human beings who inhabit the happy Eden of Mansfield Park are, *according to the novel's own system of values*, defective. The best of them, Edmund, is infatuated with a woman (Mary Crawford) who does not love or respect him. The father, Sir Thomas Bertram, is seen as entitled to respect and obedience, but is shown to be a fallible and self-deceiving parent. His wife, Lady Bertram, is a figure of comic indolence, but her comic quality does not render her immune from occasional shafts of withering irony. The other children—Tom, Maria, and Julia— misbehave in various ways, and in various degrees of gravity. Their aunt, Mrs Norris, is the epitome of selfishness, meanness and snobbery. It is this which makes the Portsmouth episode so unexpected and so challenging. Sir Thomas's ulterior motive in sending Fanny on this visit is to awaken her to the privileges of life at the social level of Mansfield Park, and thus to shock her into an awareness of the opportunity she is wasting by refusing Henry Crawford's proposal of marriage. The whole novel seems poised for a reversal, by which Sir Thomas's complacent pride in the style of life at Mansfield will be belied, and the material and social shortcomings of the impecunious Price household lost for the tender-hearted heroine in her joyful return to the spontaneous, vital, unsophisticated but innocent life of her family. That is how Dickens, for instance, would have treated the situation. But, as we have just seen, Fanny is only strengthened in her sense of belonging to Mansfield; and she even wavers in her resistance to Henry Crawford.

We are left in no doubt that Mansfield represents a more desirable order of existence than that represented by Portsmouth. In her own fashion, Jane Austen is as insistent as Mr Kingsley Amis that 'nice things are nicer than nasty things'.[4] Yet the subscription, willing or unwilling, of all members of the Mansfield Park family to a certain code of external behaviour, which is what makes Mansfield a shrine to the civilized life, is not enough to hold the family together or to make them happy. It is Fanny, the adopted outsider, who recognizes that this code must be sustained by moral passion and who thus inherits its privileges. At the end of the novel Sir Thomas realizes that 'Fanny was indeed the daughter that he wanted' (XLVIII).

Everything therefore depends on our identifying with the heroine; but Jane Austen endows her with few of the attractive and endearing qualities which the novelist is licensed to dispense to his favoured characters. Jane Austen might have written 'I am going to take a heroine whom no-one but myself will much like'[5] with far more reason of Fanny Price than of Emma Woodhouse. Fanny is almost entirely lacking in the wit, vitality, and human propensity to error which engage our sympathies for Jane Austen's other heroines. She is characterized by a humourless virtuousness, an anxious desire always to be in the right, and a censorious watchfulness over the conduct of others. She is, indeed, fully vindicated by events at the end of the story. Henry Crawford's adulterous affair with Maria, and Mary Crawford's reaction to it, prove to Sir Thomas and Edmund—the two characters in the novel whose opinions carry most weight—that Fanny's rejection of Henry Crawford, and her reservations about his sister, have been correct assessments of their characters. But these events cannot vindicate Fanny *for the reader*. She must not require vindication. We must have felt all along that Fanny was right, and feel at the end of the novel that the behaviour of the Crawfords and the Bertram girls is completely reconcilable with their characters as revealed in the main action and assessed by Fanny. Otherwise we should suspect Jane Austen of losing confidence in her moral scheme, and of seeking to re-invigorate it by a last-minute injection of spectacular sin; for she does not attempt to 'render' these scandalous goings-on at the end of the novel— they are cursorily reported and summarized.

In the greater part of the novel, however—up to Fanny's visit to Portsmouth—character is revealed in trivial actions. We are invited to make, through the consciousness of Fanny and, with qualifications, of Edmund and Sir Thomas, very serious judgments of character on the evidence of small gestures, casual remarks, and petty disagreements. The visit to Mr Rushworth's house at Sotherton provides plenty of examples: the manner in which the composition of the party, the mode of travel, the seating of the passengers, and their deployment through the estate, are determined, is pregnant with tremendous implication. But the supreme example of this feature of *Mansfield Park* is the notorious episode of the theatricals. 'I cannot understand,' says Somerset Maugham, 'why Sir Thomas Bertram should have been enraged when, on his return from overseas, he found his family amusing themselves with private theatricals.'[6] Sir Thomas is not 'enraged' —the display of passion suggested by the word would be unthinkable to him—but he does disapprove of the theatricals, as do Fanny and Edmund. Unless we understand this disapproval we shall never, perhaps, fully understand the whole novel. And here Trilling, otherwise so brilliant an interpreter of the novel, seems to falter, his anxiety to win for Jane Austen a central place in the tradition of Western literature seems to mislead him. Can we seriously ascribe to Jane Austen, 'a traditional, almost primitive feeling about dramatic impersonation . . . the fear that the impersonation of a bad or inferior character will have a harmful effect upon the impersonator; that, indeed, the impersonation of any other self will diminish the integrity of the real self'?[7] Jane Austen was neither a Platonist nor a primitive, and I find no evidence of this attitude to acting in *Mansfield Park*.

To generalize from my own first reading of the novel, I imagine many readers must find the disapproval of the theatricals entirely natural, without quite understanding why this should be so. In this respect the theatricals episode is representative of the way in which the whole novel challenges the reader on the most difficult ground the author could choose. In the rest of this essay I suggest that Jane Austen succeeds in this enterprise by schooling her readers in a vocabulary of discrimination which embraces the finest shades of social and moral value, and which asserts the prime importance, in the presented world of the novel, of exercising the faculty of judgment.

This vocabulary gets its meanings from the human behaviour to which it is applied: words like *indecorum*, *proper*, or *just*, have little meaning without a context. But the reverse is also true: human behaviour becomes intelligible by being articulated in this vocabulary. The subtle and untiring employment of this vocabulary, the exact fitting of value terms to events, the display of scrupulous and consistent discrimination, have a rhetorical effect which we cannot long resist. We pick up the habit of evaluation, and resign, for the duration of the novel at least, the luxury of neutrality.

A familiar description of Jane Austen is that she is a 'novelist of manners', but exactly what is meant by *manners* in this context is not always clear. In any context the word is a slippery one to handle. Looking through the several columns which the O.E.D. devotes to *manners*, the meanings which seem most immediately relevant to Jane Austen are, (6) 'External behaviour in social intercourse, estimated as good or bad according to its degree of politeness or of conformity to the accepted standards of propriety', and (7) 'Polite behaviour or deportment, habits indicative of good breeding'. But the meanings, (4a) 'A person's habitual behaviour or conduct, especially in references to its moral aspect; moral character, morals', and (4b) 'In a more abstract sense: Conduct in its moral aspect; also morality as a subject of study; the moral code embodied in general custom or sentiment', though they are classed as obsolete by the O.E.D., and ascribed terminal dates of 1794 and 1776 respectively, are not entirely lost in *Mansfield Park*. The novel may indeed be said to reflect a significant stage in the semantic history of the word, at which meanings (6) and (7) were becoming dominant to the exclusion of meanings (4a) and (4b). Edmund Bertram still seeks to retain the moral content of the word, as becomes clear in the scene where the meaning of *manners* is explicitly debated in a conversation between him, Fanny and Mary Crawford. They are discussing the value of the clerical calling. Mary Crawford denies that the clergy exercise any great influence over society. 'How can two sermons a week, even supposing them worth hearing, . . . do all that you speak of? govern the conduct and fashion the manners of a large congregation for the rest of the week?' Part of Edmund's reply is as follows:

'And with regard to their [the clergy's] influencing public manners, Miss Crawford must not misunderstand me, or suppose I mean to call them the arbiters of good breeding, the regulators of refinement and courtesy, the masters of the ceremonies of life. The *manners* I speak of, might rather be called *conduct*, perhaps, the result of good principles; the effect, in short, of those doctrines which it is their duty to teach and recommend'. (IX)

One of the best general definitions of *manners* has been put forward by Trilling again, in his essay 'Manners, Morals, and the Novel':

What I understand by manners, then, is a culture's buzz of implication. I mean the whole evanescent context which is made up of half-uttered or un-uttered or unutterable expressions of value. They are hinted at by small actions, sometimes by the arts of dress or decoration, sometimes by tone, gesture, emphasis, or rhythm, sometimes by the words that are used with a special frequency or a special meaning.[8]

This is a description of manners as they are embodied and apprehended in actuality. In literature, they cannot remain half-uttered or unuttered or unutterable; they have to be rendered in words, and 'the words that are used with a special frequency and a special meaning' have a particularly important function.

The relevant words in *Mansfield Park* may be divided into two classes, corresponding roughly to the two groups of meanings for *manners* cited above from the O.E.D. On the one hand an order of social or secular value is established by words like: *agreeable, appropriate, becoming, ceremony, correct, decorum, delicacy, delicate, discretion, disorder, eligible, fit, harmony, improper, impropriety, indecorous, indecorum, order, peace, proper, propriety, quiet, regularity, respectable, respectful, tranquillity, unexceptionable, unfit.* Such words cluster together thickly in the comparisons between Portsmouth and Mansfield. They assert the desirability of control and restraint in personal behaviour, the submission of the individual to the group. On the other hand, a more moral or spiritual order of value is suggested by words like *conscience, duty, evil, good, principle, right, wrong, vice*. Such words suggest the possibility of the individual having to go against the group.

The important feature of *Mansfield Park*, however, is that the two orders of value are not unambiguously distinguished or opposed. The vocabulary of moral evaluation is often applied to situations which appear to involve only secular considerations— like the projected visit of Fanny to Portsmouth:

> It had occurred to Sir Thomas, in one of his dignified musings, as a *right* and desirable measure; but before he absolutely made up his mind he consulted his son. Edmund considered it every way, and saw nothing but what was *right*. The thing was *good* in itself, and could not be done at a *better* time. (XXXVII. *My italics*.)

The italicized words are of course naturally susceptible of a secular meaning: it is the grave insistence upon them, the tone of solemn deliberation, which makes them reverberate with an almost religious significance. There is some irony at Sir Thomas's expense here, but none at Edmund's.

I do not mean to convey that Jane Austen blurs the significance of value-words. On the contrary, she insists on the most careful discrimination between, for instance, social and moral lapses. Mary Crawford finally loses Edmund's regard through a failure of discrimination, by identifying the adultery of Maria Bertram and Henry Crawford as 'folly'—'She saw it only as folly, and that folly stamped only by exposure' (XLVII)—when it is in fact 'vice'. The distinction has already been made by Sir Thomas in considering Julia's elopement with Mr Yates: 'though Julia was yet as more pardonable than Maria as folly than vice . . .' (XLVII). The rest of this sentence, however, insists on the close connection of social folly with moral vice: '. . . he could not but regard the step she had taken as opening the worst probabilities of a conclusion hereafter, like her sister's.' (*Ibid.*)

In brief, Jane Austen creates a world in which the social values which govern behaviour at Mansfield Park are highly prized (the

Mansfield: Portsmouth antithesis makes this clear) but only when they are informed by some moral order of value which transcends the social. The voice of the narrator, who sees through appearances, is insistent on this point. Of Julia, fretting because she has been separated from Henry Crawford and left to keep Mrs Rushworth company during the expedition to Sotherton, the narrator observes:

> The politeness which she had been brought up to practise as a duty, made it impossible for her to escape; while the want of that higher species of self-command, that just consideration of others, that knowledge of her own heart, that principle of right, which had not formed any essential part of her education, made her miserable under it. (IX)

Julia exemplifies *duty* divorced from *principle*. Duty animated by principle is the proper relationship between these two concepts, which are frequently invoked.

Fanny has 'all the heroism of principle' (XXVII); and this is recognized by Henry Crawford when he falls sincerely in love with her:

> Henry Crawford had too much sense not to feel the worth of good principles in a wife, though he was too little accustomed to serious reflection to know them by their proper name; but when he talked of her having such a steadiness and regularity of conduct, such a high notion of honour, and such an observance of decorum as might warrant any man in the fullest dependence on her faith and integrity, he expressed what was inspired by the knowledge of her being well-principled and religious. (XXX)

(There is an interesting suggestion here that to practise the life of virtue one needs a comprehensive vocabulary with which to describe it: Henry Crawford's vocabulary is predominantly secular—*steadiness, regularity, honour, decorum*.) For her part, Fanny formulates her reasons for rejecting his proposal by reference to his principles, or lack of them. Sir Thomas asks her:

> 'Have you any reason, child, to think ill of Mr Crawford's temper?'
> 'No, sir.'
> She longed to add, 'but of his principles I have.' (XXXII)

On another occasion she reflects:

> How evidently was there a gross want of feeling where his own pleasure was concerned—And, alas! how always known no principle to supply as a duty what the heart was deficient in. (XXXIII)*

Doing what is right is often described as *duty* in *Mansfield Park*, because doing what is right is a social as well as an individual act. Jane Austen recognizes that duty and individual inclination do not always coincide. At the end of the novel Sir Thomas recognizes his failure in educating his children in this respect:

> He feared that principle, active principle, had been wanting, that they had never been properly taught to govern their inclinations and tempers, by that sense of duty which can alone suffice. (XLVIII)

Because *duty* involves the public as well as the private world, however, its dictates are not always clear. In resisting Crawford's suit, Fanny feels that 'She must do her duty, and trust that time might make her duty easier than it now was' (XXXIII). But Lady Bertram tells her, 'You must be aware, Fanny, that it is every young woman's duty to accept such a very unexceptionable offer as this', which, we are wryly informed, 'was almost the only rule of conduct, the only piece of advice, which Fanny had ever received from her aunt in the course of eight years and a half' (XXXIII).

A code of behaviour which demands such a delicate adjustment of social and moral values is by no means easy to live up to. It demands a constant state of watchfulness and self-awareness on the part of the individual, who must not only reconcile the two scales of value in personal decisions but, in the field of human relations, must contend with the fact that an attractive or un-exceptionable social exterior can be deceptive (the Bertram sisters' 'vanity was in such good order, that they seemed to be quite free

---

* *And, alas! how always known. . . .* This is described by Chapman as 'certainly corrupt' (*op. cit.*, p. 548). The grammar is indeed elliptical, but the meaning is clear: 'And alas, how obvious it had always been that he had no principle to supply as a duty what the heart was deficient in.' The wording in the text is certainly preferable to Chapman's recommended emendation: 'And, alas! now all was known, no principle, etc.', to which there are several objections, the most important being that this is not the first occasion on which Fanny passes this judgment on Crawford.

from it' (IV)); and that morally weak characters sometimes enlist the criteria of social correctness to encompass their own selfish ends (the jealous Mrs Norris 'could not but consider it as absolutely unnecessary, and even *improper*, that Fanny should have a regular lady's horse of her own in the style of her cousins', and seeks to prevent the last-minute inclusion of Fanny in the excursion to Sotherton on the grounds that, 'It would be something so very *unceremonious*, so bordering on *disrespect* for Mrs Rushworth, whose own *manners* were such a pattern of *good breeding*' (IV and VIII respectively—*my italics*)).

In order to remain faithful to a code of conduct in which social and moral values are so delicately balanced, in order to preserve one's integrity in the face of ambiguous and sometimes conflicting notions of what is right, the faculty of *judgment* is of prime importance, as the vocabulary of *Mansfield Park* suggests. The word *judgment* itself occurs 37 times, and the associated words *judge* (noun and verb), *judicious, just, justifiable, justly, justice, injustice, injudicious, injudiciously, unjust, unjustifiable, well-judging, illjudged, ill-judging*, make up a total of 116 occurrences in all. Relatively few of these occurrences are casual and colloquial (like, 'when people are waiting, they are bad judges of time' (X)); generally they carry considerable weight and significance in forming our opinion of character and conduct—and the effect of this is to make apparently casual occurrences reverberate with a deeper significance. Thus, when Fanny is invested by the cast of the play 'with the office of judge and critic, and earnestly desired to exercise it and tell them all their faults', it is impossible to miss the irony of the request—which is, indeed, made explicit immediately afterwards: 'She believed herself to feel too much of it [disapprobation] in the aggregate for honesty or safety in particulars' (XVIII).

The faculty of judgment is, of course, possessed in a preeminent degree by the heroine of *Mansfield Park*. Fanny cultivated her own powers of judgment under Edmund's guidance ('he encouraged her taste, and corrected her judgment' (II)), and in turn becomes the teacher of her young sister Susan, encouraged to perceive 'how freely she was inclined to seek her good opinion and refer to her judgment' (XL). Edmund's own judgment is flawed by his infatuation with Mary Crawford, but his disillusionment in her is completed, as we have seen, by her failure to distinguish justly between folly and vice. (Describing their final parting to Fanny, Edmund says, 'I wished her well, and earnestly hoped that she might soon learn to think more justly' (XLVII).) Fanny condemns her mother as 'an ill-judging parent' (XXXIX); Lady Bertram is more leniently treated, perhaps, because she 'did not think deeply, but, guided by Sir Thomas, she thought justly on all important points' (XLVIII). Sir Thomas's own judgment, however, is flawed. Reflecting on his own aloof bearing towards his children, 'he saw how ill he had judged, in expecting to counteract what was wrong in Mrs Norris, by its reverse in himself' (XLVII). Mrs Norris, of course, has 'no judgment' (XLVIII).

The primary meaning of *judgment* in *Mansfield Park* is the ability to distinguish correctly between the right and wrong course of action in any given situation. Thus Fanny, having rejected Henry Crawford's suit, to the surprise and disappointment of her friends and relations, 'trusted, in the first place, that she had done right, that her judgment had not misled her' (XXXII). But such decisions usually involve the exercise of judgment in an almost legal sense—arriving at a verdict on another person,* and this can offend our modern sensibilities. G. B. Stern, for instance, observes, 'We cannot wish that [Fanny and Edmund] should be brought together at the end on their censorship of two other young people [the Crawfords].'[9] Whether we wish it or not, we can scarcely be surprised by the scene. Very early in their acquaintance with the Crawfords, Edmund and Fanny have this conversation:

'Well, Fanny, and how do you like Miss Crawford *now*?' said Edmund the next day, after thinking some time on the subject himself. 'How did you like her yesterday?'

'Very well—very much. I like to hear her talk. She entertains me; and she is so extremely pretty, that I have great pleasure in looking at her.'

'It is her countenance that is so attractive. She has a wonderful play of feature! But was there nothing in her conversation that struck you, Fanny, as not quite right?'

'Oh! yes, she ought not to have spoken of her uncle as she did.'

---

* 'We learn from her what our lives should be, and by what subtle and fierce criteria they will be judged, and how to pass judgment on the lives of our friends and fellows,' Lionel Trilling, 'Jane Austen and *Mansfield Park*', *op. cit.*, p. 129.

I was quite astonished. An uncle with whom she has been living so many years, and who, whatever his faults may be, is so very fond of her brother, treating him, they say, quite like a son. I could not have believed it!'

'I thought you would be struck. It was very wrong—very indecorous.'

'And very ungrateful, I think.'

'Ungrateful is a strong word. I do not know that her uncle has any claim to her *gratitude*; his wife certainly had; and it is the warmth of her respect for her aunt's memory which misleads her here. She is awkwardly circumstanced. With such warm feelings and lively spirits it must be difficult to do justice to her affection for Mrs Crawford, without throwing a shade on the admiral. I do not pretend to know which was most to blame in their disagreements, though the admiral's present conduct might incline one to the side of his wife; but it is natural and amiable that Miss Crawford should acquit her aunt entirely. I do not censure her *opinions*; but there certainly *is* impropriety in making them public.'

'Do you not think,' said Fanny, after a little consideration, 'that this impropriety is a reflection itself upon Mrs Crawford, as her niece has been entirely brought up by her? She cannot have given her right notions of what was due to the admiral.'

'That is a fair remark. Yes, we must suppose the faults of the niece to have been those of the aunt; and it makes one more sensible of the disadvantages she has been under. But I think her present home must do her good.' (VII)

I have thought it worth while to quote this passage at length, for it is entirely representative of the tone and preoccupations of *Mansfield Park*. One notes the deliberate, almost formal procedure of the discussion which, using quasi-judicial language—*acquit, censure, do justice to, blame*—scrutinizes the minute evidence of social behaviour to assess character, bringing *impropriety* and the *indecorous* into a context of *right* and *wrong*. One notes, too, the effort to be scrupulously fair: 'Ungrateful is a strong word . . . I do not pretend to know which was most to blame . . . That is a fair remark.' All these comments are Edmund's—he directs the discussion. Indeed, he is very much Fanny's tutor in the difficult but necessary art of judging others. For judgment in this sense is not, in *Mansfield Park*, something exercised only at the point of personal decision, but all the time, in readiness for personal decision. Thus, Fanny's judgment of Henry Crawford as a suitor is based on her many earlier judgments—not impressions—of his character. And the process of judging goes on *after* the moment of personal decision has passed—hence the long inquest of Fanny and Edmund on the Crawfords to which G. B. Stern objects. For a preoccupation with judgment is inseparable from a preoccupation with *justice*. When Henry Crawford runs off with Maria, Fanny understandably reflects, '*She* should be justified. Mr Crawford would have fully acquitted her conduct in refusing him' (XLVII). But her passion for justice goes beyond the needs of her own reputation. When Edmund has finally broken with Mary Crawford, Fanny, 'now at liberty to speak openly, felt more than justified in adding to his [Edmund's] knowledge of her [Mary's] real character, by some hint of what share his brother's state of health might be supposed to have in her wish for a complete reconciliation' (XLVII). Of all Fanny's actions, this is perhaps the hardest to swallow. It is tolerable only in a novel which so emphatically asserts the importance of exercising judgment in human affairs, and so firmly defines the strenuous effort required to do so correctly. Before passing judgment on others, one must be able to judge oneself. 'She [Fanny] would endeavour to be rational, and to deserve the right of judging of Miss Crawford's character, and the privilege of true solicitude for him [Edmund] by a sound intellect and an honest heart' (XXVII). If judging others is a responsibility which cannot be avoided, it is also a right which has to be earned.

I shall conclude this essay by examining the theatricals episode in the light of the above description of the vocabulary of *Mansfield Park*.

The reasons why the theatricals at *Mansfield Park* are wrong are quite clearly stated by Edmund, when the proposal is first made:

> I think it would be very wrong. In a *general* light, private theatricals are open to some objections, but as *we* are circumstanced, I must think it would be highly injudicious, and more than injudicious, to attempt anything of the kind. It would show great want of feeling on my father's account, absent as he is, and in some degree of constant danger; and it would be imprudent, I think, with regard to Maria, whose situation is a very delicate one, considering everything, extremely delicate. (XIII)

This last remark, of course, refers to the fact that Maria is un-officially engaged to Mr Rushworth—the public announcement being postponed till Sir Thomas's return. To these objections is added the final choice of play, Kotzebue's *Lovers' Vows*, which, because of its risqué speeches and situations, Edmund regards as 'exceedingly unfit for private representation' (XV). His opinion is anticipated by Fanny, to whom 'Agatha and Amelia appeared . . . in their different ways so totally improper for home re-presentation; the situation of one, and the language of the other, so unfit to be expressed by any woman of modesty, that she could hardly suppose that her cousins could be aware of what they were engaging in; and longed to have them roused as soon as possible by the remonstrance which Edmund would certainly make' (XIV). Though Edmund says that his father ' "could never wish his grown-up daughters to be acting plays. His sense of decorum is strict" ' (XIII), there is no objection to acting as such. Julia says to Edmund, ' "Nobody loves a play better than you do, or can have gone farther to see one," ' ' "True," ' he replies, ' "to see real acting, good, hardened, real acting; but I would hardly walk from this room to the next to look at the raw efforts of those who have not been bred to the trade: a set of gentlemen and ladies, who have all the disadvantages of education and decorum to struggle through" ' (XIII). Edmund does not of course despise the educa-tion and decorum of gentlefolk, but suggests that they cannot act without doing violence to the complex code of behaviour which regulates their lives. We are left in no doubt that the would-be actors are not seriously interested in the play as an artistic pro-duction, but as an opportunity for a feast of Misrule, for showing off and bringing themselves into various piquant and intimate relationships. Hence their difficulty in deciding upon a play:

> There were, in fact, so many things to be attended to, so many people to be pleased, so many best characters required, and above all, such a need that the play be at once both tragedy and comedy, that there did seem as little chance of a decision as anything pursued by youth and zeal could hold out. (XIV)

It is not likely that we shall feel the force of the objections to the theatricals on our pulses. But we are by this stage of the novel sufficiently schooled in the vocabulary of discrimination to understand their cogency in the world of *Mansfield Park*, and not to be surprised that, at the announcement of Sir Thomas's un-expected return, with the exception of Mr Rushworth and Mr Yates, 'every other heart was sinking under some degree of self-condemnation or undefined alarm' (XIX).

The theatricals are given great prominence in *Mansfield Park* because they produce a situation, involving all the most important characters in the book, that lends itself to a particularly full and subtle treatment of the delicate interrelationship of social and moral values. They test *manners* in every sense of the word. On the surface the objections to the theatricals appeal mainly to social values: propriety, fitness, and decorum (see the quotations above). But we are never in doubt that the moral destiny of the characters is also at stake, that the theatricals constitute, in theological language, a 'proximate occasion of sin'. And, as Walter Allen points out,[10] the decision to stage the theatricals sets in progress the series of events that culminate in Maria's disgrace and Julia's elopement. Tom Bertram, one of the prime instigators of the theatricals, later feels 'self-reproach arising from the deplorable event in Wimpole Street [Maria's affair with Crawford], to which he felt himself accessory by all the dangerous intimacy of his unjustifiable theatre' (XLVIII).

The question of whether or not to participate in the theatricals is one that pre-eminently requires the exercise of judgment. Fanny exercises her judgment correctly, Edmund compromises, while the others either have no judgment, or deliberately mis-apply it, confusing the issue and employing sophistical arguments in order to satisfy their own selfish inclinations. Mr Yates, for instance, is an absurd figure precisely because of his complete insensibility to the fact that the theatricals involve values, and therefore judgment. The possibility that there might be more than one opinion about the desirability of the theatricals never crosses his mind. When Sir Thomas, on the evening of his return, seeks to divert the conversation from the subject which so acutely embarrasses his family:

> Mr Yates, without discernment to catch Sir Thomas's meaning, or diffidence, or delicacy, or discretion enough to allow him to lead the discourse while he mingled among the others with the least obtrusiveness himself, would keep him on the topic of the theatre, would torment him with questions and remarks relative to it, and finally would make him hear the whole history of his dis-

appointment at Ecclesford.* Sir Thomas listened most politely, but found much to offend his ideas of decorum, and confirm his ill opinion of Mr Yates's habits of thinking. . . . (XIX)

As Mr Yates chatters on, Fanny intercepts a look from Sir Thomas to Edmund, which implied 'On your judgment, Edmund, I depended; what have you been about?' (XIX).

Mr Rushworth is another character who is completely lacking in judgment: enthusiastic at first because he will be able to wear a fine costume, he later turns against the theatricals out of jealousy, which ironically earns him the regard of Sir Thomas, as a 'well-judging, steady young man' (XIX)—one of Sir Thomas's own major misjudgments. The third character in this category is Mrs Norris who, on Sir Thomas's return, is not 'incommoded by many fears of Sir Thomas's disapprobation when the present state of his house should be known, for her judgment had been so blinded, that except for the instinctive caution with which she whisked away Mr Rushworth's pink satin cloak as her brother-in-law entered, she could hardly be said to shew any sign of alarm' (XIX). Lady Bertram characteristically opts out of the whole affair, falling asleep while it is being debated by Tom and Edmund (XIII), and offering only the occasional word of admonition: ' "Do not act anything improper, my dear. Sir Thomas would not like it" ' (XV).

Tom, Maria and Julia, however, are fully aware of the issues involved. Tom challenges Edmund's judgment (' "Don't imagine that nobody in this house can see or judge but yourself" ' (XIII)), while Maria and Julia adopt the technique of enlisting the social code to defend their wrong actions. 'There could be no harm in what had been done in so many respectable families, and by so many women of the first consideration' is the first defence of Maria and Julia (XIV). And when Edmund asks who is to play the female rôles in *Lovers Vows*, Maria subtly replies, alluding to Ecclesford, ' "I take the part which Lady Ravenshaw was to have done" ' (XV). All through this episode, the behaviour of Maria and Julia illustrates how notions of social correctness which are not animated by moral principle can be twisted to suit the

* Mr Yates has come to Mansfield from the country house at Ecclesford, where the presentation of a play by the assembled company was prevented by a death in the host's family. (See Chapter XIII.)

selfish purposes of the individual. Both Maria and Julia covet the part opposite Henry Crawford.

> Julia *did* seem inclined to admit that Maria's situation might require particular caution and delicacy—but that could not apply to *her*—*she* was at liberty; and Maria evidently considered her engagement as only raising her so much more above restraint, and leaving her less occasion than Julia, to consult either father or mother. (XIII)

When Edmund appeals to Maria to set an example to the others— ' "It is your place to put them right, and show them what true delicacy is. In all points of decorum, *your* conduct must be law to the rest of the party" '—Maria replies, ' "I really cannot undertake to harangue all the rest upon a subject of this kind. *There* would be the greatest indecorum I think" ' (XV).

Edmund's instinctive reaction to the proposal to stage a play is to condemn it, and he states his reasons cogently. His judgment is impaired, however, by his attraction to Mary Crawford, whose readiness to participate in the theatricals puts him in an awkward position. As Maria shrewdly observes: ' "*I* am not the *only* young woman you find, who thinks it [*Lovers' Vows*] very fit for private representation" ' (XV). His decision to take part in the theatricals is made on the grounds that, if he refuses, the situation will be made worse by the threatened introduction of an outsider to make up the cast. Accordingly, he tries to justify his decision by invoking the strongest terms of moral valuation:

> 'It does appear to me an evil of such magnitude as must, *if possible*, be prevented' (XVI).
> 'Can you mention any other measure by which I have a chance of doing equal good?' (*Ibid.*)
> 'It is an evil—but I am certainly making it less than it might be.' (*Ibid.*)

But he protests too much, and we share Fanny's opinion, that his *volte-face* 'was all Miss Crawford's doing' (XVI). Later, Edmund acknowledges to his father that 'his concession had been attended with such partial good as to make his judgment in it very doubtful' (XX). His involvement in the theatricals, however, makes him evade passing judgment on Henry Crawford, when the latter proposes to Fanny: ' "let us not, any of us, be judged by what we appeared at that period of general folly. The time of the play is a time which I hate to recollect" ' (XXXV).

Fanny is the only character who emerges with credit from the episode of the theatricals. Edmund tells his father:

> 'We have all been more or less to blame, . . . every one of us, excepting Fanny. Fanny is the only one who has judged rightly throughout; who has been consistent. *Her* feelings have been steadily against it from first to last.' (XX)

But Fanny did not find it easy to be faithful to her principles. At one point there seemed to be conflicting duties, when she was asked to fill a small but necessary rôle:

> Was she *right* in refusing what was so warmly asked, so strongly wished for? what might be so essential to a scheme on which some of those to whom she owed the greatest complaisance, had set their hearts? Was it not ill-nature—selfishness—and a fear of exposing herself? And would Edmund's judgment, would his persuasion of Sir Thomas's disapprobation of the whole, be enough to justify her in a determined denial in spite of all the rest? It would be so horrible to her to act, that she was inclined to suspect the truth and purity of her own scruples, . . . (XVI)

No passage could better illustrate Jane Austen's insight into the difficulty of judging the correct line of action in complex situations. The very scrupulosity and self-awareness which are essential for the proper exercise of judgment, may militate against it.

Paradoxically, but understandably, it is Edmund's decision to take part in the play that steadies Fanny in her own resolution not to perform. Respecting Fanny's judgment, Edmund is eager to win her approval of his decision. ' "I see your judgment is not with me," ' he says anxiously in the course of his explanation, and concludes: ' "Give me your approbation, then, Fanny. I am not comfortable without it" ' (XVI). But she cannot give it. 'Her heart and her judgment were equally against Edmund's decision: she could not acquit his unsteadiness, and his happiness under it made her wretched. She was full of jealousy and agitation' (XVII). One notes the employment of the legalistic word *'acquit'* once more. Another interesting feature of this quotation is Fanny's acknowledgment of her jealousy. Fanny is not entirely a stranger to the passions, though she can control them. Since it is often asserted that Fanny is too good to be true, it may be worth observing that she is not entirely untouched by the odium of the theatricals. She agrees to act as prompter, and looks forward to seeing Edmund and Mary Crawford acting together at the first full rehearsal 'as a circumstance almost too interesting' (XVIII). When the time comes, Mrs Grant is unable to attend the rehearsal, and Fanny is begged by all, including Edmund, to read the part. In her perturbation and embarrassment, she regrets having come to the rehearsal. 'She had known it would irritate and distress her; she had known it her duty to keep away. She was properly punished' (XVIII). She cannot reasonably refuse the request of the others, and the rehearsal begins. It is interrupted by the return of Sir Thomas.

At the end of his essay on *Mansfield Park* Lionel Trilling remarks, 'Hegel speaks of the "secularisation of spirituality" as a prime characteristic of the modern epoch, and Jane Austen is the first to tell us what this means.'[11] This may be overstating the case a little: the secularization of spirituality probably begins with the emergence of the Puritans as an influential and self-conscious social class, and is perceptible in literature as early as *Pamela*. But certainly the situation had developed and become more complicated by Jane Austen's time, and the Hegelian concept is a useful one to apply to her world, and particularly the world of *Mansfield Park*. For a world of secularized spirituality is one in which the choices and decisions, great and small, which the individual is compelled to make continually in the course of life are rendered especially difficult by the existence of two interlocking systems of value—the social (or secular) and the moral (or spiritual). The actual values with which Jane Austen is concerned may have lost some of their cogency with the passing of time, particularly the secular values; but she puts every generation of readers to school, and in learning her own subtle and exact vocabulary of discrimination and evaluation, we submit to the authority of her vision, and recognize its relevance to our own world of secularized spirituality.

II

Fire and Eyre: Charlotte Brontë's War of Earthly Elements

'I have brought you a book for evening solace,' and he laid on the table a new publication—a poem: one of those genuine productions so often vouchsafed to the fortunate public of those days—the golden age of modern literature. (XXXII)

THE 'new publication' which St John Rivers brings Jane Eyre, at that stage in her life when she is a village schoolmistress, is *Marmion* (1808), and this is, I believe, the only precise indication in the book of the date of its action. The allusion to *Marmion* suggests that, without intending to create any sense of 'period' in her novel (in which case she would have referred much more extensively to dates and historical events), Charlotte Brontë almost instinctively placed her heroine in that period whose literature she found most inspiring, the hey-day of Romanticism, the 'golden age of modern literature'.

It is inconceivable that *Jane Eyre* could have been written without the Romantic Movement. The 'gothic' elements so often noted by commentators on the novel—the Byronic hero-with-a-past, the mad wife locked up in an attic, and so on—constitute only a small part of Charlotte's debt to Romantic literature. Far more important is the characteristically Romantic theme of the novel—the struggle of an individual consciousness towards self-fulfilment—and the romantic imagery of landscape, seascape, sun, moon, and the elements, through which this theme is expressed.

On the other hand, the particular interest and strength of *Jane Eyre* is that it is not a pure expression of Romanticism. The instinctive, passionate, non-ethical drive of Romanticism towards self-fulfilment at whatever cost, is held in check by an allegiance to the ethical precepts of the Christian code and an acknowledgement of the necessity of exercising reason in human affairs. Jane's comment after Rochester's first marriage has been revealed and she realizes her duty to leave him, epitomizes the struggle within her between these two systems of value: 'conscience, turned tyrant, held passion by the throat' (XXVII).

It is clear that the dominant energies and sympathies of the novel are on the side of passion. 'Feeling without judgment is a washy draught indeed; but judgment untempered by feeling is too bitter and husky a draught for human deglutition,' Jane opines (XXI). We are frequently reminded that she herself is primarily a creature of passion and feeling. ' "[Y]ou are passionate, Jane, that you must allow" ' says Mrs Reed (IV), and she does allow it. 'I know no medium: I never in my life have known any medium in my dealings with positive, hard characters, antagonistic to my own, between absolute submission and determined revolt. I have always faithfully observed the one, up to the very moment of bursting, sometimes with volcanic vehemence, into the other' (XXXIV).

On the other hand Rochester, early in his relationship with Jane, perceives resources of reason and moral strength in her which can control the passions. Reading her character in her physiognomy (in the scene where he is disguised as a gypsy) he says her eye is ' "soft and full of feeling" ' and her mouth ' "mobile and flexible" '. But, prophesying future events, he reads a different message in the brow:

'I see no enemy to a fortunate issue but in the brow; and that brow professes to say,—"I can live alone, if self-respect and circumstances require me so to do. I need not sell my soul to buy bliss" . . . the forehead declares, "Reason sits firm and holds the reins, and she will not let the feelings burst away and hurry her to wild chasms. The passions may rage furiously, like true heathens, as they are; and the desires may imagine all sorts of vain things: but judgment shall still have the last word in every argument, and the casting vote in every decision. Strong wind, earthquake-shock, and fire may pass by: but I shall follow the guiding of that still small voice which interprets the dictates of conscience." ' (XIX)

Rochester's association of the passions with elemental disturbance has a significance I shall explore later. I am concerned immediately to draw attention to the dialogue which is sustained throughout the novel between passion and reason, feeling and judgment, impulse and conscience. At the beginning of the story Jane is an under-privileged, oppressed child. She rebels against the tyrannical authority of Mrs Reed, and experiences the romantic glow of released passion: 'My soul began to expand, to exult, with the strangest sense of freedom, of triumph, I ever felt' (IV). She is sent to Lowood School where she is more oppressed than before. But for the first time she encounters an alternative attitude to suffering and injustice, the Christian stoicism of Helen Burns (whose favourite reading is *Rasselas*, antithesis of Romantic literature). Jane says to her, ' "When we are struck at without a reason, we should strike back again very hard; I am sure we should—so hard as to teach the person who struck us never to do it again." ' To which Helen replies, ' "You will change your mind, I hope, when you grow older: as yet you are but a little, untaught girl" ', and quotes the Christian precept about loving one's enemies (VI). Inspired by the sanctity of Helen Burns, and supported by the example and encouragement of the teacher, Miss Temple, Jane patiently endures her life at Lowood. 'I had imbibed from her [Miss Temple] something of her nature and much of her habits: more harmonious thoughts: what seemed better regulated feelings had become the inmates of my mind. I had given in allegiance to duty and order; I was quiet; I believed I was content' (X). But when Miss Temple leaves the school to be married:

> I was left in my natural element, and beginning to feel the stir of old emotions . . . now I remembered that the real world was wide, and that a varied field of hopes and fears, of sensations and excitements, awaited those who had courage to go forth into its expanse, to seek real knowledge of life amidst its perils. (X)

This yearning is expressed through a characteristically Romantic gaze at the landscape:

> My eye passed all other objects to rest on those most remote, the blue peaks: it was those I longed to surmount; all within their

boundary of rock and heath seemed prison-ground, exile limits. I traced the white road winding round the base of one mountain, and vanishing in a gorge between the two: how I longed to follow it further! (X)

She follows it to Thornfield Hall, as governess to Rochester's ward. Rochester is a kindred spirit: passionate, vital, unconventional. He represents for Jane the possibility of realizing her vague, romantic aspirations in a concrete human relationship. But the life of the passions is hedged about with potential danger and disaster, personified in the haunting presence at Thornfield Hall of Rochester's mad malevolent wife.

The first great crisis of Jane's life is when she has to choose between following the law of passion by living as Rochester's mistress, and following the law of conscience and duty by renouncing him. She takes the second course, but her renunciation is only passive. St John Rivers, a reincarnation, in a much more extreme and forbidding form, of Helen Burns, and, in a less grotesque form, of Mr Brocklehurst, calls her to a life of complete renunciation—a loveless marriage to him and work in the mission fields. This is the second great crisis of Jane's life. She refuses; and is finally rewarded by being reunited with Rochester, now free to offer her a lawful love, though tamed and mutilated by the purgatorial fire of Thornfield.

In his highly perceptive and stimulating essay, 'The Brontës, or, Myth Domesticated',[1] Richard Chase remarks that *Jane Eyre* and *Wuthering Heights* end similarly: 'a relatively mild and ordinary marriage is made after the spirit of the masculine universe is controlled or extinguished.'[2] This he considers a weakness, and to some extent a betrayal of the mythical force behind both novels.

It was the Victorian period which supposed that the primeval social order consisted of a murderous old man and his company of females and weaker males and which bequeathed the idea to Freud. We may almost say that the Brontë household *was* this primeval social order. The purpose of the Brontë culture heroine is to transform primeval society into a humane and noble order of civilization. . . . Our Brontë culture heroine, then, is the human protagonist of the cosmic drama. Rochester and Heathcliff are portrayed as being at once godlike and satanic. In them the universal enemies may be set at war by a culture heroine. Then if the devil is overcome, a higher state of society will have been achieved. The tyrannical Father–God will have been displaced. The stasis will have been smashed by the creative *élan* of sex and intelligence. The Brontë heroines fail in their missions; they refuse to venture so much; they will not accept the challenge of the God–Devil. They will not accept the challenge, for fear the Devil should win. Yet when we understand these heroines in some such terms as the foregoing, they acquire a new significance: it had not occurred to us that the stakes were so great.[3]

The reservations one has about Chase's argument, which is brilliantly conducted, are the reservations one commonly has about 'myth-criticism'—that it tends to assume that a literary work accumulates more value the more closely it approximates to 'pure myth'.[4] 'The Brontës' tremendous displacement of the domestic values towards the tragic and mythical, though it falls short of ultimate achievement, gives their work a margin of superiority over that of other Victorian novelists,'[5] says Chase. This displacement is certainly the source of the enduring interest of the Brontës' work, but it does not follow that a complete displacement would have resulted in complete achievement. To leave *Wuthering Heights* aside, the domestication of the mythical or, as I would term it, the Romantic element in *Jane Eyre*, is the resolution to which the whole novel points. Such a resolution need not be a cowardly compromise. It engages with the great Faustian dilemma bequeathed by Romanticism to modern man: how to reconcile the free development of the individual consciousness with the acceptance of the checks and restraints necessary to social and individual moral health—how to buy bliss without selling one's soul. The really interesting question is how Charlotte Brontë created a literary structure in which the domestic and the mythical, the realistic world of social behaviour and the romantic world of passionate self-consciousness, could co-exist with only occasional and local lapses into incongruity.

For if we try to gather together our impressions of *Jane Eyre*, we are likely to recall two very different kinds of scene: on the one hand, the loneliness and misery of the young child in the Reed household, or the humiliations and discomforts of Lowood School, or the description of Jane, destitute and drenched with rain, peering through a window into the snug interior of Moor House; and on the other hand, the descriptions of Jane's paintings, or the scene of Rochester's proposal, when the chestnut tree is struck by lightning, or the extended image of a summer landscape invaded by icy winter through which Jane expresses her feelings when her marriage is prevented; on the one hand, writing which is firmly realistic and literal, keenly sensitive to common emotions and sensations, insisting on the value of animal comfort, domestic happiness, ordinary human affection; and on the other hand, writing which is visionary and poetic, evocative of heightened states of feeling, insisting on the value of individual self-fulfilment won from a conflict between passion and reason conducted at an extraordinary pitch of imaginative perception. I shall not be concerned in this essay, except incidentally, to demonstrate how Charlotte Brontë realizes these two orders of experience independently, but to suggest how she unites them. For she has not only to contain them within a single structure, but to persuade us that they can co-exist in a single consciousness, and that they can be reconciled.

This sense of unity pervading a novel which embraces such diverse elements, and which, when analysed in conventional terms of 'character' and 'plot', seems to reveal only glaring weaknesses and absurdities, has, I think, been acknowledged by most critics of *Jane Eyre*. 'Childish naiveté, rigid Puritanism, fiery passion, these would seem incongruous elements indeed; and it is their union which gives Charlotte Brontë's personality its peculiar distinction,' says Lord David Cecil.[6] And according to Walter Allen, 'If it were not for the unity of tone, *Jane Eyre* would be incoherent, for as a construction it is artless.'[7] 'Unity of tone' is a useful hint towards an understanding of the artistic coherence of *Jane Eyre*, yet on the surface there is a very striking variation of tone in the novel—between, for instance, this:

> I then sat with my doll on my knee, till the fire got low, glancing round occasionally to make sure that nothing worse than myself haunted the shadowy room; and when the embers sank to a dull red, I undressed hastily, tugging at knots and strings as I best might, and sought shelter from cold and darkness in my crib. (IV)

and this:

> 'And you will not marry me? You adhere to that resolution?'
> Reader, do you know, as I do, what terror those cold people can

put into the ice of their questions? How much of the fall of the avalanche is in their anger? of the breaking up of the frozen sea in their displeasure? (XXXV)

Yet there is some kind of community between these two passages.

Jane Eyre is, it will be generally agreed, a novel about the emotional life: manners and morals, the characteristic concerns of the novel-form, are of interest to Charlotte Brontë only in so far as they shape the inner life of her heroine. Adopting T. S. Eliot's well-known term for the means by which emotions are expressed in art,* I want to suggest that Charlotte Brontë succeeds in uniting the diverse elements of her novel by employing a system of 'objective correlatives' susceptible of equally diverse treatment, ranging from the prosaic and realistic to the poetic and symbolic. At the core of this system are the elements—earth, water, air, and fire; these, by a logical and linguistic association, are manifested in weather; this leads to images of nature as affected by weather, and the extensive use of the pathetic fallacy;† finally the system incorporates the sun and moon, which affect the weather, and, traditionally, human destiny.

As E.M.W. Tillyard's summary shows,[8] the Elizabethans placed the four elements in a hierarchical order, beginning at the bottom with earth (cold and dry), followed by water (cold and moist), air (hot and moist), and finally fire (hot and dry), 'the noblest element of all . . . which next below the sphere of the moon enclosed the globe of air that girded water and earth'.[9] As Shakespeare's Cleopatra says:

> I am fire and air; my other elements
> I give to baser life. (V, ii)

---

* 'The only way of expressing emotion in the form of art is by finding an "objective correlative"; in other words, a set of objects, a situation, a chain of events which shall be the formula of that *particular* emotion; such that when the external facts, which must terminate in sensory experience, are given, the emotion is immediately evoked.' 'Hamlet', *Selected Essays* (3rd edition, 1951), p. 145.

† 'All violent feelings . . . produce in us a falseness in our impressions of external things, which I would generally characterise as the "pathetic fallacy".' Ruskin, *Modern Painters*, IV, xii. Ruskin, though acknowledging the persistence of the pathetic fallacy, particularly in modern literature, and recognizing that as a literary device it must be judged by the use made of it in any particular case, regards it in general as a fault. I use the term, here and elsewhere, in a neutral, descriptive sense.

This scheme corresponds roughly with the way the elements are used in *Jane Eyre*. Earth (particularly as rock or stone) and water (particularly as ice, snow and rain) are associated with discomfort, unhappiness, alienation. Air has a punning association with the heroine. Fire is certainly the dominant element in the novel, and the one most commonly associated with happy or ecstatic states of being.

But Charlotte Brontë was not an Elizabethan; nor was she a highly self-conscious and deliberate symbolist novelist like Joyce or Conrad; and we should be mistaken in looking for a rigidly schematic system of elemental imagery and reference in *Jane Eyre*. She seeks in the natural world, not order, but a reflection of the turbulent, fluctuating inner life of her heroine. The elements have a constantly changing, and often ambivalent aspect in the novel, sustained by its basic rhythms, the alternation of night and day, storm and calm. To explore all the ramifications of this complex of elemental imagery and reference in detail would occupy too much space. I shall therefore focus attention on *fire*, which I take to have a central importance in *Jane Eyre*, and show how its meanings are developed out of the interplay of the whole complex.

Fire is a source of heat and light. It is, as the Prometheus myth tells us, necessary to civilized human life. It cheers us in the dark, when evil and unknown things threaten. It is, in the British climate, the focal point of social and domestic life—the most privileged members of the family have the seats nearest to the hearth. Fire is often applied metaphorically to the passions, particularly sexual passion. It burns and destroys as well as giving warmth and comfort. Religious, particularly Christian, concepts of spiritual purgation and eternal punishment are commonly described in terms of fire. All these denotations and connotations can be traced in *Jane Eyre*, which contains about 85 references to domestic fires (plus about a dozen separate references to 'hearths'), about 43 figurative allusions to fire, about 10 literal references to fire as conflagration (in connection with Bertha's incendiarism), and four references to Hell-fire. I intend to show that hearth-fires are important points of reference in the depiction of Jane's struggle towards a life of decent animal comfort, human acceptance, and domestic happiness, while metaphors of fire express the exciting, invigorating, frightening inner life of passionate self-fulfilment, and at the same time the disaster and punishment that wait upon an excessive indulgence in passion.

I am not aware that the imagery of fire and associated elemental imagery has been remarked on by previous critics of *Jane Eyre*, but to point it out is to engage in a fairly familiar kind of criticism. Metaphorical language naturally alerts us to the possibility of larger thematic meanings. It is less usual, perhaps, to attribute a quasi-metaphorical significance to literal descriptions of literal objects, and it may be as well to anticipate some objections to such a procedure in respect of hearth-fires in *Jane Eyre*.

The large number of references to ordinary hearth-fires in the novel is indeed explicable on a very simple environmental level. Charlotte Brontë lived in a generally cold, bleak part of England, where the open hearth fire was an essential creature comfort, shedding light as well as warmth into the dark rooms. Mrs Gaskell's account of a visit to Charlotte Brontë at Haworth late in September includes the following appreciative note:

> Then we rested, and talked over the clear bright fire; it is a cold country, and the fires were a pretty warm dancing light all over the house.[10]

Coal was relatively cheap and, as Lowood remarks in *Wuthering Heights*, fires were kept going even in summer. 'Both doors and lattices were open; and yet, as is usually the case in a coal district, a fine, red fire illuminated the chimney; the comfort which the eye derives from it renders the extra heat endurable.'[11] References to hearth-fires in *Jane Eyre*, then, have an obvious function in contributing to that effect of concrete particularity which is a staple of the novel form. They follow naturally from Charlotte Brontë's undertaking to describe realistically a certain milieu.

However, as I suggested above (pp. 44–6) no item of concrete detail in a fiction can be totally arbitrary, totally neutral in effect; and I think there are clear indications in *Jane Eyre* that hearth-fires attract a very significant cluster of emotions and values. There is, for instance, a lavishness of epithet in descriptions of fires which seems in excess of the demands of functional realism. Fires in *Jane Eyre* are 'good' (VIII), 'cheerful' (*ibid.*), 'brilliant' (*ibid.*), 'excellent' (XI), 'genial' (XII), 'superb' (*ibid.*), 'large' (XVII), 'clear' (*ibid.*), 'reviving' (XVII), 'glaring' (XXVIII), 'generous' (XXIX). There is a vivid appreciation of the effect of fires on interiors, for example:

> The hall was not dark, nor yet was it lit, only by the high-hung bronze lamp: a warm glow suffused both it and the lower steps of the oak staircase. This ruddy shine issued from the great dining room, whose two-leaved door stood open, and showed a genial fire in the grate, glancing on marble hearth and brass fire-irons, and revealing purple draperies and polished furniture in the most pleasant radiance. (XII)

(This, incidentally, is Jane's first intimation that the master of Thornfield has returned; the ritual of fire-making accompanies all significant domestic events of homecoming and reunion—cf. Jane's preparations for the return of the Rivers sisters to Moor house: ' "I shall go near to ruin you in coals and peat to keep up good fires in every room" ' . . . 'They were expected about dark, and ere dusk, fires were lit up stairs and below." (XXXIV))

The prevalence of imagery of fire in *Jane Eyre* tends to give a special resonance to literal descriptions of fires. In this respect *Jane Eyre* differs from *Wuthering Heights*, which has proportionately at least as many literal references to fires, but only half-a-dozen figurative references.* What is particularly striking in *Jane Eyre* is that the meanings of both literal and figurative references to fire are defined by a context of opposite and conflicting elemental phenomena. As I show below, the passionate relationship existing between Jane and Rochester is characterized by imagery of fire, and disruption of this relationship—whether by the separation of the two lovers or by the rival relationship offered by St John Rivers—is characterized by imagery of earth and water—stone, ice, rain, snow, etc. Literal references to domestic fires occur in the same kind of context. Let me give three examples.

We first meet Jane as a small child, excluded from the fireside circle of Mrs Reed and her children, perched on the window seat, alternately looking out at 'the drear November day. . . . Afar, it offered a pale blank of mist and cloud; near, a scene of wet lawn and storm-beat shrub, with ceaseless rain sweeping away wildly before a long and lamentable blast', and glancing at her book,

---

* This is not to imply that domestic fires in *Wuthering Heights* are unimportant: they have a significant function which overlaps at some points with their function in *Jane Eyre*, but they do not have such an important place in the thematic organization of the novel.

Bewick's *History of British Birds*, with a particular attention to the descriptions of arctic regions, ' "those forlorn regions of dreary space,—that reservoir of frost and snow, where firm fields of ice, the accumulation of centuries of winters, glazed in Alpine heights above heights, surround the pole, and concentre the multiplied rigours of extreme cold" ' (I). When Jane is reunited with Rochester at the very end of the novel, it is on a similar day—'an evening marked by the characteristics of sad sky, cold gale, and continued small, penetrating rain' (XXXVII). She finds the blinded Rochester by 'a neglected handful of fire' and her first practical gesture is to mend it:

> 'Now, let me leave you an instant, to make a better fire, and have the hearth swept up. Can you tell when there is a good fire?'
> 'Yes; with the right eye I see a glow—a ruddy haze.' (XXXVII)

The latter remark is the first hint of Rochester's recovery of his sight. In the middle of the book there is a description of Mrs Reed on her deathbed:

> . . . the patient lay still, and seemingly lethargic, her livid face sunk in the pillows: the fire was dying in the grate. I renewed the fuel, re-arranged the bed-clothes, gazed awhile on her who could not now gaze on me, and then I moved away to the window.
> The rain beat strongly against the panes, the wind blew tempestuously. 'One lies there,' I thought, 'who will soon be beyond the war of earthly elements.' (XXI)

In these passages the domestic fire is plainly associated with human vitality, and cold and damp are identified with death. Yet the value of the fire is keenly appreciated *because* of the energy of the elements opposed to it, which have their own kind of splendour and fatal fascination. This last quality is particularly evident in the account of the book the young Jane is reading in the first chapter, of which I have only quoted a small part, and which is given a prominence that is accountable only in terms of thematic suggestion. The situation of the heroine looking through a window which is a fragile barrier between domestic warmth and the raging elements is a recurrent one in *Jane Eyre*,* and in a

* Kathleen Tillotson has remarked on the recurrence of the window motif in *Jane Eyre*, in *Novels of the Eighteen-Forties* (Oxford Paperback edn., 1961), p. 300. Dorothy Van Ghent has explored the significance of windows in *Wuthering Heights* in *The English Novel: Form and Function* (Harper Torchbooks, New York, 1961), pp. 161-3.

curious way she longs to be out amidst the war of earthly elements, to engage with the forces of death. It is indeed her destiny to do so.

The section of the novel that deals with Lowood school is generally recognized as a brilliant piece of writing, based, as we know, on painfully personal experience. It, too, fits into the pattern I have been describing.

> We set out cold, we arrived at church colder: during the morning service we became almost paralysed . . . How we longed for the light and heat of a blazing fire when we got back! But, to the little ones at least, this was denied: each hearth in the schoolroom was immediately surrounded by a double row of great girls, and behind them the younger children crouched in groups, wrapping their starved arms in their pinafores. (VII)

In this context a great deal is made of the fire in Miss Temple's room, when she invites Jane and Helen Burns there for tea:

> . . . her apartment . . . contained a good fire, and looked cheerful. (VIII)
> How pretty, to my eyes, did the china and bright teapot look, placed on the little round table near the fire! (*Ibid.*)
> Tea over and tray removed, she again summoned us to the fire; (*Ibid.*)
> The refreshing meal, the brilliant fire, the presence and kindness of her beloved instructress, or, perhaps, more than all these, something in her [Helen's] own unique mind, had roused her powers within her. They woke, they kindled: first, they glowed in the bright tint of her cheek, which till this hour I had never seen but pale and bloodless, then they shone in the liquid lustre of her eyes. . . . (*Ibid.*)

In this chapter the emphasis is not so much on the physical comfort of fire, as on what it symbolizes in the way of kindness, friendship, acceptance. It is interesting, too, to note how Helen's awakening spirit is conveyed through metaphors of fire (*kindled, glowed, shone*), which seem an extension of the visible effects of firelight. Jane's second and most serious conversation with Helen took place while the latter was reading a book 'by the dim glare of the embers' of a fire (VI).

There are many other occasions in which important interviews, significant moments of communication, are lit by fires. Jane's first two interviews with Rochester—in the drawing room and dining room of Thornfield—are so characterized (XIII and

XIV). In the second of these scenes Jane takes in the appearance of her master as it is illuminated by the firelight, and when Rochester wishes to examine *her*, he stands with his back to the fire, a position which, he says ' "favours observation" '. The idea of firelight being a truth-yielding light is more elaborately exploited in the scene where Rochester, disguised as a gypsy, makes a covert declaration of his love under the pretence of telling Jane her fortune:

> An extinguished candle stood on the table; she was bending over the fire, and seemed reading in a little black book, by the light of the blaze. . . . I stood on the rug and warmed my hands, which were rather cold with sitting at a distance from the drawing-room fire. (XIX)

(Jane's distance from the fire in the drawing-room is an index of her underprivileged social standing at this point in the action.)

> I knelt within half a yard of her. She stirred the fire, so that a ripple of light broke from the disturbed coal: the glare, however, as she sat, only threw her face into deeper shadow: mine, it illumined. (*Ibid.*)
> 'Kneel again on the rug.'
> 'Don't keep me long; the fire scorches me.'
> I knelt. She did not stoop towards me, but only gazed, leaning back in her chair. She began muttering,—
> 'The flame flickers in the eye; the eye shines like dew; it looks soft and full of feeling; . . . (*Ibid.*)

The rest of this passage has already been quoted (see above, p. 115). Rochester's reading of Jane's physiognomy is a truthful one; but it is the glancing light of the fire, illuminating a strong, masculine hand and an unmistakable ring, that gives Rochester's own game away.

It is surely significant that the scene of Rochester's proposal, in which Jane is the victim of a deception more serious and more successful than the gypsy charade, is illuminated not by firelight but by moonlight—traditionally associated with deception, mystery, and evil:

> 'Will you be mine? Say yes, quickly.'
> 'Mr. Rochester, let me look at your face: turn to the moonlight.'
> 'Why?'
> 'Because I want to read your countenance; turn.'

'There: you will find it scarcely more legible than a crumpled, scratched page. Read on: only make haste, for I suffer.'

His face was very much agitated and very much flushed, and there were strong workings in the features, and strange gleams in the eyes. (XXIII)

The only fire in this scene is portentous, avenging fire: the wind rises, the chestnut tree writhes and groans, and is struck by lightning. This scene is richly Romantic, and particularly reminiscent of *Christabel*.[12] The chestnut tree, favourite Romantic image of organic life, is split in two, signifying, as has been often noted, the later separation of Jane and Rochester. The two halves are, however, still connected at the roots.

> The cloven halves were not broken from each other, for the firm base and strong roots kept them unsundered below; though community of vitality was destroyed—the sap could flow no more: their great boughs on each side were dead, and next winter's tempests would be sure to fell one or both to earth: as yet, however, they might be said to form one tree—a ruin, but an entire ruin.
>
> 'You did right to hold fast to each other,' I said: as if the monster-splinters were living things, and could hear me. 'I think, scathed as you look, and charred and scorched, there must be a little sense of life in you yet; rising out of that adhesion at the faithful, honest roots: you will never have green leaves more—never more see birds making nests and singing idylls in your boughs; the time of pleasure and love is over with you: but you are not desolate: each of you has a comrade to sympathise with him in his decay.' (XXV)

This passage plainly prefigures the eventual reunion of hero and heroine, but is touched by melancholy, hinting that when that reunion takes place Rochester will have been 'charred and scorched' by the fire of Thornfield, and that beforehand life will have been as cruel to the separated Jane and Rochester as the winter tempests will be to the riven tree. Jane utters this soliloquy in Rochester's absence immediately prior to the wedding, during which period she has seen Rochester's wife. Her emotional restlessness in Rochester's absence is expressed through her response to weather, and her solicitude for Rochester in reference to fires:

> Then I repaired to the library to ascertain whether the fire was lit; for, though summer, I knew on such a gloomy evening, Mr.

Rochester would like to see a cheerful hearth when he came in:
yes, the fire had been kindled some time, and burnt well. (XXV)
'Well, I cannot return to the house,' I thought; 'I cannot sit by
the fireside, while he is abroad in inclement weather:' (*Ibid.*)

Rochester returns and:

> When we were again alone, I stirred the fire, and then took a
> low seat at my master's knee. (*Ibid.*)

She tells him how uneasy she has been the previous night,
repeating and elaborating the pathetic fallacy as she leads up to
the apparition of Bertha:

> But, sir, as it grew dark, the wind rose: it blew yesterday evening,
> not as it blows now—wild and high—but 'with a sullen moaning
> sound' far more eerie. I wished you were at home, I came into this
> room, and the sight of the empty chair and fireless hearth chilled
> me. (*Ibid.*)

The pathetic fallacy takes on an independent metaphorical existence in the superb passage describing Jane's emotions after the
marriage service has been interrupted and prevented by the
revelation that Rochester is already married. Significantly it
begins by establishing a contrast between Jane 'ardent' (or
burning) and Jane 'cold'.

> Jane Eyre, who had been an ardent expectant woman—almost
> a bride—was a cold, solitary girl again: her life was pale, her
> prospects were desolate. A Christmas frost had come at mid-
> summer; a white December storm had whirled over June: ice
> glazed the ripe apples, drifts crushed the blowing roses; on hay
> field and cornfield lay a frozen shroud: lanes which last night
> blushed full of flowers, today were pathless with untrodden snow;
> and the woods, which twelve hours since waved leafy and fragrant
> as groves between the tropics, now spread waste, wild and white as
> pine forests in wintry Norway. (XXVI)

Jane's physical reaction to the shock is of the same kind:

> At first I did not know to what room he had borne me; all was
> cloudy to my glazed sight: presently I felt the reviving warmth of
> a fire, for, summer as it was, I had become icy cold in my chamber.
> (XXVII)

These last three quotations illustrate very clearly the remarkable
flexibility of the language of *Jane Eyre*: restricted to a relatively

narrow range of 'objective correlatives'—wind, rain, snow, ice, warmth, fire—it moves from the quasi-metaphorical to the fully metaphorical to the literal without any sense of strain. The central passage, by its astonishing audacity of conceit, its elegiac rhythms, its fluent but controlled syntax—in short, by its verbal intensity on every level—conveys the response of a keen sensibility to an extreme emotional crisis. But this essentially poetic flight grows naturally out of the literal staples of the novel. The description takes its place beside other, literal descriptions, scarcely less vivid, of the effect of weather upon landscape, so that we are not conscious of any abrupt shift from fact to fantasy: the interior landscape of Jane's emotions is no less real than the landscape she looked out on as a child in Mrs Reed's house, or the arctic landscape she read about in Bewick's *History of British Birds*— which last is, indeed, specifically recalled by the reference to 'wintry Norway'. The reverse is also true: in the third, literal passage, phrases that are potentially clichés are re-charged with expressive force by echoing the daring tropes of the previous passage. '*Icy* cold' does not seem a mechanical hyperbole after so vivid a metaphorical evocation of cold, and '*glazed* sight' puns delicately on the sense of *glazed* as 'frozen', applied to the 'ripe apples' just before.

Jane's sufferings in her voluntary exile are brought home to the reader through the same pattern of reference. While she wanders aimlessly through the countryside, penniless and homeless, she is at the mercy of the elements, content while the sun shines, but wretched when the weather is inclement. She is in a sense re-living her childhood experience of physical and emotional deprivation. Stumbling through the dark rain near Moor House, she reaches the nadir of her life, and is tempted to succumb to the forces of cold death which have always haunted her imagination:*

And I sank down where I stood, and hid my face against the ground. I lay still for a while: the night-wind swept over the hill and over me, and died moaning in the distance; the rain fell fast,

* Cf. Jane's paintings, the first of which depicts a sinking wreck and a drowned corpse, and the third a deathly head superimposed on an arctic scene, with 'the pinnacle of an iceberg piercing the polar winter sky' (XIII). These pictures derive some of their imagery from Bewick's *History of British Birds*.

wetting me afresh to the skin. Could I but have stiffened to the still frost—the friendly numbness of death—it might have pelted on: I should not have felt it; but my yet living flesh shuddered at its chilling influence. I rose ere long. (XXVIII)

She rises to follow a last hope, a glimmering light which she fears may be an '*ignis fatuus*', which is in fact a lamp burning in the window of Moor House. Standing in the pelting rain, Jane peers into a room poignantly redolent of the good life of domestic peace and warmth that has so far eluded her. It is the 'window-situation' in reverse:

> I could see clearly a room with a sanded floor, clean scoured; a dresser of walnut, with pewter plates ranged in rows, reflecting the redness and radiance of a glowing peat-fire. . . . A group of more interest appeared near the hearth, sitting still amidst the rosy peace and warmth suffusing it. (*Ibid.*)

Foreseeably, a good deal of attention is paid to fires in the succeeding description of how Jane is received into the house and restored to health.

The momentous interview in which St John Rivers reveals to Jane the truth of her origins and fortune has the kind of setting that we have by now learned to expect on such occasions:

> I had closed my shutter, laid a mat to the door to prevent the snow from blowing in under it, trimmed my fire, and after sitting nearly an hour on the hearth listening to the muffled fury of the tempest, I lit a candle, took down Marmion, . . . (XXXIII)

The entrance of St John, covered with snow, into this firelit room, establishes the basic incompatibility of their characters in a way more elaborately exploited on the metaphorical level, as I shall show later. But it is in place here to note one of Jane's attempts to formulate her antipathy to St John:

> I saw he was of the material from which nature hews her heroes —Christian and pagan—her law-givers, her statesmen, her conquerors: a steadfast bulwark for great interests to rest upon; but, at the fireside, too often a cold, cumbrous column, gloomy and out of place. (XXXIV)

It is Rochester alone who still suggests to Jane the possibility of combining the domestic warmth of Moor House, and the warmth of masculine love which it so signally lacks. At length she sets out for Thornfield, and finds it 'a blackened ruin' (XXXVI), its evil spirits exorcised by fire. Jane tracks down its master, himself purged, exorcized (or in Chase's terms, symbolically castrated) by the fire and his own heroic response to it.* ' "I am no better than the old lightning-struck chestnut-tree in Thornfield orchard" ' he says (XXXV). They are reunited, as we have seen, beside a dying fire, which Jane revives.

The above account by no means exhausts the wealth of literal references to fire in *Jane Eyre*, but it does, I hope, establish the importance of fire as the core of a cluster of emotions and values in the novel. I now turn to the figurative references to fire. Figuratively, fire is generally associated with the inner life of passion and sensibility, and this, though highly valued, is seen as morally ambivalent. Images of fire are almost entirely restricted to Jane and Rochester. They recognize the fire within each other —it is what gives meaning and value to their relationship; but they also recognize (Rochester only tardily) the perils of this fiery spirit and the necessity of controlling it.

This is well illustrated by the metaphors of fire used to express Jane's essentially rebellious temperament, which makes it difficult for her to control her anger in the face of injustice. I have previously quoted a reference to Jane's 'volcanic vehemence' (see above, p. 115). On her deathbed Mrs Reed tells Jane:

> 'You have a very bad disposition and one to this day I feel it im-possible to understand: how for nine years you could be patient and quiescent under any treatment, and in the tenth break out all fire and violence, I can never comprehend.' (XXI)

Rochester admires this fiery spirit in her—' "I have seen what a fire-spirit you can be when you are indignant" ' (XXIV)—and so do we; but we are also made to understand the cost of expend-ing this spirit. the inevitable transitoriness of anger, and of the satisfaction afforded by venting it. After her first outburst at Gateshead the young Jane, locked up in the Red Room

> grew by degrees cold as a stone, and then my courage sank. My habitual mood of humiliation, self-doubt, forlorn depression, fell damp on the embers of my decaying ire. (II)

* I.e., Rochester's unsuccessful attempt to save Bertha's life, described in Chapter XXXVI.

(Note how the elements of earth and water—'cold as a stone', 'fell damp'—are opposed to fire here; 'ire' is almost a pun.) And after her second act of rebellion the same idea is expressed in an even more striking fire image:

> A ridge of lighted heath, alive, glancing, devouring, would have been a meet emblem of my mind when I accused and menaced Mrs. Reed: the same ridge, black and blasted after the flames are dead, would have represented as meetly my subsequent condition, when half an hour's silence and reflection had shown me the madness of my conduct and the dreariness of my hated and hating position. (IV)

To control the emotional fluctuations of childhood, from vivid anger to vacant depression and despair, is a necessary condition of Jane's progress to maturity. That she does mature in this way is suggested by her thoughts on her return to Gateshead just before Mrs Reed's death:

> I still felt as a wanderer on the face of the earth; but I experienced a firmer trust in myself and my own powers, and less withering dread of oppression. The gaping wound of my wrongs, too, was now quite healed; and the flame of resentment extinguished. (XXI)

Many other aspects of Jane's character, besides her quick temper, are expressed through images of fire. She feeds her vague, romantic longings on 'a tale my imagination created, and narrated continuously; quickened with all of incident, life, fire, feeling, that I desired and had not in my actual existence' (XII). Rochester, as he himself hints to Jane in the gypsy scene, offers the possibility of releasing this fire from the subjective dream world: ' "You are cold, because you are alone: no contact strikes the fire from you that is in you" ' (XIX). He is the man to recognize and appreciate this fire

> '. . . to the clear eye and the eloquent tongue, to the soul made of fire, and the character that bends but does not break . . . I am ever tender and true.' (XXIV)

for he has it within himself:

> Strange energy was in his voice; strange fire in his look. (XV)
> . . . 'I am insane—quite insane: with my veins running fire . . .' (XXVII)

It is volcanic fire, which surges up and erupts at moments of crisis: ' "To live, for me, Jane, is to stand on a crater crust which may crack and spue fire any day" ' (XX). At Mason's interruption of the wedding, 'his face flushed—olive cheek, and hueless forehead received a glow, as from spreading, ascending heart-fire' (XXVI); and when Jane declares her intention of leaving him, 'Up the blood rushed to his face; forth flashed the fire from his eyes' (XXVII).

Jane uses a remarkable volcanic image to express her changing emotional response to Rochester from fear to desire, made all the keener at this point in the story by envy of Miss Ingram, whom she believes to be Rochester's intended:

> And as for the vague something—was it a sinister or a sorrowful, a designing or a desponding expression?—that opened upon a careful observer, now and then, in his eye, and closed again before one could fathom the strange depth partially disclosed; that something which used to make me fear and shrink, as if I had been wandering amongst volcanic-looking hills, and had suddenly felt the ground quiver, and seen it gape: that something, I, at intervals, beheld still; and with throbbing heart, but not with palsied nerves. Instead of wishing to shun, I longed only to dare—to divine it; and I thought Miss Ingram happy, because one day she might look into the abyss at her leisure, explore its secrets and analyze their nature. (XVIII)

The volcanic image is extraordinarily effective in conveying the awe that colours Jane's relationship with Rochester even after fear has been overcome by love: the sense of the danger as well as the exhilaration of exploring hidden, perhaps forbidden, daemonic, subterranean depths of the life of passion. When she wrestles, physically and spiritually, with Rochester after the prevention of the marriage, the agony of the conflict is again presented through powerful fire-imagery:

> I was experiencing an ordeal: a hand of fiery iron grasped my vitals. Terrible moment: full of struggle, blackness, burning. (XXVII)
> He seemed to devour me with his flaming glance; physically, I felt, at the moment, powerless as stubble exposed to the draught and glow of a furnace—mentally, I still possessed my soul, and with it the certainty of ultimate safety. (*Ibid.*)

This latter quotation carries Biblical echoes, particularly of Isaiah:

> Therefore as the fire devoureth the stubble, and the flame consumeth the chaff, so their root shall be as rottenness, and their blossom shall go up as dust. (Isaiah 5.25)
> Behold, they shall be as stubble; the fire shall burn them; they shall not deliver themselves from the power of the flame; there shall not be a coal to warm at, nor fire to sit before it. (47.14)

To quote these passages is to realize at once how much the whole system of elemental and natural imagery we have been exploring in *Jane Eyre* owes to the language of the Old Testament.* The second passage quoted, from the triumphant prophecy of God's judgment on Babylon and Chaldea, has a special interest in that it counterposes two kinds of fire—the avenging, consuming kind, and the domestic, comforting kind—in a manner strangely parallel to Charlotte Brontë's. The differences are, however, obvious and important. In the novelist's image of stubble, the heat emanates from a source of passionate love, not of vengeance, and the possibility of being consumed by it is as seductive as it is terrifying.

Jane Eyre is remarkable for the way it asserts a moral code as rigorous and demanding as anything in the Old Testament in a universe that is not theocentric but centred on the individual consciousness. Explicit references to the orthodox idea of Hellfire are few in *Jane Eyre*, and generally irreverent. Consider for example Mr Brocklehurst's catechism of the young Jane:

> 'Do you know where the wicked go after death?'
> 'They go to Hell,' was my ready and orthodox answer.
> 'And what is hell? Can you tell me that?'
> 'A pit full of fire.'
> 'And should you like to fall into that pit, and to be burning there for ever?'
> 'No, sir.'

* Cf. Jane's description of her desolation when her marriage to Rochester is prevented, 'I seemed to have laid me down in the dried-up bed of a great river; I heard a flood loosened in remote mountains, and felt the torrent come', an image which is explicitly connected with a quotation from the 69th Psalm, 'The waters came into my soul, I sank in deep mire: I felt no standing; I came into deep waters; the floods overflowed me' (XXVI). Charlotte Brontë's punctuation, especially her use of colons and semi-colons, rather than full-stops, between grammatically independent clauses, also seem to be modelled on the Old Testament in the Authorised Version.

'What must you do to avoid it?'

I deliberated a moment; my answer, when it did come, was objectionable: 'I must keep in good health, and not die.' (IV)

Towards the end of the book Jane recognizes a similar attempt to frighten her into obedience by St John Rivers. (He is reading from Revelations):

'. . . the fearful, the unbelieving, etc., shall have their part in the lake which burneth with fire and brimstone, which is the second death.'

Henceforth, I knew what fate St. John feared for me. (XXXV)

But if the fear of Hell is considered an unworthy motive for virtue in *Jane Eyre*, the ethical system actually proposed is very far from enlightened self-interest or humanist altruism. The sanctions of Old Testament morality—punishment by fire and water, destitution, exile, solitariness—are still very much in evidence on both the literal and metaphorical levels, but the symbolic art of the novel presents them as extensions of the individual consciousness. The relationship of Jane and Rochester appears to us not as something which, according to its lawfulness or unlawfulness, will bring punishment or reward from an external source, but as something which contains within itself extreme possibilities of fulfilment and destruction. For this reason Rochester's conventionally Christian expression of penitence at the end of the novel (XXXVII) strikes a discordant note.

One of the most fascinating examples of Charlotte Brontë's literary manipulation of the elements as objective correlatives for the inner life, is her treatment of Jane's relationship with St John Rivers. When Jane first comes to know Rivers, he is struggling against a love, which he feels to be weak, for Rosamund Oliver; and, noticing his response to Rosamund's presence, Jane attributes to him, for the first and last time, the fire of human passion:

I saw his solemn eye melt with sudden fire, and flicker with resistless emotion. Flushed and kindled thus, he looked nearly as beautiful for a man as she for a woman. (XXXI)

Rivers suppresses this passion because of his call to the missionary life, which Jane compares to a different kind of fire:

He seemed to say [to Rosamund] . . . 'I love you, and I know you prefer me. . . . If I offered my heart, I believe you would accept it. But that heart is already laid on a sacred altar: the fire is arranged round it. It will soon be no more than a sacrifice consumed.' (XXXII)

It is to this kind of consuming, sacrificial fire that Rivers later summons Jane herself, believing he recognizes in her 'a soul that revelled in the flame and excitement of sacrifice' (XXXIV). The temptation to yield is great for Jane, for her capacity for self-sacrifice and renunciation has been proved by her separation from Rochester. But St John insists that, for the sake of propriety, she must accompany him to the mission fields as his wife, and this Jane finds utterly unacceptable. She finds it unacceptable because she cannot conceive of a relationship between a man and a woman which is not one of passionate communion and domestic intimacy. These qualities she has experienced with Rochester, but she could never experience them with Rivers. For on the domestic level he is 'at the fireside a cold, cumbrous, column, gloomy and out of place' (XXXIV), while emotionally he is a man of stone and ice.*

This basic incompatibility of Jane and Rivers, the incompatibility of fire with water and earth, is intimated in the scene already alluded to where he visits her little cottage in a snow-storm, bringing her the news of her inheritance and family history:

> . . . it was St. John Rivers, who, lifting the latch, came in out of the frozen hurricane—the howling darkness—and stood before me; the cloak that covered his tall figure all white as a glacier. . . .
> I had never seen that handsome-featured face of his look more like chiselled marble than it did just now; as he put aside his snow-wet hair from his forehead and let the firelight shine free on his pale brow and cheek as pale, . . . (XXXIII)

The fireside, as usual, proves a propitious place for confidences and revelations, but Jane has to insist before Rivers makes his hints explicit. In their banter there is a significant play on 'fire' and 'ice':

> 'But I apprised you that I was a hard man,' said he: 'difficult to persuade.'
> 'And I am a hard woman,—impossible to be put off.'
> 'And then,' he pursued, 'I am cold: no fervour infects me.'
> 'Whereas I am hot, and fire dissolves ice.' (XXXIII)

* In Chapter IV Mr Brocklehurst, standing on the hearthrug, impresses the young Jane as a 'stony stranger' and a 'black pillar'.

In subsequent stages of their relationship Jane persistently returns to imagery of water and earth in forms suggestive of hardness, coldness, destructiveness—ice, rock, stone, torrents, avalanches—to express her physical and emotional alienation from Rivers.* Some of the images are casual and conventional:

> This silence damped me. (XXXIV)
> . . . his reserve was again frozen over, and my frankness was congealed beneath it. (*Ibid.*)
> I fell under a freezing spell. (*Ibid.*)
> There are no such things as marble kisses or ice kisses, or I should say, my ecclesiastical cousin's salute belonged to one of these classes; . . . (*Ibid.*)
> 'He is good and great, but severe; and, for me, cold as an iceberg.' (XXXV)

But these virtually dead metaphors are revived by, and themselves prepare for, more daring tropes drawn from the same sources:

> 'And you will not marry me? You adhere to that resolution? Reader, do you know, as I do, what terror those cold people can put into the ice of their questions? How much of the fall of the avalanche is in their anger? of the breaking up of the frozen sea in their displeasure? (XXXV)

There may be some significance in Rivers's name,† for imagery of cold, rushing water is persistently applied to him.

> '. . . he asks me to be his wife, and has no more of a husband's heart for me than that frowning giant of a rock, down which the stream is foaming in yonder gorge.' (XXXIV)
> I was tempted to cease struggling with him—to rush down the torrent of his will into the gulf of his existence, and there lose my own. (XXXV)

The latter image is particularly interesting when compared to the volcanic image applied by Jane to Rochester in Chapter XVIII

* Rochester, anticipating Jane's reaction to the news that he is married, says: ' "you will say,—'That man had nearly made me his mistress: I must be ice and rock to him;' and ice and rock you will accordingly become." ' (XXVII)

† The name of Helen Burns, the most sympathetic representative of Christianity in the novel, is nicely ambivalent, evoking both water and fire (I am indebted to Mrs Elsie Duncan-Jones for this suggestion.)

(see above, p. 133). In both cases a relationship with a man is seen as process of going down into something, being swallowed up and consumed by something. In Rochester's case the something is fire, in the case of Rivers, water. Imagery of fire keeps pace with the earth and water imagery applied to Rivers:

> . . . his wife—at his side always and always restrained, and always checked—forced to keep the fire of my nature continually low, to compel it to burn inwardly and never utter a cry, though the imprisoned flame consumed vital after vital—*this* would be unendurable. (XXXIV)
>
> To me, he was in reality become no longer flesh, but marble; his eye was a cold, bright, blue gem; his tongue a speaking instrument—nothing more.
>
> All this was slow torture to me—refined, lingering torture. It kept up a slow fire of indignation, and a trembling trouble of grief, which harrassed and crushed me altogether. I felt how—if I were his wife—this good man, pure as the deep sunless source, could soon kill me: without drawing from my veins a single drop of blood, or receiving on his own crystal conscience the faintest stain of crime. (XXXV)

It is not surprising that Charlotte Brontë has often been compared to the author of *Women in Love*.[13] Dare one suggest that she manages her transitions from the literal to the visionary rather more successfully than Lawrence?

One of the few attempts to account for the effects of Charlotte Brontë's prose fiction in terms of its iterative and controlling symbolism is Robert B. Heilman's article 'Charlotte Brontë, Reason and the Moon'[14] which I must take note of here. Heilman begins by defining the conflict in Charlotte Brontë's work 'between reason–judgment–common sense and feeling–imagination–intuition'. He identifies these two polarities with terms used by Mr Robert Graves in *The White Goddess*: 'solar reason' and 'lunar superstition', and says that 'If the movement in Charlotte Brontë's novels—the growth of her protagonists—is towards something that we can call "daylight", the field of significant action is often the dark . . . whether by plan or through an unconscious or semiconscious sense of forces at work in the world, Charlotte tends to make the "White Goddess" a presiding deity, if not over the novels as a whole, at least over moments of crisis.'[15] He proceeds to note the numerous references to the moon in Charlotte Brontë's novels, particularly in *Jane Eyre*:

> in *Jane Eyre* the moon is an aesthetic staple, at times a scenic element inherently charming to the writer, at times almost a character; at its most interesting it reveals an author groping for a cosmic symbolization of reality, or towards a reality beyond the confines of everyday reality, toward an interplay of private consciousness and mysterious forces at work in the universe.[16]

This comment supports my argument that the visionary grows very naturally out of the literal in Jane Eyre because the objective correlatives for the heroine's emotional life are susceptible of very varied treatment. Heilman seems to me, however, to overestimate and oversimplify the authority given to the White Goddess in the novel, because he does not consider the moon in the context of a larger system of elemental imagery and reference. While it is true that the two quasi-supernatural interventions which help Jane to resolve a conflict between conscience and instinct—the apparition of her mother's spirit and the telepathic call from Rochester—are attended by moonlight, the moon is not always so propitious, as Heilman admits. The first reference to the moon in the novel is a description of a picture in Bewick's *History of British Birds* which depicts a 'cold and ghastly moon glancing through bars of cloud at a wreck just sinking' (I). The moon presages Bertha's attempt on Mason's life (XX); Jane has a prophetic dream of Thornfield gutted and ruined, bathed in moonlight (XXV); Rochester, describing the crisis of his wretched married life in the West Indies says that, on the night he determined to take his own life, ' "the moon was setting in the waves, broad and red, like a hot cannon-ball—she threw her last bloody glance over a world quivering with the ferment of tempest. I was physically influenced by the atmosphere and scene" ' (XXVII). Rochester describes this scene while relating the story of his life to Jane after the interruption of the wedding service. They are sitting beside a fire; beside a fire Jane always learns the truth. I have already suggested the implications of moonlight in the scene of Rochester's proposal.

One of the most puzzling references to the moon in *Jane Eyre*, which Heilmann does not comment on, becomes fully explicable only in terms of the larger elemental context. I refer to the superficially arch and facetious scene in which Rochester teases his ward, Adèle, when she is accompanying him and Jane on a shopping expedition (to buy a trousseau). Adèle, catching a hint of Rochester's that she is to be sent away to school, asks if she is to go '*sans* mademoiselle'. Rochester then tells Adèle of his forthcoming marriage in the following manner:

> 'Yes,' he replied, 'absolutely *sans* mademoiselle; for I am to take mademoiselle to the moon, and there I shall seek a cave in one of the white valleys among the volcano-tops, and mademoiselle shall live with me there, and only me.'
>
> 'She will have nothing to eat: you will starve her,' observed Adèle.
>
> 'I shall gather manna for her morning and night: the plains and hill-sides in the moon are bleached with manna, Adèle.'
>
> 'She will want to warm herself; what will she do for a fire?'
>
> 'Fire rises out of the lunar mountains: when she is cold, I'll carry her up to a peak and lay her down on the edge of a crater.'

Rochester spins out this fable at some length, but the allegory is already plain: the flight to the moon is Rochester's proposal of marriage, and Adèle, by rejecting with 'genuine French scepticism' Rochester's fantasy, indicates that his offer of marriage is empty and deceitful. There is no fire on the moon, and no food: i.e. Jane's need for domestic happiness cannot be satisfied by the false marriage, although her more romantic longings might be, by the 'volcanic' fire of passion.

The moon, then, has a multiple and ambivalent function in *Jane Eyre*. As a prominent feature of the natural world its variable aspect is exploited *via* the pathetic fallacy to reflect inner states of being; while its ancient, mythical associations and its prominence in Romantic poetry of the supernatural make it an appropriate feature of those scenes in the novel when, for good or ill, non-rational forces command the situation.

As Heilman observes, 'the movement of the novel . . . is towards something we can call "daylight".' The sequence of night and day, day bringing relief from the trials and terrors of the night, is one of the basic rhythms of the book. But imagery of and reference to the sun is not quantitatively or qualitatively very striking in *Jane Eyre*. Generally such imagery and references are associated with the same values as are associated with domestic fires—peace, tenderness, acceptance—but they scarcely call attention to themselves by any freshness or originality. 'Even for me life had its gleams of sunshine,' observes Jane, recording an act of kindness by Bessie (IV). Rochester's smile is 'the real sunshine of feeling' (XXII), and Jane hopes that if he marries Blanche Ingram he will keep herself and Adèle 'under the shelter of his protection, and not quite exiled from the sunshine of his presence' (XXII). ' "What is the matter?" ' asks Rochester when she is disappointed by his refusal to let Adèle accompany them on the shopping expedition, ' "All the sunshine is gone" ' (XXIV). Of her life as a schoolmistress Jane observes, 'To live amidst general regard, though it be but regard of working-people, is like "sitting in sunshine, calm and sweet"; serene inward feelings bud and bloom under the ray' (XXXII). There is just one point in the novel where the sun is presented as *anti*-pathetic to Jane, and I believe that this is no trivial exception. I refer to the explicit assertion that the climate of India, where Rivers wishes to take Jane as his wife and fellow-missionary, will be death to her. When Rivers makes the proposal Jane reflects: 'I feel mine is not the existence to be long protracted under an Indian sun' (XXXIV), and her cousin Diana confirms this intuition:

> 'Madness . . . you would not live three months there, I am certain. . . . You are much too pretty, as well as too good, to be grilled alive in Calcutta.' (XXXV)

Tropical and exotic places invariably have pejorative associations in *Jane Eyre*. Rochester's disastrous first marriage takes place in the West Indies, and his misery reaches its climax in a tropical storm. A 'sweet wind from Europe' urges him to seek a solution to his problem there (XXVII). In the capitals of Europe he searches for his 'ideal woman' who had to be 'the antipodes of the Creole', and finds her at last when 'on a frosty winter afternoon, I rode in sight of Thornfield Hall' (*ibid.*). When he is prevented from marrying Jane, he tries to persuade her to run away with him—to southern Europe: ' "You shall go to a place I have in the south of France: a white-walled villa on the shores of the Mediterranean" ' (XXVII). Jane refuses and, later in the novel, when she is vindicating this decision to herself, makes an explicit connection between climate and the loss or preservation of moral integrity:

> Which is better?—To have surrendered to temptation; listened to passion; made no painful effort—no struggle;—but to have sunk down in the silken snare; fallen asleep on the flowers covering it; wakened in a southern clime, amongst the luxuries of a pleasure villa: to have been now living in France, Mr. Rochester's mistress. ... Whether it is better, I ask, to be a slave in a fool's paradise at Marseilles—fevered with delusive bliss one hour—suffocating with the bitterest tears of remorse and shame the next—or to be a village-schoolmistress, free and honest, in a breezy mountain nook in the healthy heart of England? (XXXI)

This aspect of *Jane Eyre* is connected with its author's efforts to free her literary imagination from her juvenile work, in which the exotic, tropical environment of Angria provided an appropriate setting for an excessive indulgence in the gestures of Romanticism. That Charlotte Brontë recognized the need to disengage herself from the seductive but debilitating myth of Angria has been persuasively argued by Professor Kathleen Tillotson[17] who quotes from a fragment of the Charlotte Brontë papers, speculatively dated 1839, which is very much to my purpose here:

> I have now written a great many books and for a long time I have dwelt upon the same characters and scenes and subjects. ... My readers have been habituated to one set of features ... but we must change, for the eye is tired of the picture so oft recurring and so long familiar.
>
> Yet do not urge me too fast, reader; it is not easy to dismiss from my imagination the images which have filled it so long; they were my friends and intimate acquaintances, and I could with little labour describe to you the faces, the voices, the actions, of those who peopled my thoughts by day, and not seldom stole strangely into my dreams by night. When I depart from these I feel almost as if I stood on the threshold of a home and were bidding farewell to its inmates. When I strive to conjure up new images I feel as if I had got into a distant country where every face was unknown and the character of all the population an enigma which it would take much study to comprehend and much talent to expound. Still, I long to quit for a while that burning clime where we have sojourned too long—its skies flame—the glow of sunset is always

upon it—the mind would cease from excitement and turn now to a cooler region where the dawn breaks grey and sober, and the coming day for a time at least is subdued by clouds.[18]

This is Charlotte Brontë's 'farewell to Angria'. The 'cooler region' is the physical and moral landscape of her mature work, pre-eminently *Jane Eyre*. Her imagination responded deeply to the fascination of climatic extremes—the polar cold as well as the tropical heats—but her heroine works out her destiny in a temperate—though not idyllic—zone. Extremes of heat and cold are death to Jane, we are made to feel, and paradoxically in her last great crisis, St John Rivers threatens her with both: physical death by heat and emotional death by cold.

In the war of earthly elements, in preserving a precarious equilibrium between opposing forces, Jane Eyre finds the meaning of life. Day is welcomed because it follows night, calm because it follows storm. Fire is a source of warmth and light, but it is most keenly enjoyed when snow and rain beat on the windows.

III

The Rhetoric of 'Hard Times'

'IT is the least read of all the novels and probably also the least enjoyed by those who read it,' said Humphrey House of *Hard Times* in *The Dickens World* (1941).[1] The first part of this statement, at least, has probably not been true since *The Great Tradition* was published (1948). Of *Hard Times*, it will be remembered, Dr Leavis said, '. . . of all Dickens's works, it is the one that has all the strength of his genius, together with a strength no other of them can show—that of a completely serious work of art'.[2]

There are of course two propositions here: one, that *Hard Times* is a complete and satisfactory work of art; and two, that this novel is the crown of Dickens's achievement. The latter proposition has had the greater notoriety, yet it is essentially an aside which Leavis does not attempt to argue through. The first proposition is far more susceptible of fruitful critical discussion, and as John Holloway's recent article, '*Hard Times*, a History and a Criticism',[3] is the most interesting expression of dissent it has provoked, I shall take the article as a starting point.

Holloway's case can be summarized as follows: that the Utilitarian philosophy Dickens claims to be representing in the novel is a crude travesty of the reality, shallowly conceived as a mere blind faith in statistics; that it is opposed by an equally shallow plea for 'play' and 'fancy', represented by the Slearies 'not as vital horsemen but as plain entertainers'; that Dickens's attitude to Trade Unions and labour problems is unenlightened;

that, in short, the novel as a whole is the product of a mind not prophetic and profound, but bourgeois and philistine. There is considerable force in all these arguments, and in some respects they merely consolidate points previously made by Humphrey House and Raymond Williams.[4] There are two interconnected grounds for caution in accepting Holloway's arguments, however: they are extensively documented with external evidence— such as contemporary Utilitarian works and Dickens's journalism; and they tend towards an assessment of the novel itself even lower than Holloway wishes to reach. Thus he is compelled to make a divorce between the achievements of the novel and Dickens's manifest intentions:

> The passages in *Hard Times* where Dickens is most freely himself, are not those where he is most engaged with his moral fable or intent (if we think, mistakenly that he is at all) on what Dr. Leavis has called 'the confrontation of Utilitarianism by life'.[5]

While agreeing that 'life' (with the special resonances Dr Leavis gives to that word) is far too grand a term for the values which Dickens opposes to the world of Gradgrind and Bounderby, I suggest that Dickens's achievements in the novel can no more be separated from his polemical intention than can his failures.

On every page *Hard Times* manifests its identity as a polemical work, a critique of mid-Victorian industrial society dominated by materialism, acquisitiveness, and ruthlessly competitive capitalist economics. To Dickens, at the time of writing *Hard Times*, these things were represented most articulately, persuasively, (and therefore dangerously) by the Utilitarians. It is easy to abstract the argument behind the novel, and to demonstrate its logical and practical weaknesses. The argument has two stages: (1) that the dominant philosophy of Utilitarianism, particularly as it expresses itself in education, results in a damaging impoverishment of the moral and emotional life of the individual; and (2) that this leads in turn to social and economic injustice, since individuals thus conditioned are incapable of dealing with the human problems created by industrialism. On the level of plot (1) is expounded in terms of the Nemesis which punishes Gradgrind through his children and (2) is expounded in terms of Stephen Blackpool's sufferings. That Dickens makes a connection between the two propositions and the two areas of the plot is made clear in the scene where Blackpool confronts Bounderby and Harthouse, and is challenged to offer a solution for the 'muddle' he is always complaining about. Stephen expresses himself negatively. He repudiates the employers' exploitation of their power (' the strong hand will never do't'); their reliance on *laissez faire* ('lettin alone will never do't'); their withdrawal from social contact with the working classes ('not drawin nigh to fok, wi' kindness and patience an' cheery ways . . . will never do't'); and, 'most o' aw', their mental habit of regarding the workers as soulless units in the economic machine while inconsistently accusing them of ingratitude if they protest:

> 'Most o' aw, rating 'em as so much Power, and reg'lating 'em as
> if they was figures in a soom, or machines; wi'out loves and likens,
> wi'out memories and inclinations, wi'out souls to weary and souls
> to hope—when aw goes quiet draggin' on wi' 'em as if they'd
> nowt o' th'kind, and when aw goes onquiet, reproachin' 'em for
> their want o' sitch humanly feelins in their dealins wi' yo—this
> will never do't, Sir, till God's work is onmade.' (II, v)

It is clear that Dickens is speaking through Stephen here, and what the speech amounts to in positive terms is a plea for generosity, charity, imaginative understanding of the spiritual and emotional needs of humanity.

While these values have an obvious relevance to the field of personal relations (the Gradgrind-Bounderby circle) they are less viable as a basis for reform of the body politic, because there are no sanctions to ensure their application. They are not—apart from Louisa's abortive attempt to help Stephen—shown in action in the novel vertically through the class structure: Stephen's martyr-like death bears witness to this. Yet Dickens could only offer a disembodied and vaguely defined benevolence as a cure for the ills of Coketown because he had rejected all the alternatives. In his hostile portrait of Gradgrind, Dickens repudiated not only the narrowest kind of Utilitarian rationalism, but also, as House and others have pointed out, the processes by which most of the great Victorian reforms were carried out— statistical enquiry, commissions, reports, acted on by Parliamentary legislation.[6] In his hostile portrait of Slackbridge, and his account of Stephen's ostracism because of his refusal to join the Trade Union, Dickens repudiated the workers' claim to secure justice by collective bargaining. Dickens is, then, opposed to any change in the political and economic structure of society, and places his hopes for amelioration in a change of heart, mind, and soul in those who possess power, who will then disseminate the fruits of this change over the lower echelons of society. Dickens's ideal State would be one of 'benevolent and genial anarchy'.[7]

This is an insecure basis from which to launch a critique of society, and its insecurity becomes all the more obvious when we look outside *Hard Times* to Dickens's journalism of the same period, and find him enthusing over the wonders of Victorian manufacture[8] and expressing surprised admiration for the Preston cotton-workers' conduct of their strike in 1854.[9]

And yet, when all this has been said, and the contradictions, limitations, and flaws in Dickens's argument extrapolated, *Hard Times* remains a novel of considerable polemical effectiveness. The measure of this effectiveness, it seems to me, can only be accounted for in terms of Dickens's rhetoric. This approach should recommend itself to the author of *The Victorian Sage*, a study which shows how many key Victorian writers, disarmed of logic by their opponents, resorted to non-logical methods of persuasion in order to communicate their ideas. In the criticism of fiction we have learned, notably from Wayne Booth, to use 'rhetoric' as a term for all the techniques by which a novelist seeks to persuade us of the validity of his vision of experience, a vision which cannot usually be formulated in abstract terms. But in a novel like *Hard Times*, which can be called a *roman à thèse*, rhetoric functions very nearly in its traditional rôle as the vehicle of an argument.

There is another reason why rhetoric seems a particularly useful term in discussing Dickens's work. Not only is the 'author's voice' always insistent in his novels, but it is characteristically a public-speaking voice, an oratorical or histrionic voice; and it is not difficult to see a connection between this feature of his prose and his fondness for speech-making and public reading of his works.

I shall try to show that *Hard Times* succeeds where its rhetoric succeeds and fails where its rhetoric fails; and that success and failure correspond fairly closely to the negative and positive aspects, respectively, of the argument inherent in the novel.

The very first chapter of *Hard Times* affords an excellent illustration of Dickens's rhetoric, and it is short enough to be quoted and analysed in its entirety.

HARD TIMES

BOOK THE FIRST. SOWING

CHAPTER I

THE ONE THING NEEDFUL

'Now, what I want is, Facts. Teach these boys and girls nothing but Facts. Facts alone are wanted in life. Plant nothing else, and root out everything else. You can only form the minds of reasoning animals upon Facts: nothing else will ever be of any service to them. This is the principle on which I bring up my own children, and this is the principle on which I bring up these children. Stick to Facts, Sir!'

The scene was a plain, bare, monotonous vault of a schoolroom, and the speaker's square forefinger emphasised his observations by underscoring every sentence with a line on the schoolmaster's sleeve. The emphasis was helped by the speaker's square wall of a forehead, which had his eyebrows for its base, while his eyes found commodious cellarage in two dark caves, overshadowed by the wall. The emphasis was helped by the speaker's mouth, which was wide, thin, and hard set. The emphasis was helped by the speaker's voice, which was inflexible, dry, and dictatorial. The emphasis was helped by the speaker's hair, which bristled on the skirts of his bald head, a plantation of firs to keep the wind from its shining surface, all covered with knobs, like the crust of a plum pie, as if the head had scarcely warehouse-room for the hard facts stored inside. The speaker's obstinate carriage, square coat, square legs, square shoulders—nay, his very neckcloth, trained to take him by the throat with an unaccommodating grasp, like a stubborn fact, as it was—all helped the emphasis.

'In this life, we want nothing but Facts, Sir; nothing but Facts!'

The speaker, and the schoolmaster, and the third grown person present, all backed a little, and swept with their eyes the inclined plane of little vessels then and there arranged in order, ready to have imperial gallons of facts poured into them until they were full to the brim.

This chapter communicates, in a remarkably compact way, both a description and a judgment of a concept of education. This concept is defined in a speech, and then evaluated—not in its own terms, but in terms of the speaker's appearance and the setting. Dickens, of course, always relies heavily on the popular, perhaps primitive, assumption that there is a correspondence between a person's appearance and his character; and as Gradgrind is a governor of the school, its design may legitimately function as a metaphor for his character. Dickens also had a fondness for fancifully appropriate names, but—perhaps in order to stress the representativeness of Gradgrind's views—he does not reveal the name in this first chapter.*

Because of the brevity of the chapter, we are all the more susceptible to the effect of its highly rhetorical patterning, particularly the manipulation of certain repeated words, notably *fact*, *square*, and *emphasis*. The kind of education depicted here is chiefly characterized by an obsession with facts. The word occurs five times in the opening speech of the first paragraph, and it is twice repeated towards the end of the second, descriptive paragraph to prepare for the reintroduction of Gradgrind speaking— ' "we want nothing but Facts, sir—nothing but Facts" '; and it occurs for the tenth and last time towards the end of the last paragraph. In Gradgrind's speeches the word is capitalized, to signify his almost religious devotion to Facts.

Gradgrind's concept of education is further characterized in ways we can group into three categories, though of course they are closely connected:

(1) It is authoritarian, fanatical and bullying in its application.
(2) It is rigid, abstract and barren in quality.
(3) It is materialistic and commercial in its orientation.

The first category is conveyed by the structure of the second paragraph, which is dominated by 'emphasis'. This paragraph comprises six sentences. In the first sentence we are told how the 'speaker's square forefinger emphasised his observations'. The next four, central sentences are each introduced, with cumulative

---

* Mary McCarthy has suggested that an anonymous 'he' at the beginning of a novel usually moves the reader to sympathetic identification.[10] That the effect is quite the reverse in this example shows that the effect of any narrative strategy is determined finally by the narrator's language.

force, by the clause 'The emphasis was helped', and this formula, translated from the passive to the active voice, makes a fittingly 'emphatic' conclusion to the paragraph in the sixth sentence: 'all helped the emphasis'. This rhetorical pattern has a dual function. In one way it reflects or imitates Gradgrind's own bullying, over-emphatic rhetoric, of which we have an example in the first paragraph; but in another way it helps to *condemn* Gradgrind, since it 'emphasises' the narrator's own pejorative catalogue of details of the speaker's person and immediate environment. The narrator's rhetoric is, as it must be, far more skilful and persuasive than Gradgrind's.

The qualities in category (2) are conveyed in a number of geo-metrical or quasi-geometrical terms, *wide, line, thin, base, surface, inclined plane* and, particularly, *square* which recurs five times; and in words suggestive of barren regularity, *plain, bare, monotonous, arranged in order, inflexible.* Such words are particularly forceful when applied to human beings—whether Gradgrind or the children. The metamorphosis of the human into the non-human is, as we shall find confirmed later, one of Dickens's main devices for conveying his alarm at the way Victorian society was moving.

Category (3), the orientation towards the world of commerce, is perhaps less obvious than the other categories, but it is un-mistakably present in some of the boldest tropes of the chapter: *commodious cellarage, warehouse room, plantation, vessels, imperial gallons.*

The authoritarian ring of *'imperial'* leads us back from category (3) to category (1), just as *'under-scoring* every sentence with a *line'* leads us from (1) to (2). There is a web of connecting strands between the qualities I have tried to categorize: it is part of the rhetorical strategy of the chapter that all the qualities it evokes are equally applicable to Gradgrind's character, person, ideas, his school and the children (in so far as he has shaped them in his own image).

Metaphors of growth and cultivation are of course common-place in discussion of education, and we should not overlook the ironic invocation of such metaphors, with a deliberately religious, prophetic implication (reinforced by the Biblical echo of the chapter heading, 'The One Thing Needful'[11]) in the title of the Book, 'SOWING', later to be followed by Book the Second, 'REAPING', and Book the Third, 'GARNERING'. These

metaphors are given a further twist in Gradgrind's recommendation to 'Plant nothing else and root out everything else' (except
facts).

If there is a flaw in this chapter it is the simile of the plum pie,
which has pleasant, genial associations alien to the character of
Gradgrind, to whose head it is, quite superfluously, applied.
Taken as a whole, however, this is a remarkably effective and
densely woven beginning of the novel.

The technique of the first chapter of *Hard Times* could not be
described as 'subtle'. But subtle effects are often lost in a first
chapter, where the reader is coping with the problem of 'learning
the author's language'. Perhaps with some awareness of this fact,
sharpened by his sense of addressing a vast, popular audience,
Dickens begins many of his novels by nailing the reader's
attention with a display of sheer rhetorical power, relying
particularly on elaborate repetition. One thinks, for instance, of
the fog at the beginning of *Bleak House* or the sun and shadow in
the first chapter of *Little Dorrit*. In these novels the rhetoric works
to establish a symbolic atmosphere; in *Hard Times*, to establish
a thematic Idea—the despotism of Fact. But this abstraction—
Fact—is invested with a remarkable solidity through the figurative
dimension of the language.

The gross effect of the chapter is simply stated, but analysis
reveals that it is achieved by means of a complex verbal activity
that is far from simple. Whether it represents fairly any actual
educational theory or practice in mid-nineteenth-century England
is really beside the point. It aims to convince us of the *possibility*
of children being taught in such a way, and to make us recoil
from the imagined possibility. The chapter succeeds or fails as
rhetoric; and I think it succeeds.

Dickens begins as he means to continue. Later in the novel we
find Gradgrind's house, which, like the school-room, is a function
of himself, described in precisely the same terms of fact and rigid
measurement, partly geometrical and partly commercial.

> A very regular feature on the face of the country, Stone Lodge
> was. Not the least disguise toned down or shaded off that un-
> compromising fact in the landscape. A great square house, with a
> heavy portico darkening the principal windows, as its master's
> heavy brows over-shadowed his eyes. A calculated, cast up,

balanced and proved house. Six windows on this side of the door, six on that side; a total of twelve in this wing, a total of twelve in the other wing; four and twenty carried over to the back wings. A lawn and garden and an infant avenue, all ruled straight like a botanical account-book. (I, iii)

It has been observed[12] that Dickens individualizes his characters by making them use peculiar locutions and constructions in their speech, a technique which was particularly appropriate to serial publication in which the reader's memory required to be frequently jogged. This technique extends beyond the idiosyncratic speech of characters, to the language in which they are described. A key-word, or group of key-words, is insistently used when the character is first introduced, not only to identify him but also to evaluate him, and is invoked at various strategic points in the subsequent action. Dickens's remarkable metaphorical inventiveness ensures that continuity and rhetorical emphasis are not obtained at the expense of monotony. The application of the key-words of the first chapter to Mr Gradgrind's house gives the same delight as the development of a metaphysical conceit. The observation that Mrs Gradgrind, 'whenever she showed a symptom of coming to life, was invariably stunned by some weighty piece of fact tumbling on her' (I, iv), affords a kind of verbal equivalent of knock-about comedy, based on a combination of expectancy (we know the word will recur) and surprise (we are not prepared for the particular formulation).

Bounderby offers another illustration of Dickens's use of key-words in characterization. He is first introduced as 'a big, loud man, with a stare, and a metallic laugh' (I, iv). The metallic quality is shortly afterwards defined as 'that brassy speaking-trumpet of a voice of his' (*ibid.*). His house has a front door with 'BOUNDERBY (in letters very like himself) upon a brazen plate, and a round brazen door-handle underneath it, like a brazen full stop' (I, xi). Bounderby's bank 'was another red brick house, with black outside shutters, green inside blinds, a black street door up two white steps, a brazen door-plate, and a brazen door-handle full-stop' (II, i). The buildings Bounderby inhabits take their character from him, as Gradgrind's do from him. But here the emphasis is on the brass embellishments which, by the use of the word *brazen* (rather than *brass* used adjectivally) epitomize several facets of his characters: his hardness, vanity, crude enjoyment of wealth, and, most important of all, the fact that he is a brazen liar. (We do not know for certain that he is a liar until the end of the novel; the 'brazen' fittings reinforce other hints which prepare us for the revelation.)

The failures of characterization in *Hard Times* are generally failures in using rhetorical strategies which Dickens elsewhere employs very successfully. The portrait of Slackbridge, the trade union demagogue, for instance, seeks to exploit a relationship between character and appearance in a way which is familiar in Dickens and well exemplified in the first chapter; but it does so crudely and clumsily:

> Judging him by Nature's evidence, he was above the mass in very little but the stage on which he stood. In many respects he was essentially below them. He was not so honest, he was not so manly, he was not so good-humoured; he substituted cunning for their simplicity, and passion for their safe solid sense. An ill-made, high shouldered man, with lowering brows, and his features crushed into an habitually sour expression, he contrasted most unfavourably, even in his mongrel dress, with the great body of his hearers in their plain working clothes. (II, iv)

Apart from the vividness of 'crushed', the description of Slackbridge is carelessly vague, and we miss the metaphorical inventiveness that characterizes Dickens's best descriptions of people. But the main error of the passage is the ordering of its material. The rhetorical strategy announced by the opening sentence is that Slackbridge's character is to be read in his appearance. But in fact the character is read *before* we are given the appearance. It is as if Dickens has so little confidence in his own imaginative evidence that he must inform us, over-explicitly, what conclusions we are to draw, before we come to the evidence. We know from external sources that Dickens was in a confused state of mind about the trade union movement at the time of writing *Hard Times*,[13] and we can rarely expect to receive a balanced account of organized labour from any middle-class Victorian novelist. However, the failure of understanding here reveals itself in the first place as a failure of expression; the portrait of Gradgrind, on the other hand, though it probably derives from an equivalent misunderstanding of Utilitarianism, succeeds.

Another, more significant failure of Dickens's rhetoric is to be observed in the treatment of Tom Gradgrind. In this connection, I must register my disagreement with John Holloway's opinion that 'the gradual degeneration of Tom . . . is barely (as in fact it is treated) related to Dickens's major problems in the book, though it is one of its best things'.[14] It is gradual (though not very extensively treated) up to the beginning of Book II, by which point we have gathered that Tom, so far from drawing strength of character from his repressive and rationalist upbringing, is turning into a selfish young man prepared to exploit others for his own advantage. He is still a long way, however, from the depravity that allows him to connive at the seduction of his own sister and to implicate an innocent man (Stephen Blackpool) in his own crime. This moral gap is rather clumsily bridged by Dickens in the second chapter of Book II, where he suddenly introduces a key-word for Tom: 'whelp'.

The Bounderbys are entertaining James Harthouse to dinner. Louisa does not respond to Harthouse's attempts to flirt, but when Tom comes in, late, 'She changed . . . and broke into a beaming smile. . . .'

> 'Ay, ay?' thought the visitor. 'This whelp is the only creature she cares for. So, so!'
> The whelp was presented, and took his chair. The appellation was not flattering, but not unmerited. (II, ii)

The chapter ends very shortly afterwards, but Dickens contrives to use the word 'whelp' three more times, and the title of the following chapter (II, iii), in which Tom betrays Louisa's situation to Harthouse, is entitled 'The Whelp'.

'Whelp' is a cliché, and it will be noticed that the word is first used by Harthouse, and then adopted by the novelist in his authorial capacity. When a novelist does this, it is usually with ironical intent, suggesting some inadequacy in the speaker's habits of thought.* Dickens plays on Gradgrind's 'facts' to this

---

* Compare E. M. Forster, a master of this device, in *A Room with a View* (George Emerson has been indiscreet enough to mention in company that his father is taking a bath):

> 'Oh dear!' breathed the little old lady, and shuddered as if all the winds of heaven had entered the apartment. 'Gentlemen sometimes do not realise——' Her voice faded away. But Miss Bartlett seemed to under-

effect. But in the case of Harthouse's 'whelp' he has taken a moral cliché from a character who is morally unreliable, and invested it with his own authority as narrator. This gives away the fact that Tom is being forced into a new rôle halfway through the book. For Tom's degeneration *should* be related to the major problems with which Dickens is concerned in *Hard Times*. According to the overall pattern of the novel, Tom and Louisa are to act as indices of the failure of Mr Gradgrind's philosophy of education, and should thus never be allowed to stray outside the area of our pity, since they are both victims rather than free agents. But Tom's actions do take him beyond our pity, and diminish the interest of his character.

Perhaps Dickens was misled by feeling the need to inject a strong crime-interest into his story, of which Tom was a handy vehicle; or perhaps he lost his head over the preservation of Louisa's purity (the somewhat hysterical conclusion to Chapter iii, Book II, 'The Whelp', seems to suggest this). Whatever the explanation, 'the whelp', unlike those key-words which organize and concentrate the represented character of individuals and places, acts merely as a slogan designed to generate in the reader such a contempt for Tom that he will not enquire too closely into the pattern of his moral development—a pattern that will not, in fact, bear very close scrutiny.

In the conduct of his central argument, Dickens explicitly calls our attention to a 'key-note'. The first occasion on which he does so is when introducing the description of Coketown, in Chapter v of Book I, entitled 'The Key-note':

COKETOWN, to which Messrs. Bounderby and Gradgrind now walked, was a triumph of fact; it had no greater taint of fancy in it

---

stand, and a conversation developed in which gentlemen who did not realise played a principal part.' (I, 1)

Much later in the novel. Lucy, engaged to another, is desperately fighting off the advances of George. 'What does a girl do when she comes across a cad?' she asks Miss Bartlett.

'I always said he was a cad, dear. Give me credit for that at all events. From the very first moment—when he said his father was having a bath.' ... She moved feebly to the window, and tried to detect the cad's white flannels among the laurels. (II, 16) than Mrs Gradgrind herself. Let us strike the keynote, Coketown, before pursuing our tune.

It was a town of red brick, or of brick that would have been red if the smoke and ashes had allowed it; but as matters stood it was a town of unnatural red and black like the painted face of a savage. It was a town of machinery and tall chimneys, out of which interminable serpents of smoke trailed themselves for ever and ever, and never got uncoiled. It had a black canal in it, and a river that ran purple with ill-smelling dye, and vast piles of building full of windows where there was a rattling and a trembling all day long, and where the piston of the steam engine worked monotonously up and down like the head of an elephant in a state of melancholy madness. It contained several large streets all very like one another, and many more small streets still more like one another, inhabited by people equally like one another, who all went in and out at the same hours, with the same sound upon the same pavements, to do the same work, and to whom every day was the same as yesterday and tomorrow, and every year the counterpart of the last and the next.

Dorothy Van Ghent has commented on the effects Dickens gains by investing the inanimate with animation and vice versa. 'The animation of inanimate objects suggests both the quaint gaiety of a forbidden life, and an aggressiveness that has got out of control. . . . The animate is treated as if it is a thing. It is as if the life absorbed by things had been drained out of people who have become incapable of their humanity.'[15] The description of Coketown illustrates this process. The buildings and machinery of Coketown are invested with a sinister life of their own, the life of savages, serpents, and elephants (the serpent and elephant images are reiterated at least five times in the novel).[16] The people of Coketown, on the other hand, take their character from the architecture of the town non-metaphorically conceived—'large streets all very like one another, and many small streets still more like one another'. They are reduced to indistinguishable units caught up in a mindless, monotonous, mechanical process, superbly represented in the droning repetition of sound and syntax in the last sentence of the passage quoted.

In the rest of this chapter Dickens goes on to say that, despite the efficiency of the town, it was afflicted by *malaise*, social and moral: drunkenness, idleness, irreligion. 'Is it possible,' he asks, 'that there was any analogy between the case of the Coketown populace and the little Gradgrinds?' He goes on to suggest that in both 'there was fancy in them demanding to be brought into healthy existence instead of struggling on in convulsions'.

The antithesis of 'fact and fancy' introduces the chapter (see the quotation above). It has been previously introduced in the school-room chapters, where Cissy Jupe's words, 'I would fancy——', are rudely interrupted by the government official:

> 'Ay, ay, ay! But you mustn't fancy,' cried the gentleman, quite elated by coming so happily to his point. 'That's it! You are never to fancy. . . . You are to be in all things regulated and governed . . . by fact. . . . You must discard the word Fancy altogether.' (I. ii)

A very similar interruption establishes the same antithesis in slightly different terms in Chapter viii, Book I, 'Never Wonder', where Dickens again proposes to strike the key-note:

> LET us strike the key-note again, before pursuing the tune.
>
> When she was half a dozen years younger, Louisa had been overheard to begin a conversation with her brother one day, by saying 'Tom, I wonder'—upon which Mr. Gradgrind, who was the person overhearing, stepped forth into the light, and said, 'Louisa, never wonder!'
>
> Herein lay the spring of the mechanical art and mystery of educating the reason without stooping to the cultivation of the sentiments and affections. Never wonder. By means of addition, subtraction, multiplication and division, settle everything somehow, and never wonder. Bring to me, says M'Choakumchild, yonder baby just able to walk, and I will engage that it shall never wonder.

The antithesis between fact and fancy (or wonder), is, then, the dominant key-note of *Hard Times*. It relates the public world of the novel to the private world, the *malaise* of the Gradgrind–Bounderby circle to the *malaise* of Coketown as a social community; and it draws together the two stages of the central argument of the book; the relationship between education in the broad sense and social health. In this respect Dickens is not so very far removed from the position of the Romantic critics of industrialist society. Compare Shelley:

> We have more moral, political and historical wisdom than we know how to reduce into practice; we have more scientific and

economical knowledge than can be accommodated to the just distribution of the produce which it multiplies. The poetry, in these systems of thought, is concealed by the accumulations of facts and calculating processes. . . . We want the creative faculty to imagine that which we know. . . . To what but a cultivation of the mechanical arts in a degree disproportioned to the presence of the creative faculty, which is the basis of all knowledge, is to be attributed the abuses of all invention for abridging and combining labour, to the exasperation of the inequality of mankind? From what other cause has it arisen that the discoveries which should have lightened, have added a weight to the curse of Adam? Poetry, and the principle of Self, of which money is the visible incarnation, are the God and Mammon of the world.[17]

There is a real community of feeling between Shelley and Dickens here: one might almost think that *Hard Times* takes its cue for the criticism of 'the accumulation of facts', 'calculating processes', and 'the principle of Self' from the *Defence*. But whereas Shelley opposes to these things poetry, imagination, the creative faculty, Dickens can only offer Fancy, wonder, sentiments—though he does so with the same seriousness and the same intentions as Shelley, as a panacea for the ills of modern society. It is tempting to relate the inadequacy of Dickens's concept of Fancy[18] to the discussions familiar in Romantic criticism of Fancy and Imagination. But it is on the rhetorical level that the inadequacy of Dickens's concept manifests itself. In the first 'key-note' chapter, the authorial voice inquiries, with heavy irony, whether we are to be told 'at this time of day'

that one of the foremost elements in the existence of the Coketown working-people had been for scores of years deliberately set at nought? That there was any Fancy in them demanding to be brought into healthy existence instead of struggling on in convulsions? That, exactly in the ratio as they worked long and monotonously, the craving grew within them for some physical relief—some relaxation, encouraging good humour and good spirits, and giving them a vent—some recognized holiday, though it were but for an honest dance to a stirring band of music—some occasional light pie in which even M'Choakumchild had no finger—which craving must and would be satisfied aright, or must and would inevitably go wrong, until the laws of the Creation were repealed? (I, v)

The rhetorical questions here impede and confuse the argument. The parallelism of 'which craving must and would be satisfied aright, or must and would inevitably go wrong' is tired and mechanical. A mathematical image is enlisted in arguing *against* the mathematical, calculating faculty: it is precisely Dickens's case in the novel as a whole that the 'laws of Creation' are not accountable in terms of 'ratios'. The vagueness of '*some* relaxation', '*some* recognized holiday' is by no means clarified by the unexciting offer of an 'honest dance' or a 'light pie' as specific palliatives for the people of Coketown.

Dickens is struggling to assert, here, the existence of a universal need in humanity, a need which arises from quite a different side of man's nature from that which is occupied with the mechanical processes of industrialism, a need which must be satisfied, a need distantly related to that need for poetry which Shelley asserts. But whereas Shelley's 'poetry' is a faculty which involves and enhances and transforms the total activity of man—'We must imagine that which we know'—Dickens's Fancy is merely a temporary escape from what is accepted as inevitably unpleasant. It is 'relief', 'a vent', 'a holiday'. To be cruel, one might say that Dickens offers the oppressed workers of Coketown bread and circuses: bread in the metaphorical 'light pie' and circuses in the 'honest dance'—and, of course, in Mr Sleary's circus.

The realm of Fancy is most vividly evoked by the rhetoric of *Hard Times* in what might be called the 'fairy-tale' element of the novel.* Many of the characters and events are derived from the staple ingredients of the fairy-tale, and this derivation is clearly revealed in the language.

Louisa and Tom first figure as the brother and sister who often appear in fairy-tales as waifs, exiles, victims of circumstance, hedged about with dangers (the Babes in the Woods, etc.). As they sit by the fire of their room, 'Their shadows were defined upon the wall, but those of the high presses in the room were all blended together on the wall and on the ceiling, as if the brother

---

* My attention was first directed to this (apart from the characterization of Mrs Sparsit) by a Birmingham undergraduate, Miss Margaret Thomas. Possibly it has been observed before, but I have not been able to find it in Dickens criticism.

and sister were overhung by a dark cavern' (I, viii). In their childhood their father wears the aspect of an 'Ogre':

> Not that they knew, by name or nature, anything about an Ogre. Fact forbid! I only use the word to express a monster in a lecturing castle, with Heaven knows how many heads manipulated into one, taking childhood captive, and dragging it into gloomy statistical dens by the hair. (I, iii)

Later, Louisa becomes the enchanted princess with a heart of ice, while Tom takes on the rôle of the knave. Harthouse is the demon king, popping up suddenly in the action with mischievous intent, in a cloud of (cigar) smoke:

> James Harthouse continued to lounge in the same place and attitude, smoking his cigar in his own easy way, and looking pleasantly at the whelp, as if he knew himself to be a kind of agreeable demon who had only to hover over him, and he must give up his whole soul if required. (II, iii)

Cissy tells Mrs Gradgrind that she used to read to her father 'About the fairies, sir, and the dwarf, and the hunchback, and the genies' (I, vii); and the circus folk in *Hard Times* are comparable to the chorus of benevolent, comic, grotesque, half-supernatural creatures who inhabit the world of romance and fairy-tale. They are persistently associated with legend and myth—Pegasus (I, v), Cupid (*ibid.*), Jack the Giant Killer (III, vii), etc. Mr Bounderby's mother, Mrs Pegler, 'the mysterious old woman' (III, v) is the crone who figures in many fairy tales and who brings about a surprising turn in the action. Mr Bounderby refers to her as 'an old woman who seems to have been flying into the town on a broomstick now and then' (II, viii). But the proper witch of the story, and Dickens's most effective adaptation of a stock-figure from fairy-tale, is Mrs Sparsit. 'Mrs Sparsit considered herself, in some sort, the Bank Fairy', we are told, but the townspeople 'regarded her as the Bank Dragon, keeping watch over the treasures of the mine'. Her heavy eyebrows and hooked nose are exploited for vivid effects of cruelty:

> Mr Bounderby sat looking at her, as, with the points of a stiff, sharp pair of scissors, she picked out holes for some inscrutable purpose, in a piece of cambric. An operation which, taken in connexion with the bushy eyebrows and the Roman nose, suggested

with some liveliness the idea of a hawk engaged upon the eyes of a tough little bird. (I, xvi)

She flatters Bounderby to his face, but secretly insults his portrait. She wills Louisa into Harthouse's clutches, figuring Louisa's progress as the descent of a 'Giant's Staircase', on which she keeps anxious watch (II, x). The boldest treatment of Mrs Sparsit as a witch occurs in the scene where she steals through the grounds of Mr Gradgrind's country house, hoping to catch Louisa and Harthouse together.

> She thought of the wood and stole towards it, heedless of long grass and briers: of worms, snails, and slugs, and all the creeping things that be. With her dark eyes and her hook nose warily in advance of her, Mrs Sparsit softly crushed her way through the thick undergrowth, so intent upon her object that she would probably have done no less, if the wood had been a wood of adders.
> Hark!
> The smaller birds might have tumbled out of their nests, fascinated by the glittering of Mrs Sparsit's eyes in the gloom.... (II, xi)

When a thunderstorm bursts immediately afterwards, Mrs Sparsit's appearance becomes still more grotesque:

> It rained now, in a sheet of water. Mrs Sparsit's white stockings were of many colours, green predominating; prickly things were in her shoes; caterpillars slung themselves, in hammocks of their own making, from various parts of her dress; rills ran from her bonnet, and her Roman nose. (II, xi)

Traditionally, witches are antipathetic to water. It is appropriate, therefore, that the frustration of Mrs Sparsit's spite, when she loses track of Louisa, is associated with her ludicrous, rain-soaked appearance (see the conclusion to II, xi).

We may add to these examples of the invocation of fairy tale, the repeated description of the factories illuminated at night as 'fairy palaces' (I, x; I, xi; II, i, *et passim*), and Mr Bounderby's often expressed conviction that his men 'expect to be set up in a coach and six, and to be fed on turtle soup and venison and fed with a gold spoon' (I, xi; I, vi; II, i, *et passim*). These phrases contrast ironically with the actual drab environment and existence of the Coketown people.

It is, indeed, as an *ironic* rhetorical device that the fairy-tale element operates most successfully. On one level it is possible to read the novel as an ironic fairy-tale, in which the enchanted princess is released from her spell but does not find a Prince Charming, in which the honest, persecuted servant (Stephen) is vindicated but not rewarded, and in which the traditional romantic belief in blood and breeding, confirmed by a discovery, is replaced by the exposure of Bounderby's inverted snobbery.

In other respects, however, the fairy-tale element sets up unresolved tensions in the novel. It encourages a morally-simplified, non-social, and non-historical view of human life and conduct, whereas Dickens's undertaking in *Hard Times* makes quite opposite demands. Mr Sleary's ruse for releasing Tom from the custody of Bitzer, for instance (III, viii), is acceptable on the level of fairy-tale motivation: he returns Mr Gradgrind's earlier good deed (the adoption of Cissy) and scores off an unsympathetic character (Bitzer). But the act is essentially lawless, and conflicts with Dickens's appeals elsewhere in the novel for justice and social responsibility. As long as the circus-folk represent a kind of life that is anarchic, seedy, socially disreputable, but cheerful and humane, they are acceptable and enjoyable. But when they are offered as agents or spokesmen of social and moral amelioration, we reject them. The art they practice is Fancy in its tawdriest form, solemnly defended by Mr Sleary in terms we recognize as the justification of today's mass entertainers:

> 'People mutht be amuthed. They can't be alwayth a learning, nor yet they can't be alwayth a workirg, they an't made for it. You *mutht* have uth, Thquire. (III, viii)

Cissy is meant to represent a channel through which the values of the circus folk are conveyed to the social order. But her one positive act, the dismissal of Harthouse (III, ii), depends for its credibility on a simple faith in the superiority of a good fairy over a demon king.

In other words, where Dickens invokes the world of fairy-tale ironically, to dramatize the drabness, greed, spite and injustice which characterize a society dominated by materialism, it is a highly effective rhetorical device; but where he relies on the simplifications of the fairy-tale to suggest means of redemption, we remain unconvinced.

If Dickens's notion of Fancy was attached mainly to fairy-tale and nursery rhyme (cf. the allusions to the cow with the crumpled horn and Peter Piper in I, iii), his own art is very much one of Fancy in the Coleridgean sense: 'Fancy has no other counters to play with, but fixities and definites. The Fancy is indeed no other than a mode of Memory emancipated from the order of time and space. . . .'[19] This seems an appropriate description of Dickens's method in, for instance, the first chapter of *Hard Times*, or in the description of Coketown, or in the treatment of Mrs Sparsit as a witch. To appreciate this, is to feel that Coleridge was wrong to depreciate Fancy as a literary mode; but it is also to understand why Dickens's greatest achievement as a novelist was his depiction of a disordered universe in which the organic and the mechanical have exchanged places, rather than in his attempts to trace moral and emotional processes within the individual psyche.

In *Hard Times*, Dickens expounds a diagnosis of the ills of modern industrial society for which no institutions can supply a cure: society, represented by a group of characters, must therefore change itself, learning from a group outside the social order—the circus. But Dickens's characters are incapable of change: the language in which they are embodied fixes them in their 'given' condition. They can only die (like Stephen Blackpool) or be broken (like Mr Bounderby). Mr Gradgrind may lose his 'square-ness', but he is left a shadow: he cannot become a Michelin Man, all circles and spheres. Louisa when her heart has been melted is a far less convincing character than Louisa with a heart of ice. (This can be quickly seen by comparing the scene of her interview with Gradgrind to discuss Bounderby's proposal (I, xv), rightly singled out for praise by Leavis, with the parallel scene at the end of the book where she returns to her father to reproach him for her upbringing, and where she is given the most embarrassing lines in the novel to speak (II, xii).) Dickens falters in his handling of the character of Tom Gradgrind precisely because he uses a device for fixing character (*whelp*) to express a process of change.

If *Hard Times* is a polemical novel that is only partially per-suasive, it is because Dickens's rhetoric is only partially adequate to the tasks he set himself.

IV

Tess, Nature, and the Voices of Hardy

THOMAS HARDY might be described as an 'in-spite-of' novelist. That is, he figures in literary criticism and literary history as a great novelist 'in spite of' gross defects, the most commonly alleged of which are his manipulation of events in defiance of probability to produce a tragic-ironic pattern, his intrusiveness as authorial commentator, his reliance on stock characters, and his capacity for writing badly. In my view, the last of these alleged faults involves all the others, which, considered in the abstract as narrative strategies, are not necessarily faults. If we have reservations about them in Hardy's work, it must be because of the way they are articulated—or inadequately articulated.

Does Hardy write badly? One method of trying to answer such a question is that of Practical Criticism: the critical analysis of a passage extracted from its context. I therefore begin by citing an example of Practical Criticism *avant la lettre* performed by Vernon Lee upon five hundred words taken at random from *Tess of the D'Urbervilles*.[1] The unsatisfactoriness of her conclusions, I suggest, can only be made good by returning the passage to its context— the whole novel, and by trying to define the linguistic character of the novel in terms of its literary purpose. Using the perspective thus established, I turn to the consideration of another passage from the novel, one which has attracted a good deal of conflicting commentary. My intention is primarily to try and define as clearly as possible the sense in which the author of *Tess* may be said to 'write badly'; and to show that the consideration of this question, even when based on the close examination of short extracts, must inevitably involve us in the consideration of the meaning and artistic success of the novel as a whole.

The passage discussed by Vernon Lee is from Chapter XVI, the first chapter of the third 'Phase' of the novel, entitled 'The Rally'. It follows immediately after Tess, on her journey from her home at Marlott in the Vale of Blackmoor to the dairy of Talbothays, where she hopes to make a new start after her seduction by Alec d'Urberville, breaks into the 148th Psalm; and it describes her descent into the valley of the Var:

> However, Tess found at least approximate expression for her feelings in the old *Benedicite* that she had lisped from infancy; and it was enough. Such high contentment with such a slight initial performance as that of having started towards a means of independent living was a part of the Durbeyfield temperament. Tess really wished to walk uprightly, while her father did nothing of the kind; but she resembled him in being content with immediate and small achievements, and in having no mind for laborious effort towards such petty social advancement as could alone be effected by a family so heavily handicapped as the once powerful d'Urbervilles were now.
>
> There was, it might be said, the energy of her mother's unexpended family, as well as the natural energy of Tess's years, rekindled after the experience which had so overwhelmed her for the time. Let the truth be told—women do as a rule live through such humiliations, and regain their spirits, and again look about them with an interested eye. While there's life there's hope is a conviction not so entirely unknown to the 'betrayed' as some amiable theorists would have us believe.
>
> Tess Durbeyfield, then, in good heart, and full of zest for life, descended the Egdon slopes lower and lower towards the dairy of her pilgrimage.
>
> The marked difference, in the final particular, between the rival vales now showed itself. The secret of Blackmoor was best discovered from the heights around; to read aright the valley before her it was necessary to descend into its midst. When Tess had accomplished this feat she found herself to be standing on a carpeted level, which stretched to the east and west as far as the eye could reach.
>
> The river had stolen from the higher tracts and brought in particles to the vale all this horizontal land; and now, exhausted,

aged, and attenuated, lay serpentining along through the midst of its former spoils.

Not quite sure of her direction Tess stood still upon the hemmed expanse of verdant flatness, like a fly on a billiard table of indefinite length, and of no more consequence to the surroundings than that fly. The sole effect of her presence upon the placid valley so far had been to excite the mind of a solitary heron, which, after descending to the ground not far from her path, stood with neck erect, looking at her.

Suddenly there arose from all parts of the lowland a prolonged and repeated call—

'Waow! waow! waow!'

From the furthest east to the furthest west the cries spread by contagion, accompanied in some cases by the barking of a dog. It was not the expression of the valley's consciousness that beautiful Tess had arrived, but the ordinary announcement of milking-time —half-past four o'clock, when the dairy men set about getting in the cows.

The interested reader will find it rewarding to read Vernon Lee's commentary in its entirety, but I must confine myself to extracts from it. Her basic objection to this passage is 'that we are *being told about* the locality, not what is necessary for the intelligence of the situation'[2]—the 'then', she argues, poses falsely as a connective between the description of the valley and the meditative commentary that precedes it[3]—and that even as a straightforward description it is awkwardly and untidily written:

Notice how he tells us the very simple fact of how Tess stops to look round: 'Tess . . . stood still upon the hemmed expanse of verdant flatness, like a fly on a billiard-table of indefinite length.' '*Hemmed* expanse,' that implies that the expanse had limits; it is, however, compared to a billiard-table 'of indefinite length'. Hardy's attention has slackened, and really he is talking a little at random. If he visualized that valley, particularly from above, he would not think of it, which is bounded by something on his own higher level (*hemmed*, by which he means *hemmed in*), in connection with a billiard table which is bounded by the tiny wall of its cushion. I venture to add that if, at the instant of writing, he were feeling the variety, the freshness of a valley, he would not be comparing it to a piece of cloth, with which it has only two things in common, being flat and being green; the utterly dissimilar flatness and greenness of a landscape and that of a billiard-table.

We are surely in the presence of slackened interest, when the

Writer casts about for and accepts any illustration, without realizing it sufficiently to reject it. Such slackening of attention is confirmed by the poor structure of the sentence, 'a fly on a billiard-table of indefinite length *and* of no more consequence to the surroundings than that fly.' The *and* refers the 'of no more consequence' in the first instance to the billiard-table. Moreover, I venture to think the whole remark was not worth making: why divert our attention from Tess and her big, flat valley, surely easy enough to realize, by a vision of a billiard-table with a fly on it? Can the two images ever grow into one another? is the first made clearer, richer, by the second? How useless all this business has been is shown by the next sentence: 'The sole effect of her presence upon the placid valley so far had been to excite the mind of a solitary heron, which, after descending to the ground not far from her path, stood, with neck erect, looking at her.' Leave out all about the billiard-table, and the sentences coalesce perfectly and give us all we care to know.[4]

Vernon Lee's discussion of the rest of the passage is equally severe, finding everywhere a 'general slackening of attention, the vagueness showing itself in the casual distribution of the subject matter; showing itself, as we . . . see in lack of masterful treatment of the Reader's attention, in utter deficiency of logical arrangement. These are the co-related deficiencies due to the same inactivity and confusion of thought'.[5] In her closing remarks, however, Vernon Lee glaringly declines to accept the critical conclusions which follow from her analysis:

> The woolly outlines, even the uncertain drawing, merely add to the impression of primeval passiveness and blind, unreasoning emotion; of inscrutable doom and blind, unfeeling Fate which belong to his whole outlook on life. And the very faults of Hardy are probably an expression of his solitary and matchless grandeur of attitude. He belongs to a universe transcending such trifles as Writers and Readers and their little logical ways.[6]

This disingenuous conclusion conceals either a failure of nerve before the Great Reputation, or an admission that the total effect of *Tess* is rather more impressive than the analysis of the extract suggests. I suspect that the latter is the case, and that if we consider the peculiarities of the passage in the context of the whole novel we shall arrive at a view of Hardy somewhere between the semi-illiterate blunderer exposed by Vernon Lee's commentary and the majestic figure transcending ordinary critical standards postulated in her conclusion. Such a consideration must start with an attempt to describe the function of the 'author's voice' in *Tess*, and proceed to discuss the attitudes of that author to Nature.

Underlying all Vernon Lee's criticism we can detect a prejudice against omniscient narration and in favour of Jamesian 'presentation'; against 'telling' and in favour of 'showing'. Just how dangerously narrowing and exclusive such prescriptive interpretation of Jamesian precept and practice can be, has been fully and persuasively argued by Wayne Booth in *The Rhetoric of Fiction*. But to note the existence of this element in Vernon Lee's approach to Hardy by no means disposes of her objections, for a candid appraisal of *Tess* will reveal a fundamental uncertainty about the author's relation to his readers and to his characters, an uncertainty which is betrayed again and again in the language of the novel.

Tess, we are told, 'spoke two languages: the dialect at home, more or less; ordinary English abroad and to persons of quality' (III). To some extent the same is true of Hardy as narrator. There is the Hardy who can recreate dialect speech with flawless authenticity, who shows how closely he is in touch with the life of an agrarian community through being in touch with its idiom; and there is the Hardy speaking to 'the quality' in orotund sentences of laboured syntax and learned vocabulary, the Hardy who studied *The Times*, Addison, and Scott to improve his style.[7] It is probably the second Hardy who is responsible for the most spectacular stylistic lapses. But to regard the second Hardy as a regrettable excrescence superimposed upon the first, 'true', Hardy would be mistaken. For while one aspect of the novelist's undertaking in *Tess* demands a quality of immediacy, of 'felt life', achieved through his empathetic identification with his characters, particularly his heroine—in other words, the voice of the first Hardy—other aspects demand a quality of distance, both of time and space, through which the characters can be seen in their cosmic, historical, and social settings—in other words, the voice of the second Hardy. And some of the most effective passages in the book—the description of the mechanical thresher, for instance (XLVII)—are articulated by this second Hardy.

Several accents are mingled in this voice. The author here is a combination of sceptical philosopher, and local historian, topographer, antiquarian, mediating between his 'folk'—the agricultural community of Wessex—and his readers—the metropolitan 'quality'. About the sceptical philosopher critics have had much to say, and most of them have regretted his presence. But if we reject such intrusions *qua* intrusions, we must reject other kinds of intrusion in the novel, in which case we shall not be left with very much in our hand. On the whole I think it will be found that these intrusions offend when they are crudely expressed. The sentence in Vernon Lee's passage, 'While there's life there's hope is a conviction not so entirely unknown to the "betrayed" as some amiable theorists would have us believe', for example, alienates rather than persuades the reader because it attempts to overthrow a social–moral cliché (that sexual betrayal is irredeemable) by nothing more potent than a proverbial cliché ('while there's life there's hope') and an ironic cliché ('amiable'). Compare the bitingly effective comment on the burial of Tess's child:

> So the baby was carried in a small deal box, under an ancient woman's shawl, to the churchyard that night, and buried by lantern-light, at the cost of a shilling, and a pint of beer to the sexton, in that shabby corner of God's allotment where He lets the nettles grow, and where all unbaptized infants, notorious drunkards, suicides and others of the conjecturally damned are laid. (XIV)

There is much to admire in this sentence. It begins with a subdued literal description of the pathetic particulars of the child's burial. A hint of irony appears in the shilling and the pint of beer. This becomes overt in the axis of the sentence which marks the transition from impersonal narration to comment—'That shabby corner of God's allotment where He lets the nettles grow'— where, through the conventional idea that the churchyard is ground dedicated to God, He is held responsible for the behaviour of His earthly representatives—is presented, in fact, as a cynically careless smallholder, a stroke which has particular appropriateness in the agrarian environment of the story. The irony is sustained and intensified in the conclusion of the sentence, in the grouping of unbaptized infants with drunkards and suicides, and in the juxtaposition of the cool 'conjecturally' with the uncompromising 'damned', which effectively shocks us into awareness of the arrogance and inhumanity of presuming to forecast the eternal destiny of souls.

The author of *Tess* as local historian has received less attention than the author as sceptical philosopher, but his presence is unmistakable. The title-page tells us that the story of Tess is 'Faithfully Presented by Thomas Hardy'; and the explanatory note to the first edition of 1891 describes the novel, rather equivocally, 'as an attempt to give artistic form to a true sequence of things'. Although no dates are specified in the novel, we are often made to feel that Tess's story is not taking place in a continuum in which author and reader keep pace with the action and, so to speak, discover its outcome with the protagonists; but that it is already finished, that it took place in living memory, and is being reported to us by someone who lived in the locality, who knew her, though only slightly, who has received much of his information at second-hand, and whose account is one of imaginative reconstruction:

> The name of the eclipsing girl, whatever it was, has not been handed down. (II)
>
> '. . . the stopt-diapason note which her voice acquired when her heart was in her speech, and which will never be forgotten by those who knew her. (XIV)
>
> It was said afterwards that a cottager of Wellbridge, who went out late that night for a doctor, met two lovers in the pastures, walking very slowly, without converse, one behind the other, as in a funeral procession, and the glimpse he obtained of their faces seemed to denote that they were anxious and sad. (XXXV)

This voice of the author as local historian, dependent upon secondary sources, is in a state of uneasy co-existence with the voice of the author as creator and maker, as one acquainted with the deepest interior processes of his characters' minds. The uneasiness manifests itself notably in Hardy's hesitation about how far to attempt an imitation of the verbal quality of Tess's consciousness. Often he does not attempt it at all: the morning after Angel's sleep-walking, for instance, we are told that, 'It just crossed her mind, too, that he might have a faint recollection of his tender vagary, and was disinclined to allude to it from a conviction that she would take amatory advantage of the opportunity it gave her of appealing to him anew not to go' (XXXVII). That Hardy was not entirely happy about using vocabulary and syntax so far removed from Tess's natural idiom is suggested by this quotation: 'She thought, *without actually wording the thought*, how strange and godlike was a composer's power, who from the grave could lead through sequences of emotion, which he alone had felt at first, a girl like her who had never heard of his name. . . .' (XIII—*my italics*). Of course, in the strict sense, there is no 'real' Tess, and everything we know about her proceeds from the same source. But in terms of literary illusion, the distinction between Tess's consciousness and the author's articulation of it is a real one. Consider for example the account of her disappointment at the appearance of Alec D'Urberville:

> She had dreamed of an aged and dignified face, the sublimation of all the d'Urberville lineaments, furrowed with incarnate memories representing in hieroglyphic the centuries of her family's and England's history. But she screwed herself up to the work in hand, since she could not get out of it, and answered—
> 'I came to see your mother, sir.' (V)

The first sentence is a consciously literary paraphrase of Tess's vague, romantic expectations; whereas the second sentence is tough, simple and idiomatic, precisely rendering the verbal quality of Tess's consciousness. Each sentence is written in a mode which is legitimate and effective. But the transition between the two is too abrupt: a slight disturbance and confusion is created in the movement of the language, of a kind which we experience persistently in Hardy. It is particularly noticeable when he employs free indirect speech, for it would appear that the novelist who uses this device is obliged to be particularly faithful to the linguistic quality of his character's consciousness— the omission of the introductory verb 'he thought', 'he said', etc., seems to break down the literary convention by which we accept that the writer and his characters operate on quite different levels of discourse. Here is an example: 'Was once lost always lost really true of chastity? she would ask herself. She might prove it false if she could veil bygones. The recuperative power which pervaded organic nature was surely not denied to maidenhood alone' (XV). The structure of the last sentence indicates that it is a rendering, in free indirect speech, of Tess's thought; but its vocabulary belongs to the voice of the authorial commentator.

This duality in the presentation of Tess's consciousness is

paralleled in the treatment of Nature (understanding Nature in its general cosmic sense and more specific sense of landscape, the earth, flora and fauna). Ian Gregor has commented acutely on the contradiction that exists in *Tess* between a 'Rousseauistic view of Nature' as essentially life-giving, healthy, opposed to the inhibiting, destructive forces of society and convention which alone generate human misery, and the 'deterministic [view] which Hardy runs alongside it', in which the world appears as a 'blighted star' and the three dairymaids in love with Angel 'writhed feverishly under the oppressiveness of an emotion which they neither expected nor desired'.[8] This contradiction applies not only to generalizations about Nature, but also to the treatment of landscape, and Gregor's own assertion that 'at every stage of the tale interior states are visualized in terms of landscape'[9] must be qualified. It would be difficult to refute Vernon Lee's point that in the passage she quotes the description of the landscape does *not* reflect Tess's interior state of mind. On the other hand, we must not assume that such a relationship between character and setting is a necessary feature of imaginative prose, or that Hardy failed to establish it through incompetence. The truth of the matter is rather more complex.

No attentive reader can fail to note how persistently Tess is associated and identified with Nature, on several different levels. On the social level, in terms of the rural/urban or agrarian/industrial antithesis on which the values of the novel are largely based, she is a 'daughter of the soil' (XIX), almost timeless and anonymous—'Thus Tess walks on; a figure which is part of the landscape, a fieldswoman pure and simple, in winter guise' (XLII) (the present tense here having an effect of timelessness rather than of immediacy)—a quasi-symbolic 'object . . . foreign to the gleaming cranks and wheels' of the railway engine (XXX). In religious or spiritual terms, Tess is a Nature-worshipping pagan. Her beliefs are 'Tractarian as to phraseology' 'but Pantheistic as to essence' (XXVII). ' "You used to say at Talbothays that I was a heathen," says Tess to Angel, as she lies on a stone 'altar' at Stonehenge, ' "So now I am at home" ' (LVIII). ' "Did they sacrifice to God here?" ' she asks later. ' "No . . . I believe to the sun," ' he replies (LVIII). And we may recall here, that at their second embrace at Talbothays the sun had shone through the window 'upon her inclining face, upon the blue veins of her temple, upon her naked arm, and her neck, and into the depths of her hair' (XXVII).

This schematic association of Tess with Nature is enforced by insistent allusion, literal and figurative, to flora and fauna. Early in the novel she appears with 'roses at her breast; roses in her hat; roses and strawberries in her basket to the brim' (VI). Her hair is 'earth-coloured' (V), her mouth 'flower-like' (XIV), and her breath tastes 'of the butter and eggs and honey on which she mainly lived' (XXXVI). She is compared to a 'plant' (XXVII) and a 'sapling' (XX); the dew falls on her as naturally as on the grass (XX). To Angel, 'her arm, from her dabbling in the curds, was cold and damp to his mouth as new-gathered mushrooms' (XXVIII). While her physical appearance finds its metaphorical equivalents in the vegetable world, her behaviour is often compared to that of animals, particularly cats and birds. She 'wears the look of a wary animal' (XXXI). 'There was something of the habitude of the wild animal in the unreflecting instinct with which she rambled on' (XLI). She is as unresponsive to sarcasm as a 'dog or cat' (XXXV). She listens to Angel's harp like a 'fascinated bird', and moves through an overgrown garden 'as stealthily as a cat' (XIX). After sleep, 'she was as warm as a sunned cat' (XXVII). When she is happy her tread is like 'the skim of a bird which has not quite alighted' (XXXI). She faces D'Urberville with 'the hopeless defiance of the sparrow's gaze before its captor twists its neck' (XLVII).

This network of imagery and reference encourages us to think of Tess as essentially 'in touch' with Nature. Her character is defined and justified by metaphors of flora and fauna, and the changing face of the earth both directs and reflects her emotional life. At such moments we are least conscious of the literary *persona* of the author, and of his distance from the story. But it is equally true that Nature is quite indifferent to Tess and her fate. It is simply 'there', the physical setting against which the story takes place, described by the local historian with a wealth of geological and topographical detail, its moral neutrality emphasized by the sceptical philosopher.

This is surely the case in the passage quoted by Vernon Lee, particularly the two paragraphs beginning, 'The marked difference, in the final particular, between the rival vales now showed itself.' These paragraphs have the very tone of the guide-book, the tone of the parallel description of the Vale of Blackmoor: 'It is a vale whose acquaintance is best made by viewing it from the summits of the hills that surround it—except perhaps during the droughts of summer. An unguided ramble into its recesses in bad weather is apt to engender dissatisfaction with its narrow, tortuous, and miry ways' (II). But this earlier description is deliberately and clearly detached from the narrative, most obviously by its use of the present tense. Whereas in the passage quoted by Vernon Lee there is a fumbling attempt to relate the guide-book view to Tess. It is true that the two valleys might present themselves to Tess as in some sense 'rivals', but not in such impersonal, topographical terms.

A similar problem is raised by the simile of the fly, of which Vernon Lee asks, 'Why divert our attention from Tess and her big, flat valley, surely easy enough to realise, by a vision of a billiard table with a fly on it?' The answer surely is that Hardy, having got Tess into the valley, wants to give us, not a horizontal picture of the situation from her point of view, but a vertical, bird's eye picture; and he wants to do so in order to bring out her defencelessness, her isolation, her insignificance, in the eye of impersonal nature. (One is reminded of the later description of Flintcombe, in which the earth and the sky are compared to two vacant faces, 'the white face looking down on the brown face, and the brown face looking up at the white face, without anything standing between them but the two girls crawling over the surface of the former like flies' (XLIII), and even of the lines from *Lear* quoted in the Preface to the Fifth and later editions: 'As flies to wanton boys are we to the gods;/They kill us for their sport.') The trouble, once again, is that the structure of the sentence is confused and misleading. 'Not quite sure of her direction Tess stood still . . .' arouses expectations that any subsequent image will define her sense of uncertainty, whereas it does nothing of the sort. This confusion in the handling of the point of view, with its consequent disturbance of tone and meaning, is the essential basis of Vernon Lee's criticism; and I do not see how it can be dismissed, here or elsewhere in the novel.

On the other hand her critique can be challenged on two grounds. Firstly, she does not seem to have given her text the careful attention which close criticism demands. Her transcription of the passage (from an unspecified 'cheap edition') runs together the three paragraphs beginning 'Tess Durbeyfield, then', 'The marked difference', and 'The river had stolen', and adds on the following sentence to make one paragraph ending with 'fly'. This considerably increases the confusion in the point of view. For in my text the first of these three paragraphs stands as a self-contained statement of Tess's mood and action, which seems to have a sufficient logical connection with the preceding commentary to justify the use of the connective 'then'; and the third stands as a self-contained statement of the geological history of the valley. The attempt to provide some transition between the two in the second paragraph remains, however, a muddle.*

A more significant limitation of Vernon Lee's critique is her assumption that landscape in fiction must be vividly realized in sensuous terms, and reflect characters' states of consciousness. The fly and billiard table image does neither of these things, and is dismissed as the mechanical gesture of a nodding writer. She does not consider the possibility that it is a deliberately homely and bathetic image, designed to dissociate us from Tess at this point, to check any tendency to find reassurance in the identification of Tess's renewed hope with the fertile promise of the valley.

Ruskin called such identification the 'pathetic fallacy', and Hardy's ambiguous treatment of Nature throughout *Tess* might be formulated as his inability to decide whether the pathetic fallacy was fallacious or not. For of course it is Hardy himself who has encouraged us to make this kind of identification between Tess and her environment. A page or two before the passage quoted by Vernon Lee, we have the following description of Tess on a summit overlooking the valley into which she later descends:

> The bird's eye perspective before her was not so luxuriantly beautiful, perhaps, as that other one which she knew so well; yet it was more cheering. It lacked the intensely blue atmosphere of the rival vale, and its heavy soils and scents; the new air was clear, bracing, ethereal. The river itself, which nourished the grass and cows of these renowned dairies, flowed not like the streams in Blackmoor. Those were slow, silent, often turbid; flowing over

* Vernon Lee also omits from her transcription the line 'Waow! waow! waow!'; and when quoting the sentence with the fly simile a second time, she omits the comma after *length*, which removes the grammatical ambiguity of which she complains.

beds of mud into which the incautious wader might sink and vanish unawares. The Froom waters were clear as the pure River of Life shown to the Evangelist, rapid as the shadow of a cloud, with pebbly shallows that prattled to the sky all day long. There the water-flower was the lily; the crowfoot here.

Either the change in the quality of the air from heavy to light, or the sense of being amid new scenes where there were no invidious eyes upon her, sent up her spirits wonderfully. Her hopes mingled with the sunshine in an ideal photosphere which surrounded her as she bounded along against the soft south wind. She heard a pleasant voice in every breeze, and in every bird's note seemed to lurk a joy. (XVI)

Here we have the 'rivalry' of the two valleys defined in a quite different way, a way that is verbally related to Tess's sensuous and emotional experience (the pedantic 'photosphere' striking the only incongruous note). The suggestions of hope and recovery are unmistakable, and appropriate to the first chapter of a 'Phase' of the novel entitled 'The Rally'. And yet, as Tess descends this same valley, the 'Froom waters . . . clear as the pure river of life shown to the Evangelist', become a river exhausted by aeons of geological activity, and we are sharply reminded that Tess was of not the slightest consequence to her natural surroundings, that the sudden burst of sound 'was not the expression of the valley's consciousness that lovely Tess had arrived.' 'Who in his senses would have thought that it was?' asks Vernon Lee. The answer is surely, a Romantic poet—Wordsworth, perhaps, to whom Hardy twice alludes in sarcastic asides elsewhere in the novel (III and LI). Hardy's undertaking to defend Tess as a pure woman by emphasizing her kinship with Nature* perpetually drew him towards the Romantic view of Nature as a reservoir of benevolent impulses, a view which one side of his mind rejected as falsely sentimental. Many Victorian writers, struggling to reconcile the view of Nature inherited from the Romantics with the discoveries of Darwinian biology, exhibit the same conflict, but it is particularly noticeable in Hardy.

A passage which seems especially revealing in this respect is that which describes Tess's gloomy nocturnal rambling in the

* In the Preface to the 5th edition (1895), Hardy says of readers who had objected to the description of Tess as a 'pure' woman: 'They ignore the meaning of the word in Nature.'

weeks following her seduction, where she is explicitly shown entertaining the pathetic fallacy, and her mistake explicitly pointed out by the author:

> On these lonely hills and dales her quiescent glide was of a piece with the element she moved in. Her flexuous and stealthy figure became an integral part of the scene. At times her whimsical fancy would intensify natural processes around her till they seemed a part of her own story. Rather they became a part of it; for the world is only a psychological phenomenon, and what they seemed they were. The midnight airs and gusts, moaning among the tightly-wrapped buds and bark of the winter twigs, were formulae of bitter reproach. A wet day was the expression of irremediable grief at her weakness in the mind of some vague ethical being whom she could not class definitely as the God of her childhood, and could not comprehend as any other.
>
> But this encompassment of her own characterization, based on shreds of convention, peopled by phantoms and voices antipathetic to her, was a sorry and mistaken creation of Tess's fancy—a cloud of moral hobgoblins by which she was terrified without reason. It was they that were out of harmony with the actual world, not she. Walking among the sleeping birds in the hedges, watching the skipping rabbits on a moonlit warren, or standing under a pheasant-laden bough, she looked upon herself as a figure of Guilt intruding into the haunts of Innocence. But all the while she was making a distinction where there was no difference. Feeling herself in antagonism she was quite in accord. She had been made to break an accepted social law, but no law known to the environment in which she fancied herself such an anomaly. (XIII)

Here we have two paragraphs, one describing Tess's subjective state of mind, and the second describing the objective 'reality'. We are meant to feel that the second cancels out the first, that 'guilt' is a fabrication of social convention, something unknown to the natural order which Tess distorts by projecting her own feelings into it. It seems to me, however, that there is an unresolved conflict in Hardy's rhetoric here. Not only are the 'midnight airs and gusts, moaning amongst the tightly wrapped buds and bark of the winter twigs' images of sorrow and remorse too moving and impressive to be easily overthrown by the rational arguments of the second paragraph; we are explicitly told that 'the world is only a psychological [i.e. subjective] phenomenon', in which case the view expressed in the second paragraph is as 'subjective' as that expressed in the first, and has no greater validity. If Tess felt herself in antagonism she *was* in antagonism. But in fact 'antagonism' is a clumsy formulation of the experience so delicately expressed in the first paragraph. That Nature should present its most sombre aspect to Tess when she is most desolate is, in a way, evidence of how deeply she is 'in accord' with Nature. There are many other places in the book where Hardy 'intensifies natural processes around Tess till they seem part of her story', without suggesting that she is deceiving herself, e.g.—

> She was wretched—O so wretched. . . . The evening sun was now ugly to her, like a great inflamed wound in the sky. Only a solitary cracked-voiced reed-sparrow greeted her from the bushes by the river, in a sad, machine-made tone, resembling that of a past friend whose friendship she had outworn. (XXI)

There is further ambiguity about the 'actual world' of nature with which, according to the author, Tess is in accord without realizing it. Is she mistaken in thinking herself guilty, or Nature innocent, cr both? Elsewhere in the novel it is true to say that when Nature is not presented through Tess's consciousness, it is neither innocent nor guilty, but neutral; neither sympathetic nor hostile, but indifferent. When Tess and her young brother are driving their father's cart through the night, 'the cold pulses' of the stars 'were beating in serene dissociation from these two wisps of human life' (IV). The birds and rabbits skip happily and heedlessly round the defenceless Tess at her seduction (XI); and the Valley of the Var has no interest in her arrival. Is not Tess more human in preferring a sad but sympathetic Nature to a gay but indifferent one?

Hardy, then, here undermines our trust in the reliability of Tess's response to Nature, which is his own chief rhetorical device for defending her character and interesting our sympathies on her behalf. Without this winterpiece, which the author dismisses as a delusion of Tess's mind, we would lose the significance of Tess's renewal of energy in the spring which urges her towards the Valley of the Var and her 'rally':

> A particularly fine spring came round, and the stir of germination was almost audible in the buds; it moved her, as it moved the wild animals, and made her passionate to go . . . some spirit within

her rose automatically as the sap in the twigs. It was unexpended youth, surging up anew after its temporary check, and bringing with it hope, and the invincible instinct towards self-delight. (XV)

But of course the instinct is, in the event, vincible . . . and so we return to the basic contradiction pointed out by Ian Gregor, of which he says: 'the small measure in which this confusion, which is central to the theme of the novel, really decreases its artistic compulsion, suggests how effectively the latter is protected against the raids of philosophic speculation'.[10] I find myself in some disagreement with this verdict for, as I have tried to show, the confusion is not merely in the abstractable philosophical content of the novel, but inextricably woven into its verbal texture.

John Holloway has also noted the duality in Hardy's view of life, and defends him on the grounds that 'Hardy has a good deal more to say about the quality of events, the feel of them, than about their course'.[11] In a novel, however, no representation of reality can be entirely neutral and objective: it must always be mediated through the consciousness of a character or a narrator. The reader must be able to identify this consciousness, and he does so by responding correctly to the language used. The case against Hardy is that he regularly confuses the reader with a number of conflicting linguistic clues. I shall offer one further illustration of the difficulties of interpretation and evaluation this creates.

In Chapter XIX there is a description of Tess walking in the garden of Talbothays Dairy at dusk:

It was a typical summer evening in June, the atmosphere being in such delicate equilibrium and so transmissive that inanimate objects seemed endowed with two or three senses, if not five. There was no distinction between the near and the far, and an auditor felt close to everything within the horizon. The soundlessness impressed her as a positive entity rather than as the mere negation of noise. It was broken by the strumming of strings.

Tess had heard those notes in the attic above her head. Dim, flattened, constrained by their confinement, they had never appeared to her as now, when they wandered in the still air with a stark quality like that of nudity. To speak absolutely, both instrument and execution were poor; but the relative is all, and as she listened Tess, like a fascinated bird, could not leave the spot. Far from leaving she drew up towards the performer, keeping behind the hedge that he might not guess her presence.

The outskirt of the garden in which Tess found herself had been left uncultivated for some years, and was now damp and rank with juicy grass which sent up mists of pollen at a touch; and with tall blooming weeds emitting offensive smells—weeds whose red and yellow and purple hues formed a polychrome as dazzling as that of cultivated flowers. She went stealthily as a cat through this profusion of growth, gathering cuckoo-spittle on her skirts, cracking snails that were underfoot, staining her hands with thistle-milk and slug-slime, and rubbing off upon her naked arms sticky blights which, though snow-white on the apple-tree trunks, made madder stains on her skin; thus she drew quite near to Clare, still unobserved of him.

Tess was conscious of neither time nor space. The exaltation which she had described as being producible at will by gazing at a star, came now without any determination of hers; she undulated upon the thin notes of the second-hand harp, and their harmonies passed like breezes through her, bringing tears into her eyes. The floating pollen seemed to be his notes made visible, and the dampness of the garden the weeping of the garden's sensibility. Though near nightfall, the rank-smelling weed-flowers glowed as if they would not close for intentness, and the waves of colour mixed with the waves of sound.

I am particularly concerned, here, with the meaning of the third of these four paragraphs,* of which John Holloway has said, 'This passage is almost uniquely significant for understanding Hardy. The scene is centrally important in *Tess* itself, and among the most intensely realized the author ever wrote.'[12] He quotes the paragraph (with a few small omissions[13]) to illustrate the multiplicity of Hardy's universe:

It is Nature's expanse, as much as anything, which gives Hardy opportunity for portraying Nature's variety. He carefully drew attention to the profusion of different, unexpected, and oddly contrasted events occurring simultaneously in the natural world. The varying reactions of plants and animals, birds and even insects,

---

* There is a remarkable parallel between this description, and Dickens's description of Mrs Sparsit creeping through the undergrowth in *Hard Times* (II, xi). But to compare them is to appreciate how utterly different in effect is the 'same' action or event in different literary contexts.

all made their contribution. . . . As Tess wanders through the garden at the Talbothays Dairy, and listens to Angel playing on the harp, Hardy is careful to amass the trivial and also the bizarre details of the scene. . . . One cannot possibly miss how distinctive was the sense of Man and Nature which, at such a crisis, relied for point upon details so unexpected.[14]

This is a perceptive, but perhaps slightly tame account of a passage so centrally important. Does not the intensity of the language in this paragraph encourage us to read it as symbolic action?

Robert Liddell takes this to have been Hardy's intention, but holds that it was frustrated by the very concrete particularity Holloway admires. Hardy's 'close observation of nature' says Liddell, 'may tempt him to a pre-raphaelite accuracy in depicting her, and when he chooses some of her more uncomfortable features to depict like this, the result may be unintentionally comic. For example, there are the various country messes with which Tess covered herself.' And after quoting the paragraph, he comments:

> Such a chapter of accidents, such a series of booby tricks played upon Tess by Nature, well enough parallel the booby tricks which Destiny plays on her, and on so many of Hardy's characters. But he never saw that such an accumulation of disasters was farcical, not tragic—part of the technique of the comic pantomime, rather than of the serious novel.[15]

I feel that a comic or farcical effect can be obtained from the passage only by the importation of irrelevant associations. Mrs Dorothy Van Ghent would agree, but she follows Mr Liddell in seeing Tess as a victim in this passage. Her characteristically ingenious interpretation runs as follows:

> The weeds, circumstantial as they are, have an astonishingly cunning and bold metaphorical function. They grow at Talbothays, in that healing and procreative idyll of milk and mist and passive biology, and they too are bountiful with life, but they stain and slime and blight; and it is in this part of Paradise (an 'outskirt of the garden'—there are even apple trees here) that the minister's son is hidden, who, in his conceited impotence, will violate Tess more nastily than her sensual seducer; who but Hardy would have dared to give him the name Angel, and a harp too?[16]

I will now offer another reading of the paragraph which differs considerably from those cited. To me, the remarkable feature of the paragraph, the source of that 'unexpected' quality noted by Mr Holloway, is that in it the conventional response (of revulsion) invited by concepts like 'rank', 'offensive smells', 'spittle', 'snails', 'slug-slime', 'blights', 'stains', etc., is insistently checked by an alternative note which runs through the language, a note of celebration of the brimming fertility of the weeds and the keen sensations they afford. This note is conveyed cognitively in words like 'juicy', 'mists', 'blooming', 'dazzling', 'profusion'; but it also seems to invade the very language in which the conventionally noisome features of the garden are described. There is a kind of sensuous relish, enforced by the rhythm and alliteration, in the thickening consonants of 'cuckoo-spittle', 'cracking snails', 'thistle-milk', and 'slug-slime', which is strangely disarming. A linguist would no doubt regard this argument with suspicion; and it is indeed difficult to give a satisfactory account of verbal effects at this depth. But it must be conceded, I think, that if Hardy intended to stress the *unpleasantness* of the garden, he has gone about his task in a curious way.

Even if the reader recoils from the overgrown garden, there is no suggestion that Tess does. She seems at home in it. She moves through the undergrowth 'as stealthily as a cat'—an image which, taken in conjunction with the 'fascinated bird' simile in the preceding paragraph, catches up the whole web of natural imagery and reference applied to Tess throughout the novel. The participles *gathering, cracking, staining,* and *rubbing off,* of which the grammatical subject is Tess, as well as imitating her physical movement, stress the active nature of her relationship with the natural world. She seems to collaborate in the transformation of her appearance rather than suffer it. (Mrs Van Ghent mis-represents the grammar of the passage by saying that 'the weeds . . . stain and slime and blight'.) We are twice reminded that Clare is unaware of Tess's behaviour ('keeping behind the hedge that he might not guess her presence'—'still unobserved of him'). There are good reasons, therefore, for thinking that in so far as the paragraph has metaphorical implications, it throws light not, as Mrs Van Ghent suggests, on Clare and what he will do to Tess, but on Tess herself, revealing a facet of her character of which he is significantly ignorant.*

* This does not affect the value of Mrs Van Ghent's insight concerning Hardy's use of the Genesis myth. Angel, however, despite his Christian name

This interpretation becomes more attractive as soon as we consider the differences between the characters of Tess and Clare, the nature of their relationship, and the part played in its development by the natural environment.

Talbothays is situated in 'the Valley of the great Dairies, the valley in which milk and butter grew to rankness' (XVI), 'a green trough of sappiness and humidity' (XXVII). When Clare, returning from a visit to his parents, 'began to descend from the upland to the fat, alluvial soil below, the atmosphere grew heavier; the languid perfume of the summer fruits, the mists, the hay, the flowers, formed therein a vast pool of odour which, at this hour, seemed to make the very bees and butterflies drowsy ... he could not help being aware that to come here, as now, after an experience of home-life, affected him like throwing off splints and bandages' (XXVII). The 'note' of the valley is, then, one of fertility running almost to excess, indulging the senses, relaxing or suspending conscience. In this environment humanity is helpless in the grip of its instincts and passions. In Tess, conscience and scruple are inexorably overwhelmed by ' "the appetite for joy " which pervades all creation' (XXX); and 'Amid the oozing fatness and warm ferments of the Froom Vale, at a season when the rush of juices could almost be heard below the hiss of fertilization, it was impossible that the most fanciful love should not grow passionate' (XXIV). There is a relishing of sound in the language of these passages which associates them with the 'weeds' paragraph.

(which is not in fact, used in this passage) and his harp, is cast primarily as Adam—a somewhat priggish, Miltonic Adam—and Tess as Eve. In the early mornings at the dairy, they experience 'a feeling of isolation, as if they were Adam and Eve' (XX); after an embrace, 'she regarded him as Eve at her second waking might have regarded Adam' (XXVII)—what a powerful, though discreet, erotic charge that 'second' has! D'Urberville with his numerous disguises, his unpredictable appearances and his malicious tricks, has the role of Satan: 'You are Eve and I am the old Other One come to tempt you in the disguise of an inferior animal,' he says to Tess in the firelit potato-planting scene (L), and goes on to quote from *Paradise Lost*. Hardy exploits the story of the Fall without accepting the idea of sin. The first two Phases of the novel (in the Valley of Blackmoor and the Chase) correspond to Eve's seduction by Satan, the third and fourth Phases (in the Valley of the Var) to Adam's participation in Eve's action, and the fifth and sixth Phases (Flintcombe and Salisbury Plain) to their banishment from the Garden to pain, labour, and death.

The 'fanciful love' is, of course, Clare's, and the qualification is important. 'He loved her dearly, though perhaps rather ideally and fancifully than with the impassioned thoroughness of her feeling for him' (XXXII). We are told of Clare's father that 'to the aesthetic, sensuous, pagan pleasure in natural life and lush womanhood which his son Angel had lately been experiencing in Var Vale, his temper would have been antipathetic in a high degree' (XXV). In fact this pleasure is always something of an affectation on the part of Angel, a kind of compensation for his exclusion from the busy civilized world of the nineteenth century, a swaggering advertisement of his free-thinking. His reaction to Tess's confession later in the novel demonstrates conclusively that his temperament is essentially puritanical and conventional— ' "My position—is this" he said abruptly. "I thought—any man would have thought—that by giving up all ambition to win a wife with social standing, with fortune, with knowledge of the world, I should secure rustic innocence as surely as I should secure pink cheeks; . . .' (XXXVI). From the beginning it is clear that Tess is an assurance to Angel that the 'aesthetic, sensuous, pagan pleasure' of the Var Valley is respectable and innocent in the conventional moral sense. ' "What a fresh and virginal daughter of Nature that milkmaid is," ' he thinks, on first taking notice of Tess (XVIII). Later, 'It seemed natural enough to him now that Tess was again in sight to choose a mate from unconstrained Nature, and not from the abodes of Art' (XXVII), and yet he is constantly trying to dignify the homely pastoral in which he is involved—the country wooing of a milkmaid—by Art, by talking to her about 'pastoral life in ancient Greece' and calling her by classical names (XX), thus demonstrating that he is not really prepared to accept a mate from unconstrained Nature.

The paragraph describing the overgrown garden might be aptly described as an image of 'unconstrained nature'. It reminds us of the wild, exuberant, anarchic life that flourishes on the dark underside, as it were, of the cultivated fertility of the valley. Does it not reveal something similar about Tess—that she is 'a child of Nature' in a sense that extends far beneath the surface of conventional pastoral prettiness and innocence which that phrase denotes to Angel? Let us examine one item in the description in the light of this interpretation:

184

. . . rubbing off upon her naked arms sticky blights which, though snow-white on the apple-tree trunks, made madder stains on her skin.

There is clearly an antithesis here between *snow-white* and *madder*, which is given a cautionary or ironic note by the *though*: i.e., though the blights looked pretty and pure on the tree trunks, they produced a red stain on Tess's naked arms when she rubbed against them. *Snow-white* has associations with chastity and virginity. Red (the colour of some of the weed-flowers earlier in the passage) is the colour of passion, and of blood (with which Tess is ominously splashed at the death of the horse, Prince—IV). And it is difficult to avoid seeing an Empsonian ambiguity in the word *madder*—no doubt many readers have, like myself, taken it to be the comparative form of *mad* on first reading, not the name of a vegetable dye. Thus, although one cannot paraphrase meanings so delicately hinted, I submit that the force of this connection between Tess and the natural world is to suggest the 'mad' passionate, non-ethical quality of her sensibility.

This dimension of Tess's character makes her life a peculiarly vulnerable one. It lays her open to seduction by D'Urberville—it is important to realize that she is seduced, not raped;* and Tess herself is frightened by the intensity of her passion for Angel:

> Her idolatry of this man was such that she herself almost feared it to be ill-omened. She was conscious of the notion expressed by Friar Lawrence: 'These violent delights have violent ends.' It might be too desperate for human conditions—too rank, too wild, too deadly. (XXXIII)

Yet this vulnerability is something we value in Tess. Ironically it is valued by Clare, without his understanding the reason. He is intrigued and impressed by a quality of imaginative thoughtfulness in her speech which he finds surprising in one so young. 'Not guessing the cause,' comments Hardy, 'there was nothing to remind him that experience is as to intensity, and not as to

---

* 'She had dreaded him, winced before him, succumbed to adroit advantages he took of her helplessness; then, temporarily blinded by his ardent manners, had been stirred to confused surrender awhile' (XII). In the serialised version of the novel Hardy felt obliged, in deference to his readers' requirements, to make Tess the victim of a false marriage—which of course makes nonsense of her character. Cf. Gregor, *op. cit.*, pp. 133–4.

duration. Tess's passing corporeal blight had been her mental harvest' (XIX). The play on 'blight' and 'harvest' here, and the metaphorical application of 'rank' and 'wild' to Tess's passion in my previous quotation, give further encouragement for a reading of the weeds paragraph as a metaphorical expression of Tess's character. But I offer it tentatively, because it does not account for everything in the paragraph and its immediate context.

The readings of Mr Liddell and Mrs Van Ghent require us to see the paragraph as ironic, the irony being directed against Tess, who does not realize how she is being smirched and stained. Mr Holloway seems to take a similar view, since he compares the passage to another in *A Pair of Blue Eyes* in which 'the humans seem to be blundering unconsciously through Nature; but these are the details which show what Nature is really like'.[17] The cat simile in the *Tess* passage, however, shows Tess at ease in her surroundings. And the clause 'in which Tess *found* herself' (*my italics*) in the opening sentence suggests that she is aware of these surroundings. One's reading of the whole paragraph depends very importantly on whether we take the observing consciousness to be primarily Tess's or primarily the author's. But it is very difficult to decide. The information that the garden had been uncultivated for some years, and the comparison of the weeds with cultivated flowers must come from the narrator. But the lines 'damp and rank with juicy grass which sent up mists of pollen at a touch; and with tall blooming weeds emitting offensive smells' seem to describe directly the sensations of Tess; it is surely her touch which sends up the mists of pollen, and her eye which observes them.

The opening sentence of the succeeding paragraph seems to favour a view of the weeds paragraph as authorial, for we are told that Tess was conscious of neither time nor space. Yet reading on, we discover that this state of mind did not exclude observation of the physical attributes of the overgrown garden, but included and transfigured them through the pathetic fallacy: 'The floating pollen seemed to be his notes made visible, and the dampness of the garden the weeping of the garden's sensibility. Though near nightfall, the rank-smelling weed-flowers glowed as if they would not close for intentness, and the waves of colour mixed with the waves of sound.' This introduces quite a new view of the overgrown garden—an image neither of soiling nastiness nor of wild, unconstrained nature, but of beauty perceived through emotion. This can be seen as an extension of either of the two former views (but scarcely of both), depending on our evaluation of Tess's ecstatic response to the music. The poor quality of the instrument and the musician is twice remarked upon. Are we, then, to see Tess as 'taken in' by Clare's musicianship, as she is taken in subsequently by his declaration of love? In which case we are meant to 'see through' the pathetic fallacy at the end of the passage, to feel that the transfiguration of the, in fact, noisome weeds is an index of her delusion. Or is her ecstatic experience to be valued independently of the music which provokes it? Is her inclusion in this experience of the homely and conventionally unaesthetic particulars of her environment a moving testimony to an 'undissociated sensibility' to which nothing natural is alien? Hardy's aside 'but the relative is all' (like his earlier comment that 'the world is a psychological phenomenon') does not help us to decide.

There is no end to such questions, because Hardy presents us with such a confusion of linguistic clues. What an astonishing diversity of tone is displayed in the four paragraphs! The first shows Hardy in his most ponderous, generalizing authorial style,, with which Tess herself is incongruously saddled in the penultimate sentence. The second paragraph establishes her keen sensuous response to the music with the striking image of nudity, and the simile of the fascinated bird, but qualifies this effect by some slightly patronizing reference to the absolute and the relative. The third paragraph assaults us with an astonishing *tour de force* of concretely realized sensation. And the final paragraph leads us into a world of romantic synaesthesia. It is as if Hardy, bewildered by the rich possibilities of the scene, has confused himself and us by trying to follow out all of them at the same time.

Hardy is a peculiarly difficult novelist to assess because his vices are almost inextricably entangled with his virtues. We value him for the breadth, variety, and unexpectedness of his vision; his mind plays over his characters and their actions so as to place them in constantly shifting perspectives which are never without interest. The nature of the undertaking provokes comparison with the very greatest writers, but it creates enormous demands upon his control of his verbal medium which he does not consistently satisfy. That is, he shows himself capable, on different occasions, of realizing all the effects for which he was striving, but he cannot be relied upon to do so. Sometimes his various 'voices' subtly make their points and modulate smoothly into one another; at other times they seem to be interrupting and quarrelling between themselves. Alternately dazzled by his sublimity and exasperated by his bathos, false notes, confusions, and contradictions, we are, while reading him, tantalized by a sense of greatness not quite achieved.

V

Strether by the River

HENRY JAMES is distinguished from the novelists discussed above in that he naturally invites, and has received, criticism which concerns itself with his use of language. There has never been any doubt that he had a 'style', or that an assessment of his total achievement is inseparable from a consideration of the way he uses language. Few other novelists, indeed, can have received so much attention in this respect.* If, therefore, my approach has seemed to possess any novelty elsewhere in this book, it will not do so in this chapter.

Nevertheless, there seem to be good reasons for devoting at

---

* Apart from incidental comment on style in nearly all criticism of James, more specialized studies include: R. W. Short, 'The Sentence Structure of Henry James', *American Literature*, XVIII (1946), pp. 71–88, and the same author's 'Henry James's World of Images', *P.M.L.A.*, LXVIII (1953), pp. 943–60; John Henry Raleigh, 'Henry James: the Poetics of Empiricism', *P.M.L.A.*, LXVI (1951), pp. 107–23; Charles R. Crow, 'The Style of Henry James: *The Wings of the Dove*', *Style in Prose Fiction*, English Institute Essays 1958, ed. Harold C. Martin (New York, 1959), pp. 172–89; Robert L. Gale, *The Caught Image: figurative language in the fiction of Henry James*, (Chapel Hill, 1964); Alexander Holder-Barell, *The Development of Imagery and its Functional Significance in Henry James's Novels* (Basel, 1959); Dorothea Krook, 'Principles and Method in the Late Works of Henry James', *London Magazine*, I (1954), pp. 54–70; John Paterson, 'The Language of Adventure in Henry James', *American Literature*, XXXII (1960), pp. 291–301. I have already referred to Ian Watt's excellent article, 'The First Paragraph of *The Ambassadors*', *Essays in Criticism*, X (1960), pp. 250–74; and Vernon Lee has a sensitive commentary on a passage from the same novel in *The Handling of Words* (pp. 241–51).

least one chapter to an author whose conscious verbal artistry can be assumed, and Henry James is a particularly interesting example of this kind of novelist. I suggested earlier that modern criticism pays attention to a novelist's language most readily when it approximates to the language of poetry—when, that is, it can be described in terms of modern symbolist poetics. While James's art and aesthetic theory certainly have affinities with the symbolist movement, he draws back at the brink of a total commitment to it. One way of formulating this, is to say that he is more of a nineteenth-century novelist than a twentieth-century one, an explorer of the intelligence rather than of the sub-conscious. Another, is to say that his language allows the maximum degree of play to the complexity of experience that is compatible with the retention of a logically ordered discourse. As Charles R. Crow observes, 'What James will not do, one sees, is let intensity be entire. His style is a prose style. If the compressions, the strainings of poetry do enter, they are brought to conform.'[1] It is the struggle between the 'strainings of poetry' and the logical discipline of prose which, of course, makes the late novels so demanding on the reader. In almost any sentence in these books, James is likely to be juggling with so many ideas, sensations, actions, persons, and images at once that his syntax, and our understanding, are strained to their limits to preserve a sense of both the distinctions and the connections between them.

Modern criticism of James may fairly claim to have exonerated him from the charge of a perverse mannerism in the late style, and to have shown that, in the words of Ian Watt, 'all or at least nearly all the idiosyncrasies of diction or syntax are fully justified by the emphases they create'.[2] There is no need, in other words, to defend James at this time of day, against the imputation that in his later work he was getting senile, or careless, or falling a victim to the habit of dictation. But there is a more profound argument against the method of the late James which continues to be a live issue in the criticism of his work, and which has been most memorably stated by Dr Leavis in his comment on *The Ambassadors*:

> *The Ambassadors* . . ., which he seems to have thought his greatest success, produces an effect of disproportionate 'doing'—of a technique the subtleties and elaborations of which are not sufficiently controlled by a feeling for value and significance in living.

What, we ask, is this, symbolized by Paris, that Strether feels himself to have missed in his own life? Has James sufficiently inquired? Is it anything adequately realised? If we are to take the elaboration of the theme in the spirit in which we are meant to take it, haven't we to take the symbol too much at the glamorous face-value it has for Strether? Isn't, that is, the energy of the 'doing' (and the energy demanded for the reading) disproportionate to the issues—to any issues that are concretely held and presented?[3]

In some respects, this argument can never be rebutted. Whether James displays a sense of what is valuable and significant in living, and whether he demands a disproportionate effort from the reader, are questions that can only be answered in a spirit of religious witness. But the strategy of a possible defence of James can be established by attempting to answer the other rhetorical questions posed by Dr Leavis.

What . . . is this, symbolized by Paris, that Strether feels himself to have missed in his own life? James, of course, deliberately abstains from giving it a name, but if we need one, Christof Wegelin's 'Social Beauty' will do.[4] 'Strether's new vision,' says Wegelin, 'consists in the awareness that there is a virtue which cannot be measured by the bundles of moral "notions with which he started from home" '.[5] It is a virtue which Strether finds supremely in Madame de Vionnet. Explaining to Maria Gostrey at the end of the novel the 'basis' of his conduct, Strether observes:

> 'A basis seemed to me just what her beauty of person supplied.'
> 'Her beauty of person?'
> 'Well, her beauty of everything. The impression she makes. She has such variety and yet such harmony.' (XII, iii)

But Strether also finds this virtue, this social beauty, in such small things as Chad's manner of coming into a theatre box.

> He had never in his life seen a young man come into a box at ten o'clock at night, and would, if challenged on the question in advance, scarce have been ready to pronounce on different ways of doing so. But it was in spite of this definite to him that Chad had had a way that was wonderful: a fact carrying with it an implication that, as one might imagine it, he knew, he had learned, how. (III, ii)

The novel is full of such 'epiphanies' of social beauty, but the most important one is the distinguished gathering at Gloriani's house, where Strether explicitly confesses to little Bilham his sense of having missed something in his own life, in the famous 'Live!' speech (V, ii). Later, little Bilham reminds Strether of his outburst when encouraging him to see the association between Chad and Madame de Vionnet in the most favourable light:

> 'Well, it's very strange!' Strether presently remarked with a sighing sense of fulness.
> 'Very strange indeed. That's just the beauty of it. Isn't it very much the kind of beauty you had in mind,' little Bilham went on, 'when you were so wonderful and inspiring to me the other day?' (VI, iii)

Has James himself sufficiently inquired? I take this question to imply, has James considered the objective nature of this social beauty, or (since objectivity is scarcely a property of things in the Jamesian world), does he show himself aware of other perspectives in which it might be seen and evaluated, other than the perspective of Strether in Gloriani's garden? The answer must surely be, yes. For the crucial scene in Gloriani's garden is balanced by the equally crucial scene when Strether meets Chad and Madame de Vionnet on the river, and realizes belatedly that their relationship is, after all, a common illicit liaison. Having committed himself completely to the idea of social beauty, Strether faces the painful truth that it is sustained by people who are human beings, with all the vulgar weaknesses of human beings. Having cut loose from the crude moral system of Woollett, he discovers that this system fits the facts more truthfully than his own idealizing vision. Not that this is enough to make him renounce his vision, to throw him back into the arms of Woollett: Strether does not repudiate his alliance with Madame de Vionnet, with Chad, with Paris. But after the river-scene his appreciation of these things is mingled with a wry mockery of his own previous innocence. This reversal in Strether's heuristic progress does not diminish him in our eyes—we feel that he is ennobled as well as chastened by his disillusionment, that the trouble with his vision is not so much that it is false as that it is too good for anyone but himself to live up to. But it shows that James had 'inquired' into the validity of the Paris 'symbol' and ruefully acknowledged that 'the glamorous face value it has for Strether' is partially deceiving.

Is it anything adequately realized? 'Realized' I take it, denotes here the literary qualities of sensuous concreteness, of immediacy, of particularity, which compel assent or recognition in the reader. The language of the late James is, of course, notoriously abstract, but this is generally compensated for by a richness of imagery and symbolism. Such compensation is not, however, striking in *The Ambassadors* which, as Ian Watt notes, 'is written with considerable sobriety and has, for example, little of the vivid and direct style of the early part of *The Wings of the Dove*, or of the happy symbolic complexities of *The Golden Bowl*'.[6] It appears odd, too, that a novel which pins so much of its meaning to a *place*, should be so signally lacking in specificity. Here is a typical passage, describing Madame de Vionnet's house:

> The court was large and open, full of revelations, for our friend, of the habit of privacy, the peace of intervals, the dignity of distances and approaches; the house, to his restless sense, was in the high homely style of an elder day, and the ancient Paris that he was always looking for—sometimes intensely felt, sometimes more acutely missed—was in the immemorial polish of the wide waxed staircase and in the fine *boiseries*, the medallions, mouldings, mirrors, great clear spaces, of the greyish-white salon into which he had been shown. He seemed at the very outset to see her, in the midst of possessions not vulgarly numerous, but hereditary cherished charming. (VI, i)

What one notices immediately about this passage is the precedence of abstract nouns or near-abstract nouns (like *intervals* and *approaches*) over concrete nouns, and the use of plurals where singulars might have been expected. The effect of both devices is to dissipate the sense of particular time and place and to synthesize the discrete items of local detail into a confused but evocative impression of an historical way of life. This effect is sustained by running together groups of nouns or adjectives, by exploiting alliteration and by omitting punctuation:* *high homely*;

---

* The omission of commas is a recurrent device in *The Ambassadors*. Cf. 'a great stripped handsome red-haired lady' (II, i) and the description of Mlle de Vionnet as 'bright gentle shy happy wonderful' (V, ii). The effect is to abolish any logical order or variation of emphasis in the series, and to suggest a complex but instantaneous response. It anticipates the attempts of later experimental novelists, like Joyce and Gertrude Stein, to impose simultaneity upon the linear medium of language.

wide waxed; *medallions*, *mouldings*, *mirrors*; *hereditary cherished charming*. It is in fact a deliberately *vague* description; and *vague* is the word Strether uses to characterize his illusions about the Chad–Madame de Vionnet relationship after they have been exposed by the meeting on the river.

> he almost blushed, in the dark, for the way he had dressed the possibility of a sexual liaison in vagueness, as a little girl might have dressed her doll. (XI, iv)

I suggest that what is being realized in the greater part of *The Ambassadors* is the experience of a man who has himself not fully 'realized' the total implications of that experience; and that what might seem inadequate realization in terms of our customary demands on literature, in fact displays a perfect adjustment of means to an end in terms of the overall design of this particular book.* I do not imply, of course, that James bores or dissatisfies us for ten books of the novel and recovers himself in the eleventh. Strether's 'impressions' are sufficiently sensitive, sufficiently beautiful, sufficiently discriminating (particularly when played off against the responses of the Woollett circle) to engage our sympathetic interest from the very beginning. But if we feel a certain impatience with him, if we long for him to encounter some brute fact that cannot be beaten into a shimmering tissue of impressions, is this not precisely how we should feel? Is this not precisely the point of the joke about the vulgar domestic utensil manufactured by the Newsomes, which Strether refuses to name? Is this not the necessary effect of the whole narrative tone, a tone of humorous, affectionate irony?[7] Is it not this which gives the recognition scene on the river (considered merely as an action, the most genteel of dénouements) its tremendous force? For in that scene we find no vagueness at all.

My argument keeps returning to the scene on the river, and I should confess that it began with a wish to account for my enormous admiration for the way that scene is done. I propose to

---

* Dr Leavis has himself acutely remarked of a passage of Shakespeare: 'One might, by way of emphasising that "realisation" is not offered as a technical term, an instrument of precision, put it this way: it is in the incomplete realisation of the metaphors that the realising gift of the poet and the "realised" quality of the passage are manifested.' 'Education and the University (III): Literary Studies,' *Scrutiny*, IX (1941), p. 315.

devote the rest of this essay to a detailed examination of its opening. One would have to go on quoting much more extensively to bring out the full flavour of the episode—the wry comedy of the embarrassed meal, and of the more embarrassed journey back to Paris, the polite pretence that Chad and Madame de Vionnet were, like Strether, simply out for the day becoming increasingly absurd with every moment, and poor Madame de Vionnet's poise and self-possession, so much admired by Strether, collapsing in ruins. But the first two paragraphs are enough—too much in fact—to cope with.

James, particularly the late James, was so self-conscious an artist, so zealous for the 'grace of intensity'[8] so scrupulous in maintaining a consistent tone, that the analysis of any passage selected at random is likely to reveal more reliable evidence about his method than would be the case with most novelists. However, even a passage by James needs to be judged and interpreted in its context; and this particular one has been selected with its context very much in mind. My main object is to show that the opening paragraphs of Book XI, Chapter iv, are knitted into the fabric of the novel by a number of linguistic threads, but that these connections are ironical, and serve to point up the function of the scene as a *peripeteia*.

The immediate context of the scene is, of course, Strether's expedition into the French countryside near Paris. It is something of a sentimental journey, prompted by a consciousness that, as his days in France are 'numbered', he should 'give the whole of one of them to that French ruralism, with its cool special green, into which he had hitherto looked only through the little oblong window of the picture-frame' (XI, iii). One particular picture is alluded to—a small landscape by Lambinet which Strether, characteristically, *nearly* purchased in his youth. His ramble through the countryside is delightfully described through the conceit of his exploring a framed landscape. At the end of the day he comes to a small inn, the Cheval Blanc, and orders himself a supper. There follows this important passage:

> He had walked many miles and didn't know he was tired; but he still knew he was amused, and even that, though he had been alone all day, he had never yet so struck himself as engaged with others and in the midstream of his drama. It might have passed for finished, his drama, with its catastrophe all but reached: it had,

however, none the less been vivid again for him as he thus gave it its fullest chance. He had only had to be at last well out of it to feel it, oddly enough, still going on.

For this had been all day at bottom the spell of the picture—that it was essentially more than anything else a scene and a stage, that the very air of the play was in the rustle of the willows and the tone of the sky. The play and the characters had, without his knowing it till now, peopled all his space for him, and it seemed somehow quite happy that they should offer themselves, in the conditions so supplied, with a kind of inevitability. It was as if the conditions made them not only inevitable, but so much more nearly natural and right as that they were at least easier, pleasanter, to put up with. The conditions had nowhere so asserted their difference from those of Woollett as they appeared to him to assert it in the little court of the Cheval Blanc while he arranged with his hostess for a comfortable climax. They were few and simple, scant and humble, but they were *the thing*, as he would have called it, even to a greater degree than Madame de Vionnet's old high salon where the ghost of the Empire walked. 'The' thing was the thing that implied the greatest number of other things of the sort he had had to tackle; and it was queer of course, but so it was—the implication here was complete. (XI, iii)

This is a taxing passage to follow, complicated by the juggling with theatrical and pictorial imagery, but its meaning is clear: Strether's expedition, undertaken in a spirit of escape from the human problems of his ambassadorship, has ended by reminding him more completely than ever of his involvement in them, and by placing a further sanction on his chosen role. The 'beauty' by which he has justified Chad and Madame de Vionnet takes on a more than 'social' dimension—they are blessed by the French countryside as seen in the perspectives of art. Their relationship, considered in these 'conditions' seems not only inevitable but 'so much more natural and right'; and the conditions are epitomized by the situation and appointments of the little inn, which impresses Strether in the same way as Madame de Vionnet's home, but more intensely.

Dorothea Krook has commented on the philosophical language of this passage,[9] but the most striking phrase in it, *'the thing'* belongs not to philosophical discourse, but to a type of discourse that might be described as heightened cliché. It is one of the most distinctive traits of James's late style. All his most sensitive

characters speak and to some extent think in this way. It is a kind
of in-group game which consists in managing to discuss, or at
least to suggest, infinite complexities and discriminations in a
vocabulary that is on the face of it remarkably impoverished,
giving expressive force to platitudes and dead metaphors by
devices of intonation, stress, placing, and repetition. One could
find an illustration anywhere, but I shall select one that also
illuminates Strether's situation; Miss Barrace is speaking:

> 'We're all looking at each other—and in the light of Paris one
> sees what things resemble. That's what the light of Paris seems al-
> ways to show. It's the fault of the light of Paris—dear old light!'
> 'Dear old Paris!' little Bilham echoed.
> 'Everything, every one shows,' Miss Barrace went on.
> 'But for what they really are?' Strether asked.
> 'Oh, I like your Boston "reallys"! But sometimes—yes.'
> 'Dear old Paris then!' Strether resignedly sighed while for a
> moment they looked at each other. (V, i)

Here Strether—not for the first time—hesitantly seals his complicity with Chad's set by adopting their language—'Dear old
Paris'—and by accepting their mockery of his Boston 'really'.

The value attached to this kind of discourse is equivocal.
Clearly, James admires it as a form of linguistic virtuosity which
has the social usefulness of enabling delicate subjects to be discussed publicly—a problem which preoccupied him as a professional writer; and on a more profound level he undoubtedly
held that there were few things that were both true and simply
statable. On the other hand the language of heightened cliché is a
treacherous medium of communication, concealing as much as it
reveals. It is certainly a double-edged weapon in the hands of an
innocent like Strether.

The O.E.D. gives the following meanings for *the thing*:
'(Colloquial, emphatic) a. The correct thing; what is proper,
benefiting, or fashionable; also of a person, in good condition, or
"form", "up to the mark", fit (physically or otherwise); b. the
special, important, or notable point; *esp.* what is specially required.' This is the cliché which is heightened in Strether's use of
it by being loaded with all his sensitive impressions. It does not
indicate any lack of discrimination on his part; but the fact that
he uses a morally neutral and signally vague word as a term of the
highest praise suggests the precariousness of his elected stance.

We are now at least partly prepared to consider the first two paragraphs of the next chapter (XI, iv). To facilitate reference, I number the sentences in each paragraph.

(1) What he saw was exactly the right thing—a boat advancing round the bend and containing a man who held the paddles and a lady, at the stern, with a pink parasol. (2) It was suddenly as if these figures, or something like them, had been wanted in the picture, had been wanted more or less all day, and had now drifted into sight, with the slow current, on purpose to fill up the measure. (3) They came slowly, floating down, evidently directed to the landing-place near their spectator and presenting themselves to him not less clearly as the two persons for whom his hostess was already preparing a meal. (4) For two very happy persons he found himself straightway taking them—a young man in shirt-sleeves, a young woman easy and fair, who had pulled pleasantly up from some other place and, being acquainted with the neighbourhood, had known what this particular retreat could offer them. (5) The air quite thickened, at their approach, with further intimations; the intimation that they were expert, familiar, frequent—that this wouldn't at all events be the first time. (6) They knew how to do it he vaguely felt—and it made them but the more idyllic, though at the very moment of the impression, as happened, their boat seemed to have begun to drift wide, the oarsman letting it go. (7) It had by this time none the less come much nearer—near enough for Strether to dream the lady in the stern had for some reason taken account of his being there to watch them. (8) She had remarked on it sharply, yet her companion hadn't turned round; it was in fact almost as if our friend had felt her bid him keep still. (9) She had taken in something as a result of which their course had wavered, and it continued to waver while they just stood off. (10) This little effect was sudden and rapid, so rapid that Strether's sense of it was separate only for an instant from a sharp start of his own. (11) He too had within the minute taken in something, taken in that he knew the lady whose parasol, shifting as if to hide her face, made so fine a pink point in the shining scene. (12) It was too prodigious, a chance in a million, but, if he knew the lady, the gentleman, who still presented his back and kept off, the gentleman, the coatless hero of the idyll, who had responded to her start, was, to match the marvel, none other than Chad.

(1) Chad and Madame de Vionnet were then like himself taking a day in the country—though it was as queer as fiction, as farce,

that their country could happen to be exactly his; and she had been the first at recognition, the first to feel, across the water, the shock —for it appeared to come to that—of their wonderful accident. (2) Strether became aware, with this, of what was taking place—that her recognition had been even stranger for the pair in the boat, that her immediate impulse had been to control it, and that she was quickly and intensely debating with Chad the risk of betrayal. (3) He saw they would show nothing if they could feel sure he hadn't made them out; so that he had before him for a few seconds his own hesitation. (4) It was a sharp fantastic crisis that had popped up as if in a dream, and it had only to last the few seconds to make him feel it as quite horrible. (5) They were thus, on either side, *trying* the other side, and all for some reason that broke the stillness like some unprovoked harsh note. (6) It seemed to him again, within the limit, that he had but one thing to do—to settle their common question by some sign of surprise and joy. (7) He hereupon gave large play to these things, agitating his hat and his stick and loudly calling out—a demonstration that brought him relief as soon as he had seen it answered. (8) The boat, in midstream, still went a little wild—which seemed natural, however, while Chad turned round, half springing up; and his good friend, after blankness and wonder, began gaily to wave her parasol. (9) Chad dropped afresh to his paddles and the boat headed round, amazement and pleasantry filling the air meanwhile, and relief, as Strether continued to fancy, superseding mere violence. (10) Our friend went down to the water under this odd impression as of violence averted—the violence of their having 'cut' him, out there in the eye of nature, on the assumption that he wouldn't know it. (11) He awaited them with a face from which he was conscious of not being able quite to banish this idea that they would have gone on, not seeing and not knowing, missing their dinner and disappointing their hostess, had he himself taken a line to match. (12) That at least was what darkened his vision for the moment. (13) Afterwards, after they had bumped at the landing place and he had asssisted their getting ashore, everything found itself sponged over by the mere miracle of the encounter. (XI, iv)

The phrase 'the right thing' in the first line, obviously recalls all the allusion to *'the thing'*, ' "The" thing' and 'other things' in the passage quoted above from the preceding chapter. The appearance of the boat seems 'the right thing' to Strether because it accords with his sense of the total harmony of everything—his surroundings, 'his drama', his own immediate contentment—and this harmony is expressed by returning to the aesthetic image of 'the picture' which has been used throughout the preceding chapter. But, of course, what appears to be 'the right thing' in this idealized vision turns out to be altogether the wrong thing when the couple in the boat come into sharper focus, and prove to be not two vague figures in a composition, but particular people in particular circumstances which concern Strether very closely. And the effect of this is surely to undermine the authority of '*the thing*' and the whole language of heightened cliché to which it belongs.

I shall return to this point in due course. I want immediately to indicate the ironic double-effect of Strether's impressions. While these impressions are attached to two anonymous figures, they are only agreeable, but when the figures turn out to be Chad and Madame de Vionnet the same impressions become evidence of moral turpitude. Strether is in fact betrayed into full knowledge of the unpleasant truth by his own characteristic habit of 'watching . . . and overscoring with thought' (X, i). For when Strether recognizes Chad and Madame de Vionnet it is against the background of his earlier, unguarded deduction that this couple had used this particular 'retreat' before, and thus he cannot avoid the conclusion that his friends have been deceiving him for some time. Strether does not explicitly formulate this conclusion until the end of the chapter, but it is implicit even in the first of our two paragraphs, in for instance the change of tone that occurs halfway through it.

The first six sentences display Strether's consciousness in its customary mood of sensitive but indulgent appreciation, which approvingly recognizes in the young couple, in their assurance, their practical skill, their visual harmony with the surroundings, their appropriately casual dress, their air of relaxed contentment, yet another example of that 'beauty' which has haunted him throughout his stay in Europe, and never more so than on this particular excursion. The drifting wide of the boat at the end of sentence 6, however, disturbs this impression—the 'though' makes this clear—and prepares for the recognition of Chad and Madame de Vionnet. The account of this recognition includes an ironic recapitulation of the details which had so charmed Strether just before. Thus the pink parasol, formerly a purely pictorial element, is now a device of deception—'shifting as if to hide her face' (sentence 11). The equivocation of the grammar beautifully catches Strether's complex feelings at this point: recognizing the motive of concealment, he tries to attribute it to the inanimate parasol. The latter still preserves its pictorial value—it 'made so fine a pink point in the shining scene' (sentence 11); but this phrase echoes another (a favourite one of James's), 'not to put too fine a point on it', often the colloquial introduction to an unpleasant truth. (James himself, of course, generally uses the phrase to introduce a very fine point indeed.) Similarly 'the young man in shirt-sleeves' (sentence 4) becomes 'the gentleman, the coatless hero of the idyll' in sentence 12. A coatless gentleman in James's supremely 'dressed' world* is a gentleman caught off his guard. Whereas 'in shirt-sleeves' had suggested only appropriate casualness and freedom, the negative formulation 'coatless' suggests incongruity, indiscretion, vulnerability. 'Hero' in this context becomes a mock-heroic description—this hero 'presented his back, and kept off'—and makes 'idyll' (recapitulating 'it made them but the more idyllic' in sentence 6) deeply ironic. And there is further irony in the fact that these observations on Chad occur in a sentence that begins with the suggestion of a pleasant surprise—'it was too prodigious, a chance in a million'—and continues in a rhythm which, so to speak, parodies the expression of delight. So that in this sentence we get a premonition of that tension between what all the parties know to be the truth, and the agreeable appearance which they try to put upon it, which is a main source of comedy and irony in the sequel.

The shift of tone I have remarked in this paragraph can be matched with the formal structure of its language. The first six sentences which display Strether's consciousness in what I have called his customary mood of sensitive but indulgent and idealizing appreciation (the 6th typically begins with his 'vaguely' feeling something) conform to the general pattern which has been observed by other critics who have studied the language of *The Ambassadors*, but sentences 7 to 12 deviate in certain ways from this pattern.

R. W. Short has estimated the average length of the sentences in II, ii, of *The Ambassadors* as 35 words;[10] and Ian Watt found the

---

* E. M. Forster has complained of James's characters that 'their clothes will not take off'. *Aspects of the Novel* (Penguin edition, 1962), p. 162.

average length of the sentences in the opening paragraph of the novel to be 41 words. In the first paragraph of XI, iv, the sentences 1–6 have a length of 32, 42, 34, 46, 28, 41 respectively, giving an average of just over 37; and sentences 7–12 have a length of 35, 28, 24, 27, 34, 48, respectively, giving an average of just under 33. What pushes up the latter average is the long sentence 12, in which Strether is struggling to regain his former equilibrium, to work up some pleasure at the turn of events. His actual apprehension of the odd, disturbing behaviour of the couple in the boat is appropriately conveyed in short, alert sentences (8, 9, and 10).

In his analysis of the opening paragraph of the novel, Ian Watt noted the following distinctive features: 'a preference for non-transitive verbs, many abstract nouns; much use of "that"; a certain amount of elegant variation to avoid piling up personal pronouns and adjectives such as "he", "his", and "him"; and the presence of a great many negatives and near negatives.'[11] As I suggested earlier, opening paragraphs of novels are not necessarily linguistically representative; but Watt's description will accord with most readers' general impression of the language of the late James. It is interesting, therefore, that where comparison is possible, it matches the first six sentences of the first paragraph of XI, vi, more closely than the last six.

By 'non-transitive verbs', Watt means copulatives (e.g. *was*), intransitive verbs, and the use of the passive voice. He counted 14 such verbs in the indicative in the opening paragraph of the novel, as against only 6 transitive verbs. In sentences 1–6 of the first paragraph of XI, vi, I find exactly the same ratio—14 non-transitive verbs and 6 transitive—but in sentences 7–12 there is a much more even balance—12 non-transitive and 10 transitive. These counts exclude infinitives, participles and gerunds, James's extensive use of which is associated by Watt with his preference for non-transitive verbs in the indicative. In sentences 1–6 there are 13 such verbs, but in sentences 7–12 only 7.

The paragraph from Book XI is not notable for its use of abstract nouns, but the ones most characteristic of James's account of consciousness in *The Ambassadors*—*intimations, intimation, impression*—occur in the first six sentences. The occurrence of *that* is not significant—twice in the first six sentences and twice in the last six.

Elegant variation in *The Ambassadors* does not very much affect the point I am making about this particular paragraph. However, it is interesting to note that James subdues the effect of 'elegance' here in order to place us more immediately in Strether's consciousness. He has to use the device a great deal, for he is describing three actors, two of whose names he cannot reveal until the end of the paragraph. But either the variations are natural enough to be unobtrusive—*spectator* (sentence 3), *oarsman* (6), *companion* (8)—or else they are like the variation from *man* to *gentleman*—charged with special meaning. The only obvious example of elegant variation—*our friend* (8)—has the effect of identifying us with Strether at the very moment that the couple in the boat seem to be forming an alliance against him.

There are two negative expressions in the first six sentences and three in the last six. But the first couple are stylistically the more significant. *Not less clearly* (3) and *wouldn't at all events be the first time* (5) are characteristic of Strether's hesitant, elaborately qualified trains of thought. 'None the less' (7), 'hadn't turned round' (8) and 'none other than' (12) don't have this emphasis.

The comparison of verb-usage seems most significant, especially when linked with Watt's observation that James's preference for non-transitive, participial, infinitive, and gerundial verbs in his late work is associated with an abatement of the active nature of the subject–verb–object sequence, and with an avoidance of concrete and particular subjects.[12] This is generally true of the first six sentences: the subjects are vague and tentative—

What he saw . . . (1)
It was as if . . . (2)

or are delayed by the word-order—

For two happy young people he found himself straightway taking them . . . (3)
They knew how to do it he vaguely felt . . . (6)

In sentences 8–11 we have a succession of regular subject–verb–object constructions, with in three cases particular, concrete subjects:

She had remarked on it . . . (8)
She had taken in . . . (9)
This little effect was sudden . . . (10)
He too had within the minute taken in something . . . (11)

We may say, then, that if the latter part of the paragraph displays Strether's consciousness violated by facts which, in his absorption in beauty, he has hitherto failed to recognize, this is conveyed by the partial violation, at the moment of recognition, of the linguistic norms of the novel (norms which are, of course, themselves highly idiosyncratic). Watt relates the normative linguistic form of *The Ambassadors* to James's concern with a mental rather than with a physical continuum, which frees the narrative from particular time and place, and tends to 'express states of being rather than particular actions affecting objects'.[13] These comments can be applied to the first six sentences of my paragraph; but in the last six we are very much in a physical continuum, very much aware of particular actions affecting particular objects. We are still of course in a mental continuum—Strether's consciousness—but events stand out in it with a stark unadorned clarity which is unique in the novel.

It is worth considering how James produces this effect of clarity although he is dealing with very complicated material. It is complicated because it concerns not only Strether's consciousness, but Strether's consciousness of the other characters' consciousness, and all these consciousnesses are undergoing a process of rapid change and adjustment. His method is, characteristically, to impose logical order—and therefore chronology—upon mental processes that are intuitive and partly synchronized. He spreads out lineally the over-lapping responses and actions of the characters involved so that we are able to distinguish clearly between them and follow the sequence of cause and effect. The passing of time is registered, but the words and phrases denoting time—*moment* (6), *sudden and rapid* (10), *instant* (10), *within the minute* (11)—emphasize the brevity of the time-span. The passage achieves lucidity without any dissipation of immediacy, and the principal agent of this success is James's subtle manipulation of tense.

The staple tense is the past:

> They *knew* how to do it he vaguely *felt*—and it *made* them the more idyllic, though at the very moment of the impression, as *happened*, their boat *seemed* to have begun to drift wide, the oarsman letting it go. (Sentence 6.)

The two verbal groups, *to have begun* (which is, I suppose, a present perfect infinitive) and the participle *letting . . . go*, bring the movement of the boat more 'up to date' than the other verbs in the sentence. The first verb in the next (7th) sentence is in the past perfect tense:

It *had* by this time *come* none the less nearer

indicating a lapse of time, time for Strether to have perceived

that the lady in the stern *had* for some reason *taken* notice of him

and that

She *had remarked* on it sharply, yet her companion *hadn't turned* round; . . . (8)

The sentence continues:

it *was* in fact almost as if our friend *had felt* her bid him keep still.

The past tense of *was* keeps us in touch with Strether's state of mind, while the past perfect *had felt* places his perception correctly in time. Strether goes on to recapitulate and interpret the action so far in the past perfect:

She *had taken* in something as a result of which their course *had wavered*

But this is followed in turn by an up-to-date logging of the boat's position in the past tense:

and it *continued* to waver while they just *stood* off.

So the passage goes on, looping between past and past perfect, taking in both the sequence and the simultaneity of events; while the repetition of certain words—*nearer, near enough* (sentence 7), and *rapid, so rapid* (sentence 10), *taken in, taken in* (sentence 11),—establishes these events in the mental continuum of Strether's consciousness.

The encounter between Strether and Chad and Madame de Vionnet on the river is an event of pure chance. Yet it occurs to no reader of *The Ambassadors*, I suspect, to question the artistic propriety of James's reliance on coincidence at so crucial a point in the action; and it is worth inquiring why this should be so.

Of course, James takes the usual evasive action of a novelist in his situation by anticipating, and thus deflecting the reader's objections: 'It was too prodigious, a chance in a million . . .'

(para 1, sentence 12); 'it was as queer as fiction, as farce . . .' (para 2, sentence 1). Further, it is not impossible that the reader is sub-consciously prepared for the revelation of the identity of the couple in the boat by certain undertones in the initial description of them. The metaphor 'thickened' has ominous associations ('the plot thickens', 'night thickens' etc.); while some of the epithets— *easy* (4), *expert* (5), *familiar* (5)—suggest that social *savoir faire* which Strether has persistently admired in Chad and Madame de Vionnet, and at the same time have a remote sexual allusiveness. It might be added that the phrase, 'they knew how to do it' recalls the observation—quoted earlier—on Chad's way of entering an opera-box: 'he knew, he had learned, how.'

I suggest, however, that the scene acquires its effect of aesthetic logic and inevitability by virtue of its place in a larger pattern. At least two critics[14] have noted the wealth of water imagery in *The Ambassadors*, but neither of them has connected it with the scene on the river. Yet one such image occurs very near the scene, and obviously prepares for it. It has already been quoted:

> though he had been alone all day, he had never yet so struck him-
> self as engaged with others and in the midstream of his drama. It
> might have passed for finished, his drama, with its catastrophe all
> but reached: it had, however, none the less been vivid for him as
> he gave it its fuller chance. He had only had to be at last well out
> of it to feel it, oddly enough, still going on. (XI, iii)

This is ironically prophetic. Strether's sense that his drama is not finished is not mistaken, but the catastrophe is to be very different from the one he imagines, and it is to occur literally 'in midstream'.

The connection between the river-scene and the water-imagery in *The Ambassadors* becomes clearer when we consider that many of these images are explicitly concerned with boats, e.g.:

> She [Mme de Vionnet] had settled in Paris, brought up her
> daughter, steered her boat. It was no very pleasant boat—especially
> there—to be in; but Madame de Vionnet would have headed
> straight. (V, iii)

There is a highly significant passage in which Strether's commit-ment to Madame de Vionnet's 'side' is elaborately expressed in terms of his being drawn, rather against the counsels of prudence, into her 'boat'. It is the scene where Madame de Vionnet first introduces herself to Sarah Pocock (who is herself pulling Mrs

Newsome's boat, as Strether remarks to Chad (VIII, i)). When Strether enters, Madame de Vionnet takes the opportunity publicly to establish him as her ally:

> as she thus publicly drew him into her boat she produced in him such a silent agitation as he was not to fail afterwards to denounce as pusillanimous. . . . It would be exactly *like* the way things always turned out for him that he should affect Mrs. Pocock and Waymarsh as launched in a relation in which he had really never been launched at all. They were at this very moment—they could only be—attributing to him the full licence of it and all by the operation of her own tone with him; whereas his sole licence had been to cling with intensity to the brink, not to dip so much as a toe into the flood. But the flicker of his fear on this occasion was not, as may be added, to repeat itself; it sprang up, for its moment, only to die down and then go out for ever. To meet his fellow visitor's invocation and, with Sarah's brilliant eyes upon him, answer, *was* quite sufficiently to step into her boat. During the rest of the time her visit lasted he felt himself proceed to each of the proper offices, successively, for helping to keep the adventurous skiff afloat. It rocked beneath him, but he settled himself in his place. He took up an oar and, since he was to have the credit of pulling, pulled.' (VIII, iii)

The image of the boat, it may be remarked, is a good example of what I have called the language of heightened cliché, for it is developed out of the colloquialism, 'in the same boat'. The example just quoted is especially interesting as being one of those relatively rare occasions in *The Ambassadors* where James invests a metaphor with that startling concreteness of elaboration which we associate particularly with *The Golden Bowl*. The effect is rather like that of the heroic simile in epic poetry, where the 'tenor' recedes from sight, and the 'vehicle' takes on an independent poetic life. Strether is indeed formulating his situation in heroic terms: he addresses himself to his voyage in the 'adventurous skiff' in the spirit of an Argonaut.[15] The way in which the image is handled, however, produces something more akin to a mock-heroic effect. This is partly because Strether himself does not regard his situation with a completely straight face—he is far from being a totally deluded hero. But there does seem to be a joke lurking in the passage of which Strether is not aware. In the phrase 'not to dip so much as a toe into the flood', he seems to picture himself as a figure on a comic postcard. But the striking of this note ensures that when we come to the final elaboration of the stepping-into-the-boat image, our attention is as much occupied with its comic as with its heroic possibilities. It always seems possible that Strether might miss his footing and tumble into the water. To invoke Dr Leavis again, there *is* here a kind of disproportion between the energy of the doing and the issues at stake, but this disproportion is deliberately exploited to 'place' Strether's character and situation.

Holder-Barrell describes the primary meaning of the water symbolism in *The Ambassadors* in these terms: 'Woollett appears as the place of safety, the shore, the secure ground, whereas Europe is pictured as the mighty stream with dangerous currents.'[16] How appropriate it is, therefore, that Strether, at the climax of an experience which he has consistently likened to swimming in or navigating a watery medium,* at the very point where he has to reassess this experience and acknowledge the partial correctness of the Woollett interpretation of events, should be returned to the Woollett stance on the shore, and recognize the deviousness of Chad's and Madame de Vionnet's conduct, as they come drifting down the current of a river in a boat. The development of the iterative metaphor into a literal event supports the function of the river-scene as a *peripeteia* in which Strether's vision is violated by fact.

To analyse the linguistic structure of the second paragraph would be to reiterate many observations made above: the uncharacteristic preference for a subject–verb–object structure, and the manipulation of tense, for instance, perform much the same

---

* E.g. 'Waymarsh himself, for the occasion, was drawn into the eddy; it absolutely, though but temporarily, swallowed him down, and there were days when Strether seemed to bump against him as a sinking swimmer might brush a submarine object' (IV, ii). 'If Madame de Vionnet, under Sarah's eyes, had pulled him into her boat, there was by this time no doubt whatever that he had remained in it and that what he had really most been conscious of for many hours together was the movement of the vessel itself' (IX, i). 'They were touching bottom assuredly tonight' (X, i). ' "Our general state of mind had proceeded, on its side, from our queer ignorance, our queer misconceptions and confusions—from which, since then, an inexorable tide of light seems to have floated us into our perhaps still queerer knowledge".' (Strether to Sarah, X, iii.)

function in this paragraph as in the first. I shall confine myself, therefore, to indicating how this second paragraph extends and develops the situation established in the first, and, like the first, ironically echoes notes struck earlier in the novel.

The tension, which I remarked on earlier, between what all the parties know to be the truth and the agreeable appearance they try to put upon it, is intensified in the second paragraph. Strether's embarrassment, discomfiture, pain, become sharper as he perceives the true nature of the situation, and to compensate he gropes for more and more emphatic formulae of pleasure and surprise. But the darkening sequence of *queer, shock, crisis, horrible, harsh,* and *violence,* only makes the invocation of *wonderful, surprise and joy, gaily, amazement, pleasantry,* and *miracle,* hollow and mocking. The hypocrisy, as James of course intended, is rendered, not stated. The forced quality of Strether's 'sign of surprise and joy' is perfectly conveyed in the selection and arrangement of words in:

> He hereupon gave large play to these things, agitating his hat and his stick and loudly calling out. (7)

There is a heavy flatness in the syntax, a note of deliberation in 'hereupon', an excessiveness of effort about 'agitating', which betray the insincerity of Strether's gestures.

Like the first paragraph, the second is knitted into the fabric of the novel by a number of finely-spun threads. The double repetition of *violence,* for instance, echoes Strether's musings in Book VI on his deepening complicity with Madame de Vionnet and Chad:

> He failed quite to see how his situation could clear up at all logically except by some turn of events that would give him the pretext of disgust. He was building from day to day on the possibility of disgust, but each day brought forth meanwhile a new and more engaging bend of the road. That possibility was now ever so much further from sight than on the eve of his arrival, and he perfectly felt that, should it come at all, it would have to be at best inconsequent and violent. (VI, ii)

Though Strether's reaction to the discovery of Chad's relationship with Madame de Vionnet is not one of 'disgust'—that kind of response belongs to the moral world of Woollett which he has abandoned for ever—his situation is 'cleared up' by an event which is 'inconsequent' and in which 'violence' is narrowly averted.

The phrase 'queer as . . . farce' catches up all the theatrical imagery and allusion in *The Ambassadors*. According to R. W. Short, theatrical images in James generally 'stand for the unnatural, the meretricious, the over-ingenious, the glittering front, the false ritual, the social perversion'.[17] Throughout the major part of *The Ambassadors*, however, the theatre does not carry such unambiguously derogatory associations. The legitimate theatre is in fact one of the novel's touchstones for indicating fineness or crudity of sensibility, the acceptance or rejection of European culture and the idea of social beauty. Strether, under the tutelage of Maria Gostrey, becomes a keen theatregoer, and presumably Chad has already become one, since he knows so well how to enter a box. Waymarsh, on the other hand, rejects Strether's invitation to go to a theatre: 'he had seen plays enough, he signified, before Strether had joined him—an affirmation that had its full force when his friend ascertained by questions that he had seen two and a circus' (II, i). Waymarsh later takes Sarah to a circus, while Strether resignedly escorts Jim Pocock to the Varieties. It is not surprising, therefore, that Strether's sense of the interest and excitement of his situation is often articulated in theatrical imagery: the passage from Chapter iii of Book XI, which I have already referred to several times, contains a particularly striking example of Strether relishing his 'drama'. The drama, however, becomes a 'farce': the word, in its context, has associations of extravagance, vulgarity, and poor taste. And on the next occasion when Strether resorts to a theatrical metaphor, it carries a definite connotation of deception and pretence:

> It had been a performance, Mme de Vionnet's manner [on the return journey to Paris], and though it had to that degree faltered toward the end, as though her ceasing to believe in it, as though she had asked herself, or Chad had found a moment surreptitiously to ask her, what after all was the use, a performance it had none the less quite handsomely remained, with the final fact about it that it was on the whole easier to keep up than to abandon. (XI, iv)

One of the most interesting phrases in the second paragraph is 'their wonderful accident', for *wonderful* is a word that rings through the whole novel. Usually it belongs to what I have called the language of heightened cliché. I have noted 36 occurrences, and there are probably many more. It seems to start with Maria Gostrey agreeing with Strether that the things he has to deal with in Paris will be 'wonderful' (III, ii). But at Gloriani's party the word becomes associated with Miss Barrace, perhaps the most sinister and morally dubious character in the novel. In light conversation with Strether, she remarks of Waymarsh,

> 'He'll resist even Miss Gostrey: so grand is it not to understand. He's wonderful.' (V, i)

A little later, Strether queries her response to the mention of Madame de Vionnet:

> 'Then why did you a minute ago say "Oh, oh, oh!" at the name?'
> She easily remembered. 'Why, just because——! She's wonderful.'
> 'Ah she too?'—Strether had almost a groan. (V, i)

This exchange, like the one quoted above about 'dear old Paris' (which it immediately follows), shows Strether offering a certain resistance to the new language and the new system of values it embodies. But by the next chapter he has already adopted the new word:

> The only thing he was clear about was that, luckily, nothing indiscreet had in fact been said, and that Chad himself was more than ever, in Miss Barrace's great sense, wonderful.' (V, ii)

Henceforward, the word is thrown about with more and more abandon. Everyone, everything, it seems, is 'wonderful': either because, like Gloriani and Madame de Vionnet, they embody Europe, or because like Waymarsh they don't understand it, or because like Strether they appreciate it, or because like Chad they have learned from it, or like Mamie Pocock they are quite alien to it. 'Wonderful' becomes the supreme 'in-group' word, which those who are 'in' apply honorifically to each other and patronizingly to those who are 'out'. It is a word which blurs distinctions of value and opinion by its soothing flattery, its easy extravagance. There are moments when Strether resists the habit:

> He found himself on the point of telling her [Mme de Vionnet] that she was, as Miss Barrace called it, wonderful, but catching himself up, he said something else instead. (VI, i)

There are moments when he suspects the innocent surface of the word. (Chad is speaking of Madame de Vionnet):

> 'She's under arms,' Chad laughed again; 'she's prepared.'
> Strether took it in; then, as if an echo of Miss Barrace were in the air: 'She's wonderful.' 'You don't begin to know *how* wonderful!' There was a depth in it, to Strether's ear, of confirmed luxury —almost a kind of unconscious insolence of proprietorship; but the effect of this glimpse was not at this moment to foster speculation: there was something so conclusive in so much graceful and generous assurance. (VIII, i)

And there are moments when he associates the word with his own imprudence:

> 'It's quite true. I'm extremely wonderful just now. I daresay in fact I'm quite fantastic, and I shouldn't be at all surprised if I were mad.' (VII, iii)

It is appropriate, therefore, that the river-scene, which forces Strether to revise his vision of social beauty, should invoke the word *wonderful* in such a way as to reduce its over-inflated meaning. The 'accident' of the encounter is 'wonderful' because it is surprising, but not at all because it is pleasant. In the context of the novel 'wonderful accident' is a kind of oxymoron, juxtaposing the supreme value-word of European social beauty and a word suggestive of disaster, misfortune, indecorum, error. After this scene, Strether cannot invoke 'wonderful' with the old enthusiasm. ' "I . . . should have liked to seem to you—well, sublime!" ', says Madame de Vionnet at their last interview:

> He could only, after a moment, re-echo Miss Barrace. 'You're wonderful.' (XII, iii)

In one of the last scenes in the novel, Strether and Maria Gostrey discuss his failure to perceive the truth about the relationship between Chad and Madame de Vionnet:

> 'What I see, what I saw,' Maria returned, 'is that you dressed up even the virtue. You were wonderful—you were beautiful, as I've had the honour of telling you before; but, if you wish really to know,' she sadly confessed, 'I never quite knew *where* you were. There were moments,' she explained, 'when you struck me as grandly cynical; there were others when you struck me as grandly vague.' (XII, iii)

We know that Strether was never grandly cynical. He was always grandly vague. 'Grandly' because his vision of social beauty was a noble one; 'vague' because it failed to take into account some of the brutal facts of human nature. Hence, this vision is conveyed in a special language, a grandly vague style. The way in which James, in the river-scene, disperses the vision, and modifies the style, on which he had lavished such loving skill, is a testimony to his greatness as an artist.

VI

'Tono-Bungay'
and the Condition of England

T<small>HE</small> famous quarrel between Henry James and H. G. Wells, so
ably documented by Leon Edel and Gordon N. Ray,[1] takes
on, in the critic's contemplation of it, an almost allegorical
quality. It was a classic encounter between a great theorist and
exponent of the aesthetically 'pure', modern, international novel,
and a redoubtable spokesman for and practitioner of the rambling,
discursive, aesthetically 'impure' novel of the traditional English
type. At the time of their breach Wells must have seemed the
victor, for he was riding the wave of popular acclaim, while the
'major phase' of James was misunderstood and neglected. Time
and changing literary taste have brought about a reversal of this
situation; now it is Wells who is neglected and even despised,
while James sits in glory on Parnassus. Just recently this movement of the scales has been checked by a renewal of interest in
Wells's early scientific romances, an interest promoted particularly
by Bernard Bergonzi's excellent study *The Early H. G. Wells*
(Manchester, 1961). But most modern critics would still endorse
Mark Schorer's words: 'as James grows for us . . . Wells dis-
appears'.[2]

The Edel–Ray book can only confirm this process. On the
purely human level, James probably emerges with more credit;
and he certainly has the best of the literary debate. The eloquence
of his *credo* in the final letter, 'It is art that *makes* life, makes interest,

makes importance, for our consideration and application of these things, and I know of no substitute whatever for the force and beauty of its process'³—is overwhelming. However, as in most literary quarrels, James and Wells were too involved in their own literary destinies to do each other justice; and Wells was plainly irritated by James's mandarin gestures into doing *himself* injustice, affecting a literary barbarism which the skill of his own work belies.

I am not going to argue that Wells was as great a novelist as James, but I am going to argue that *Tono-Bungay* (1909) is a much better novel than it is commonly supposed to be. Clearly, we shall never reach this conclusion if we read the novel as we read a novel by James, in the way James has taught us to read him, and to read other novelists. *Tono-Bungay* sins, deliberately, against most of the Jamesian commandments: it is picaresque, full of apparent digressions in the form both of episodes, and of expository comment on politics, economics, history, and society. It is told in the first person, and rejoices in 'the terrible *fluidity* of self-revelation'⁴ which James saw as the great weakness of that mode of narration. Its characters are largely of the 'flat', humorous variety. Plainly, *Tono-Bungay* will not offer the same satisfactions as *The Ambassadors*. But I suggest that if we read *Tono-Bungay* with an open mind, with attention to its language, to the passages where that language becomes most charged with imaginative energy, we shall find that it is an impressive, and certainly coherent, work of art.

At first sight, this may seem a surprising recommendation, because insensitivity to language is one of the commonest complaints made by critics of Wells. In the essay in which he calls for closer attention to language in novel-criticism, Mark Schorer invokes Wells as an example of a novelist whose severe limitations will be exposed by such an approach.⁵ Norman Nicholson says, 'as for style, he had none, if by style we mean the shaping of sentences which will be a pleasure in themselves'.⁶ Vincent Brome says, 'words were not weighed and flavoured with care in *Tono-Bungay*'.⁷ Arnold Kettle says:

> Wells himself achieved in his novels no satisfactory artistic expression of his own vision of life. Part of the trouble would seem to be in his incurably slap-dash, slip-shod method of composition. He does not give himself time to search for the right word, let alone organize his total material.⁸

There is a certain amount of truth in these criticisms, but the weight they should be given in assessing the novel needs to be carefully measured. One can certainly find scattered through *Tono-Bungay* examples of loose grammar and careless punctuation which obscure meaning and serve no perceptible expressive function. But such faults—although they remain faults—cause less disturbance than they would in a novel by, for example, James, because Wells's undertaking in *Tono-Bungay* does not require the elegant, harmonious, intricate kind of language adopted by James, but a language that is hurried, urgent, groping. This is not to say that we can ever excuse 'bad' writing—writing that consistently fails to meet the legitimate expectations of the reader. But such expectations must arise out of the novel itself.

More than 'style', in Nicholson's sense, is at stake here. Kettle, for instance, complains that Wells fails 'to people adequately the world of the novel. There are almost no characters in *Tono-Bungay* who grip the imagination of the reader.'[9] But what if Wells set out to grip the imagination of the reader in other ways? This, after all, was the point at issue between him and James:

> The important thing which I tried to argue with Henry James was that the novel of completely consistent characterisation, arranged beautifully in a strong and rounded story, and painted deep and round, no more exhausts the possibilities of the novel, than the art of Velasquez exhausts the possibilities of the painted picture.[10]

But if *Tono-Bungay* is not a novel of the Jamesian type, of what type is it? It is confessional in form. 'I want to tell—*myself*' says the narrator, George Ponderevo, at the outset; but adds immediately: 'and my impressions of the thing as a whole, to say things I have come to feel intensely of the laws, traditions, usages and ideas we call society' (I, i, 2). He feels qualified to do so because his career has led him through an 'extensive cross-section of the British social organism' (I, i, 1).

The Victorians had a name for this kind of undertaking in fiction: the 'Condition of England novel'. This description was often applied to novels which sought to articulate and interpret, in the mode of fiction, the changing nature of English society in an era of economic, political, religious, and philosophical revolution. In *Coningsby* (1844) Disraeli refers to 'that Condition of England question, of which our generation hears so much'.[11]

Other novels of this type include Disraeli's own *Sybil* (1845), Mrs Gaskell's *Mary Barton* (1848), and *North and South* (1855), Dickens's *Hard Times* (1854), Charles Kingsley's *Alton Locke* (1850), and *Yeast* (1851), and George Eliot's *Felix Holt* (1866). And there were a host of justly-forgotten minor novels in the *genre*. The central issue for most of these writers was the economic one. Carlyle begins his *Past and Present* (1843):

> The condition of England question, on which many pamphlets are now in the course of publication, and many thoughts unpublished are going on in every reflective head, is justly regarded as one of the most ominous, and withal one of the strangest, ever seen in this world. England is full of wealth, of multifarious produce, supply for human want in every kind; yet England is dying of inanition.[12]

The voice of Carlyle reminds us however, that the condition of England question was not merely an economic one, but part of the continuous cultural debate about the place of human values in a society given over to materialism, a debate which has been sustained from the Industrial revolution to the present day, and which has been so well surveyed by Raymond Williams in *Culture and Society*. Not only is the question still alive for Wells's generation—the very phrase is still alive. And the phrase is important: it invites us to consider England as a social organism whose health is suspect, which, as I shall try to show, is precisely Wells's perspective in *Tono-Bungay*. In the very same year that *Tono-Bungay* appeared (1909), C. F. G. Masterman* published *The Condition of England*, a book of social criticism in the tradition of Carlyle and Arnold, which it is fascinating to read in conjunction with *Tono-Bungay*. Masterman had read the page proofs of Wells's novel while preparing his own book,[13] and clearly he was very excited by it, for he frequently alludes to it.

'The hero of [Wells's] greatest novel,' says Masterman, 'reveals an experience fragmentary and disconnected in a tumultuous world.'[14] With this may be coupled a passage from Wells's *An Experiment in Autobiography*, in which Wells argues that the fact

---

* C. F. G. Masterman was born in 1873 and died in 1923. He was a Junior Minister in Asquith's 1908 Government, and subsequently held a series of other important political posts. He was a journalist, and had many contacts with the radical literary world.

that the English novel matured at a time of social fixity inevitably tilted the novelist's interests in the direction of individual characters reacting and conflicting within a comfortably stable social framework. He says that the novel's 'standards were established within that apparently permanent frame and the criticism of it began to be irritated and perplexed when, through a new instability, the splintering frame began to get into the picture'.[15] Wells's literary history, as is often the case with practising writers, is somewhat over-dramatized by his own sense of artistic purpose: Wells was not as revolutionary as he thought. But the comment yields an important clue to the understanding of *Tono-Bungay*. For here the frame does get into the picture; one might almost say the frame *is* the picture. That is, the main vehicle of Wells's social analysis of the condition of England in *Tono-Bungay* is not the story or the characters, but the descriptive commentary which, in most novels, we regard as the frame. I refer to the descriptions of landscape and townscape, of architecture and domestic interiors, and the narrator's reflection on them, which occupy so prominent a place in the novel.

The function of these descriptions seems to me different from the function of description in other novels discussed in this book—different from Charlotte Brontë's real and visionary landscapes, different from Hardy's double-sided Nature, different from James's Paris. It comes closest to Dickens's Coketown, as we might expect, for that is the setting of another Condition of England novel. But Coketown *is* a setting, a 'frame'. The England of *Tono-Bungay* is not merely an appropriate setting for the gestures of Wells's characters, not merely a means of symbolizing their inner lives—not, in other words, something which gets its meaning from the individual lives which inhabit it. It is simply the central character of the novel, as England is the central character of Shakespeare's history plays.

A summary of Wells's diagnosis of the Condition of England in *Tono-Bungay* might be formulated as follows: Late Victorian and Edwardian England is a country dedicated to aimlessness and waste. The social and political principles of 1688 have not been replaced by any new theories, although society has been economically transformed by the Industrial Revolution. Consequently, capitalism has been allowed to burgeon without control, creating 'the most unpremeditated, subtle, successful, and aimless plutocracy that ever encumbered the destinies of mankind' (III, ii, 7); and forcing the mass of mankind into living conditions of barbarous dreariness. If things continue to drift in this way, they can only get worse.

This pessimistic analysis of the Condition of England is conveyed partly in the main narrative line, which concerns the rise of Edward Ponderevo, George's uncle, to the financial heights, and his abrupt collapse into bankruptcy and dishonour. It is an effective parable of modern capitalism, but it is not the organizing principle in the design of *Tono-Bungay*. Nor are the episodes in George's life which are unrelated to his uncle and which mainly concern the unsatisfactory nature of his relationships with women. The organizing principle of *Tono-Bungay* is to be found in the web of description and commentary by which all the proliferating events and characters of the story are placed in a comprehensive political, social, and historical perspective. In the characteristic manner of the novelist, Wells develops this role of description out of the routine devices of concrete particularity and specificity. Houses, rooms, furnishings, townscapes, landscapes, and landscaped landscapes, are observed and described with a shrewd eye, placing the characters in a recognizable realistic environment, and serving as indices of their social status, tastes, and temperaments. But the language of the novel, like Dickens's language for Coketown, invests these inanimate objects and collections of objects with a strange and sinister life of their own, more powerful than the life of any individual character. It is, however, a diseased life. Running through the whole novel there is a strain of disease and decay imagery which establishes its theme and draws the episodic narrative into a coherent design. Seen in this perspective, the fact that 'Tono-Bungay', the foundation of Ponderevo's immense fortune, should be a quack *medicine*, which falsely claims to cure all the ills of modern society, from boredom, fatigue, and strain, to falling hair and ageing gums, has a more than fortuitous appropriateness; George's failure to achieve a satisfactory and mature sexual relationship becomes a symptom of the universal disorder ('Love,' he says, 'like everything else in this immense process of social disorganization in which we live, is a thing adrift, a fruitless thing broken away from its connections' (IV, ii, 2)); and the 'quap' episode, which many critics have taken to be an afterthought designed merely to give a flagging story a lift, earns its place in the novel as a logical, though daring piece of symbolic action.

It is the language of the novel which binds it into a unified whole, setting up verbal echoes which establish connections between the many disparate subjects of George's discourse, and giving that discourse a consistent and individual tone of voice. To summarize: George sees life in terms of society, and society as an *organism* or *system* which is often spatially conceived in terms of architecture or topography, and which is involved in a *process* of *change* and *growth* characterized by negative qualities of *confusion, disorder, disarrangement, disturbance, degeneration, dissolution, disproportion, muddle,* and *waste,* and more concretely, by *cancer, disease, decay, festering, swelling,* and *rot.* The spectacle is *huge, immense, stupendous*—hence all the more *strange* and *sinister.* These words, or words with associated meanings, recur in the most heightened passages of the novel, and suggest that Wells used language with more discrimination and a firmer sense of artistic purpose and design than critics have usually given him credit for.

Clearly, however, Wells's undertaking in *Tono-Bungay* is not compatible with the canons of the aesthetically pure and symmetrical novel; and he takes steps to deflect an appeal to such canons in the prefatory remarks of his narrator. Indeed, Wells seems to be rehearsing his debate with James in such passages as these:

> I warn you that this book is going to be something of an agglomeration. I want to trace my social trajectory (and my uncle's) as the main line of my story, but as this is my first novel and almost certainly my last, I want to get in, too, all sorts of things that struck me, things that amused me and impressions I got—even though they don't minister directly to my narrative at all. . . . My ideas of a novel all through are comprehensive rather than austere. (I, i. 1)
>
> I've read an average share of novels and made some starts before this beginning, and I've found the restraints and rules of the art (as I made them out) impossible for me. . . . I fail to see how I can be other than a lax, undisciplined story-teller. I must sprawl and flounder, comment and theorise, if I am to get the thing out I have in mind. (I, i, 2)

This is not an admission of failure on Wells's part, but a rhetorical device to prepare the reader for the kind of novel *Tono-Bungay* is—

a case of artlessness concealing art. The major technical problem confronting the Condition of England novelist—as nineteenth-century examples show—is how to accommodate within an imaginative structure an abundance of material of a kind which is usually treated discursively. Wells's solution is to use a narrator who asserts at the outset his intention of commenting, describing, and theorizing, and to invest his most powerful literary resources in this area of the novel.

George Ponderevo begins his chronicle, in the conventional way, with an account of his boyhood and early impressions 'in the shadow of Bladesover House', Lady Drew's stately home, where his mother was employed as a housekeeper.

> Bladesover lies up on the Kentish Downs, eight miles perhaps from Ashborough; and its old pavilion, a little wooden parody of the temple of Vesta at Tibur, upon the hill-crest behind the house, commands in theory at least a view of either sea, of the Channel southward and the Thames to the north-east. The park is the second largest in Kent, finely wooded with well-placed beeches, many elms and some sweet chestnuts, abounding in little valleys and hollows of bracken, with springs and a stream and three fine ponds and multitudes of fallow deer. The house was built in the eighteenth century, it is of pale red brick in the style of a French chateau, and save for one pass among the crests which opens to blue distances, to minute, remote, oast-set farm-houses and copses and wheatfields and the occasional gleam of water, its hundred and seventeen windows look on nothing but its own wide and hand-some territories. A semi-circular screen of great beeches masks the church and village, which cluster picturesquely about the high-road along the skirts of the great park. (I, i, 3)

This seems a fairly unexceptional descriptive set-piece. But, apart from the faintly ironic and decidedly unawed tone of the narrator ('parody', 'in theory') the detail of the windows, the self-regarding eyes of Bladesover, placed in an emphatic position at the end of a long sentence, and the noting of the careful concealment from these eyes of the lesser buildings dependent upon Bladesover, suggest that the scene has a more than pictorial significance. This becomes explicit in the next paragraph:

> Now, the unavoidable suggestion of that wide park and that fair large house, dominating church, village and the country-side, was

that they represented the thing that mattered supremely in the world, and that all other things had significance only in relation to them. They represented the Gentry, the Quality, by and through and for whom the rest of the world, the farming folk, and the labouring folk, the tradespeople of Ashborough and the upper servants and the lower servants and the servants of the estate, breathed and lived and were permitted. And the Quality did it so quietly and thoroughly, the great house mingled so solidly and effectually with earth and sky, the contrast of its spacious hall and saloon and galleries, its airy housekeeper's room and warren of offices with the meagre dignities of the vicar, and the pinched and stuffy rooms of even the post-office people and the grocer, so enforced these suggestions, that it was only when I was a boy of thirteen and fourteen . . . that . . . I began to question the final rightness of the gentlefolks, their primary necessity in the scheme of things. (I, i, 3)

Already, what one might call the 'architectural rhetoric' of *Tono-Bungay* begins to make itself felt. Reduced to logical terms, what Wells is saying is that the great estates, like Bladesover, were designed by people who enjoyed a privileged position in an élitist society. But the concentration on the physical features of the estate, rather than on the people who inhabit it (it is the former which are particularized by epithets) attributes to these physical features, themselves the creation of man, an unnatural power over men; and this unnaturalness in the relationship between men and their physical environment is one of Wells's primary illustrations of the disorder in society as a whole. That the architecture and layout of Bladesover can continue to dominate the surrounding country long after the social order on which it was built has become obsolete, eloquently represents the failure of society to come to terms with the changes it has experienced. The social fabric of England is undergoing a process of change and decay, a process of which the inhabitants are ironically and fatally unaware. The idea comes out in an autumnal image:

There are times when I wonder whether any but a very inconsiderable minority of English people realise how extensively this ostensible order has even now passed away. The great houses stand in the parks still, the cottages cluster respectfully on their borders, touching their eaves with their creepers . . .

(note the bold anthropomorphism here—the cottages stand in for cottagers touching their forelocks)

> . . . the English countryside—you can range through Kent from Bladesover northward and see—persists obstinately in looking what it was. It is like an early day in a fine October. The hand of change rests on it all, unfelt, unseen; resting for awhile, as it were half reluctantly, before it grips and ends the thing for ever. One frost and the whole face of things will be bare, links snap, patience end, our fine foliage of pretences lie glowing in the mire. (I, i, 3)

George recalls this image in the very last chapter of the novel:

> Other people may see this country in other terms; this is how I have seen it. In some early chapter in this heap I compared all our present colour and abundance to October foliage before the frosts nip down the leaves. That I still feel was a good image. Perhaps I see wrongly. It may be that I see decay all about me because I am, in a sense, decay. To others it may be a scene of achievement and construction radiant with hope. I, too, have a sort of hope, but it is a remote hope, a hope that finds no promise in this Empire or in any of the great things of our time. (IV, iii, 1)

There may be an element of anarchic glee in the contemplation of this inevitable decay. But it is very far from being a revolutionary spirit. Misgiving, fear, even regret for lost beauty, are the dominant overtones in these images. We find in *Tono-Bungay* in fact, that submission of Wells's professed radical optimism to the more pessimistic intuitions of his imagination, which Bernard Bergonzi has located as a prime source of the enduring interest of Wells's science fiction. Whereas Wells the scientific propagandist is associated in our minds with facile optimism and Progress-worship, *The Time Machine* is one of the most desolating myths in modern literature. And it is worth invoking at this point Robert Conquest's definition of science fiction as a distinct genre: 'science fiction ranges over every type of story in which the centre of attention is on the results of a possible, though not actual, change in the conditions of life'.[16] In *Tono-Bungay* Wells is concerned with the actual rather than with the possible (though he crosses the frontier in the quap episode). But the important point is that he is concerned with change in the 'conditions of life'—a concern that, as Conquest points out, necessarily conflicts with the traditional concerns of the novel form, 'the variations of human feelings and actions within contexts which are taken for granted'.[17]

Though George recognizes that Bladesover is given over to change, the nature of the change invests the old obsolete Bladesover with a kind of virtue. George jumps forward in time, at the end of the first Book of the novel, to describe a visit, much later in his life, to Bladesover under the tenancy of Sir Reuben Lichtenstein. Bladesover under Lady Drew, he reflects, although obsolete and reactionary, had enshrined certain values. 'About that park there were some elements of a liberal education . . . there was mystery, there was matter for the imagination' (I, i, 5). And the big saloon had housed books which, even if unread by their owners, helped a servant's son to a surreptitious education. Against the description of Lady Drew's saloon and its literary treasures is deliberately contrasted a description of the same room under the Lichtensteins:

> When I came back at last to the real Bladesover on an inconsequent visit, everything was far smaller than I could have supposed possible. It was as though everything had shivered and shrivelled a little at the Lichtenstein touch. The harp was still in the saloon, but there was a different grand piano with a painted lid and a metrostyle pianola, and an extraordinary quantity of artistic litter and *bric à brac* scattered about. There was the trail of the Bond Street showroom over it all. (I, ii, 8)

The detailed description continues for many lines. We are never at any point informed about the Lichtensteins as individuals. George passes directly from the account of their domestic furnishings to generalizations about their class. Bladesover is thus made into an *exemplum* of the decay of the social organism as a whole.

> The Lichtensteins and their like seem to have no promise in them at all of any fresh vitality for the kingdom. I do not believe in their intelligence or their power—they have nothing new about them at all, nothing creative or rejuvenescent, no more than a disorderly instinct of acquisition, and the prevalence of them and their kind is a phase in the broad slow decay of the great social organism of England. They could not have made Bladesover, they cannot replace it; they just happen to break out over it—saprophytically. (I, ii, 8)

The final, arresting metaphor (a saprophyte is 'any vegetable organism which lives on decayed vegetable matter'—O.E.D.) makes vividly concrete the sustained image of England as an organism in which growth has become decay. On this note the first Book of *Tono-Bungay* ends.

The analysis of the condition of England in *Tono-Bungay* is dramatized throughout as a heuristic process in the narrator. As a child he did not question the fixed and stratified society represented by Lady Drew's Bladesover. 'When I was a little boy I took the place with the entirest faith as a complete authentic microcosm. I believed that the Bladesover system was a little working model—and not so very little either—of the whole world' (I, i, 3). Even when he is permitted to be a playmate of the Honourable Beatrice Normandy, the two children play with a microcosm of the microcosm, 'the great doll's house that the Prince Regent had given Sir Harry Drew's first born (who died at five), that was a not ineffectual model of Bladesover itself, and contained eighty-five dolls and had cost hundreds of pounds' (I, i, 7). Although George quickly discovers that Lady Drew's Bladesover is not a microcosm of the modern world, its importance as a clue to the social anatomy of England is not diminished:

> . . . in a sense Bladesover has never left me; it is, as I said at the outset, one of those dominant explanatory impressions that make the framework of my mind. Bladesover illuminates England; it has become all that is spacious, dignified, pretentious, and truly conservative in English life. It is my social datum. That is why I have drawn it here on so large a scale. (I, ii, 8)

George's first realization that there is an uglier, more sinister aspect of English life than that represented by Bladesover, comes when he is exiled to Chatham, after he has disgraced himself by fighting Beatrice's half-brother Archie. This realization is partly formed by George's misery in the mean, dismal life of his chapel-going cousins, the Frapps (one of whom, George says, 'I am now convinced, had some secret disease that drained his vitality away' (I, i, 1)); but the dominant impression is of Chatham, and its neighbour Rochester, as *places*, as the antithesis of Bladesover. The large, free, assured handling of townscape in this section, while at the same time sustaining a polemical argument, is characteristic of *Tono-Bungay*. But Wells reserves his most powerful effects in this mode for London.

In Kent, the great estates have managed to keep the ugliness and squalor of industry at a distance; but in London, as George sees, once more in architectural terms, the two forces are engaged at close quarters. As a young student, George explores the city, and out of this exploration, he says, 'there has grown up in me a kind of theory of London' (II, i, 1). It is a theory that again takes Bladesover as its starting point, and is again darkened by allusion to disease:

> . . . I do think I see lines of an ordered structure out of which it [London] has grown, detected a process that is something more than a confusion of casual accidents, though indeed it may be no more than a process of disease.
>
> I said at the outset of my first book that I find in Bladesover the clue to all England. Well, I certainly imagine it is the clue to the structure of London. There have been no revolutions, no deliberate restatements or abandonments of opinion in England since the days of the fine gentry; since 1688 or thereabouts, the days when Bladesover was built; there have been changes, dissolving forces, replacing forces if you will; but then it was that the broad lines of the English system set firmly. And as I have gone to and fro in London, in certain regions the thought has recurred, this is Bladesover House, this answers to Bladesover House. The fine gentry may have gone; they have indeed largely gone, I think; rich merchants may have replaced them, financial adventurers or what not. That does not matter; the shape is still Bladesover. (II, i, 1)

He then traces out what he regards as the 'Great-House region' of London, the residential areas around the West End Parks. It is an enlargement of Bladesover—the National History museum corresponding to the cases of stuffed birds on the Bladesover staircase, the Art Museum to the Bladesover curios and porcelain, and so on.

> It is this idea of escaping parts from the seventeenth-century system of Bladesover, of proliferating and overgrowing elements from the Estates, that to this day seems to me the best explanation, not simply of London, but of all England. England is a country of great Renaissance landed gentlefolk who have been unconsciously outgrown and overgrown. (II, i, 1)

The landed gentlefolk have been outgrown and overgrown by the new rich, who have preserved, if vulgarized, the architectural fabric they have parasitically occupied. ('In the meanwhile the old shapes, the old attitudes remain, subtly changed and changing still, sheltering strange tenants' (I, i, 3).) But both orders are threatened 'by the presence of great new forces, blind forces of invasion, of growth.'

> The railway termini on the north side of London have been kept as remote as Eastry had kept the railway station from Wimblehurst, they stop on the very outskirts of the estates, but from the south, the South Eastern railway had butted its great stupid rusty iron head of Charing Cross station—that great head that came smashing down in 1905—clean across the river, between Somerset House and Whitehall. The south side had no protecting estates. Factory chimneys smoke right over against Westminster with an air of carelessly not having permission, and the whole effect of industrial London and of all London east of Temple Bar and of the huge dingy immensity of London port, is to me of something disproportionately large, something morbidly expanded, without plan or intention, dark and sinister toward the clean clear social assurance of the West End. And south of this central London, south-east, south-west, far west, north-west, all round the northern hills, are similar disproportionate growths, endless streets of undistinguished houses, undistinguished industries, shabby families, second-rate shops, inexplicable people who in a once fashionable phrase, do not 'exist'. All these aspects have suggested to my mind at times, do suggest to this day, the unorganized, abundant substance of some tumourous growth-process, a process which indeed bursts all the outlines of the affected carcass and protrudes such masses as ignoble comfortable Croydon, as tragic impoverished West Ham. To this day I ask myself will those masses ever become structural, will they indeed shape into anything new whatever, or is that cancerous image their true and ultimate diagnosis . . .? (II, i, 1)

Speaking as a Londoner, I can think of few writers who have succeeded as well in constructing a comprehensive image of the metropolis as Wells in this passage. The passing of time has affected its validity to a very small extent. There are still tragic and impoverished areas of London, still comfortable and ignoble areas. The endless streets of undistinguished houses still depress the eye and bewilder the mind. Above all, the architectural contrasts around the banks of the Thames, which Wells renders so vividly, still seem to embody the confusion and conflict of values in the capital, and in society as a whole.

The movement of the passage illustrates very well how in *Tono-Bungay* Wells's analytic, Fabian radicalism is transposed into a literary and imaginative key. Beginning with a *datum* of social history (the locations of the London railway termini) we are swiftly introduced to a vision of boldly anthropomorphized architecture and engineering (the Charing Cross railway station, the South Bank chimneys) in which these material objects seem to be more alive than the people that use them. The parallel with Dickens's Coketown is striking. But Wells exploits the unnaturalness of the contrast more deliberately, in order to reintroduce his thematic image of decay. Wells, as one would expect, chooses his pathological metaphors with care. Cancer is the perfect metaphorical diagnosis of the condition of England, for cancer has an organic life of its own, which is however unnatural and malignant. It is also a disease which often goes long undetected by those who suffer from it. To quote the *O.E.D.* again, cancer is 'a malignant growth or tumour, that tends to reproduce itself; it corrodes the part concerned, and generally ends in death'. This image thus draws together the two predominant strains in the language of descriptive comment in the novel: words suggestive of growth, change, and movement; and words suggestive of decay and death.

On the narrative level, the principal vehicle of Wells's critique of modern capitalism is the story of Edward Ponderevo's rise and fall. Wells demonstrates wittily and persuasively how bold and unscrupulous methods of sales-promotion applied to a worthless and indeed mildly injurious product can obtain for a man of no real ability, immense power, wealth, and prestige. Kettle complains that Wells does not condemn Ponderevo with adequate severity.[18] But it is surely Wells's point that Ponderevo is a foolish, childishly innocent man, that it is society, which puts this collossal power into his hands, which is ultimately responsible. 'This irrational muddle of a community in which we live gave him that [his wealth], paid him at that rate for sitting in a room and scheming and telling it lies' (III, i, 2). George does not attempt to soften his contempt for Ponderevo's enterprises and his own part in them:

> he created nothing, he invented nothing, he economised nothing. I cannot claim that a single one of the great businesses we organised added any real value to human life at all.

The 'frame' of architectural and topographical description 'gets into the picture' of Ponderevo's career in a very significant way. When for example, in the early days of 'Tono-Bungay', George is hesitating between his uncle's offer of a partnership and the arduous and demanding career of a scientist, he goes for a solitary walk in London to meditate:

> And as I walked along the Embankment, the first effect was all against my uncle. He shrank—for a little while he continued to shrink—in perspective until he was only a very small shabby little man in a dirty back street, selling off a few hundred bottles of rubbish to foolish buyers. The great buildings on the right of us, the Inns and the School Board place—as it was then—Somerset House, the big hotels, the great bridges, Westminster's outlines ahead, had an effect of grey largeness that reduced him to the proportions of a busy black beetle in a crack in the floor.
> And then my eye caught the advertisements on the south side of 'Sorber's Food', of 'Cracknell's Ferric Wine', very bright and prosperous signs, illuminated at night, and I realised how astonishingly they looked at home there, how evidently they were part of the whole thing. (II, ii, 3)

This passage draws for its effect upon the more elaborate description of London quoted above: in both, the new world of vulgar commerce jauntily confronts the old order across the Thames. And as George walks on, he realizes that a bridgehead has been established across which the new forces are already swarming. Again and again, on hoardings in Adelphi terrace and Kensington High Street, the strident advertisements for 'Tono-Bungay' catch his eye. With a helpless shrug, he dismisses his dreams of the good society and joins his uncle.

Each stage in Ponderevo's rapid rise to fame and wealth is marked by an account of his changing domestic environment, conducted in such a way as to provide an ironic comment upon the absurdity of Ponderevo's career. That Ponderevo should use his newly acquired wealth to improve his domestic environment is natural. But his constant moving from house to house (described mainly in the long second chapter of Book III, 'Our Progress from Camden Town to Crest Hill') is motivated less and less by considerations of comfort, convenience, and suitability, and more and more by a desire to emulate Bladesover. This desire is only partly conscious in Ponderevo, and is to some extent resisted by his more sensible and sympathetic wife; but it is inescapable and insatiable, an infection of the utter confusion of values in which they live.

As soon as the first money from Tono-Bungay begins to roll in, the Ponderevos move to a flat in Gower Street. George notes on his first visit: 'the furniture of the room struck upon my eye as almost stately. The chairs and sofa were covered with chintz, which gave it a dim remote flavour of Bladesover' (II, ii, 6). Soon Ponderevo buys a villa in Beckenham, 'with a conservatory and a shrubbery, a tennis-lawn, a quite considerable vegetable garden, and a small disused coach-house' (III, ii, 1). No sooner, however, has Susan Ponderevo begun to settle happily in Beckenham society, than she is uprooted to Chislehurst.

> The Chislehurst mansion had 'grounds' rather than a mere garden, and there was a gardener's cottage and a little lodge at the gate. (III, ii, 3)

But no imitation of Bladesover can satisfy Ponderevo. In Lady Grove he acquires a Bladesover of his own. George's leisurely, appreciative description recalls his account of Bladesover:

> Lady Grove, you know, is a very beautiful house indeed, a still and gracious place, whose age-long seclusion was only effectively broken with the toot of the coming of the motor-car. . . . An old Catholic family had died out in it, century by century, and was now altogether dead. . . . Its terrace is its noblest feature, a very wide broad lawn it is, bordered by a low stone battlement, and there is a great cedar in one corner under whose level branches one looks out across the blue distances of the Weald—blue distances that are made extraordinarily Italian in quality by virtue of the dark masses of that single tree. . . . One turns back to the still old house, and sees a gray and lichenous façade with a very finely arched entrance. It was warmed by the afternoon light and touched with the colour of a few neglected roses and pyrancanthus. . . . And there was my uncle holding his goggles in a sealskin glove, wiping the glass

with a pocket-handkerchief, and asking my aunt if Lady Grove
wasn't a 'Bit of all Right'. My aunt made him no answer. (III, ii,
6)

'Numbers go down in the competition,' says Masterman, in *The
Condition of England*, 'then the country estates are sold and pass
into the hands of South African millionaires or the children of the
big traders, or the vendors of patent medicines.'[19]

Ill at ease among the ghosts of Lady Grove, Ponderevo will
not rest until he has not only emulated but exceeded Bladesover,
until he has built himself a new Bladesover, 'a Twentieth Century
house' (III, ii, 10): Crest Hill. Crest Hill marks the climax of
Ponderevo's career, epitome of his inflated wealth, his irresponsi-
bility and his delusions of grandeur:

> There he stands in my memory, the symbol of this age for me,
> the man of luck and advertisement, the current master of the
> world. There he stands upon the great outward sweep of the
> terrace before the huge main entrance, a little figure, ridiculously
> disproportionate to that forty-foot arch, with the granite ball
> behind him—the astronomical ball, brass coopered, that repre-
> sented the world. . . . There he stands, Napoleonically grouped
> with his retinue . . . below are hundreds of feet of wheeling planks,
> ditches, excavations, heaps of earth, piles of garden-stone from the
> Wealden ridges. On either hand the walls of his irrelevant un-
> meaning palace rise. At one time he had working in that place—
> disturbing the economic balance of the whole countryside by their
> presence—upwards of three thousand men. . . .
> So he poses for my picture amidst the raw beginnings that were
> never to be completed. He did the strangest things about that place,
> things more and more detached from any conception of financial
> scale, things more and more apart from sober humanity. He
> seemed to think himself at last quite released from any such limita-
> tions. He moved quite a considerable hill, and nearly sixty mature
> trees were moved with it to open his prospect eastward, moved it
> about two hundred feet to the south. At another time he caught a
> suggestion from some city restaurant and made a billiard-room
> roofed with plate glass beneath the waters of his ornamental lake.
> He furnished one wing while its roof still awaited completion. He
> had a swimming bath thirty feet square next to his bedroom up-
> stairs, and to crown it all he commenced a great wall to hold all his
> dominions together, free from the invasion of common man. It
> was a ten-foot wall, glass-surmounted, and had it been completed

as he intended it, it would have had a total length of nearly eleven miles. Some of it towards the last was so dishonestly built that it collapsed within a year upon its foundations, but some miles of it still stand. I never think of it now but what I think of the hundreds of eager little investors who followed his 'star', whose hopes and lives, whose wives' security and children's prospects are all mixed up beyond redemption with that flaking mortar. (III, ii, 10)

Wells needs to be quoted at length, for his effects are broad and cumulative. He did not, like James, pursue 'the grace of intensity'. But the language of this passage has its own kind of expressive effectiveness. The rather loose, conversational syntax of the second paragraph, its rather clumsy repetitions (*moved* in the fourth sentence, *it* in the eighth and ninth), and its abundance of figures and measurements, establish the tone of a man who is striving to make a fantastic event credible, to compel our assent to this particular event.* But the mock portentous repetition of 'there he stands . . .' supports the invitation to see Ponderevo as a symbolic figure, symbolic not only of commercial vulgarity but of commercial megalomania. While Ponderevo's previous vanities had been merely comic, his activities at Crest Hill have a lunatic unnatural quality, 'a quality,' as George puts it, 'of unforseeing outrage upon the peace of nature' (III, ii, 10) which is implied in Ponderevo's re-shaping of the landscape. The disturbance of nature echoes the disturbance of the economic balance; the dishonestly-built walls reflect Ponderevo's dishonestly-earned fortune; and their collapse foreshadows his financial collapse. Characteristically, the emblematic description becomes fully metaphorical in the next paragraph:

It is curious how many of these modern financiers of chance and bluff have ended their careers by building. It was not merely my uncle. Sooner or later they all seem to bring their luck to the test

* Masterman describes an 'England where millionaire company promoters, on their hectic path between poverty through prosperity to prison or suicide [*sic*], will purchase so many miles of good English land, build round it a great wall ten feet high, construct billard rooms under a lake, move a hill that offends the view' (*op. cit.*, p. 28). It is difficult to tell whether Masterman is alluding to Crest Hill here, or to the source of Wells's description in real life—the folly built by the financier Whittaker Wright, whose career served in several respects as a model for Ponderevo's. (See Ingvald Raknem, *H. G. Wells and His Critics* (1962) pp. 255-61.)

of realisation, try to make their fluid opulence coagulate out as
bricks and mortar, bring moonshine into relations with a weekly-
wages sheet. Then the whole fabric of confidence and imagination
totters—and down they come. . . . (III, ii, 10)

Wells brilliantly rounds off the architectural commentary upon
Ponderevo's career in the scene of his death, in which irony and
pathos are so skilfully mingled. In his last delirium Ponderevo
raves of a still more grandiose building, a financier's new
Jerusalem:

'What is this great place, these cloud-capped towers, these airy
pinnacles? . . . Ilion. Sky-y-pointing . . . Ilion House, the resi-
dence of one of our great merchant princes . . . Terrace above
terrace. Reaching to the Heavens . . . Kingdoms Caesar never
knew. . . . A great poet, George. Zzzz. Kingdoms Caesar never
knew. . . . Under entirely new management. (IV, i, 7)

This recalls another visionary city in *Tono-Bungay*: the City of
Women envisaged by Ewart, George's bohemian, idealistic, revolutionary friend as an answer to the sexual problems of the age:

'I seem to see—I seem to see—a sort of City of Women,
Ponderevo. Yes . . . a walled enclosure—good stone-mason's
work—a city wall, high as the walls of Rome, going about a
garden. Dozens of square miles of garden—trees—fountains—
arbours—lakes. Lawns on which the women play, avenues in
which they gossip, boats. . . . And no man—except to do rough
work perhaps,—ever comes in. . . . The homes of the women,
Ponderevo, will be set in the walls of their city. . . . Built into the
wall—and a little balcony. . . . And men will stroll up and down
there when they feel the need of feminine company. . . . And each
woman will have this; she will have a little silken ladder she can
let down if she chooses—if she wants to talk closer. . . . (II, iv, 3)

Thus the architectural 'frame' gets into the picture of the sexual
relationships of the novel. That George's marriage to Marion is
doomed is conveyed from the start by the home in which he finds
her, and the house and furnishings Marion insists upon when
they are married. 'All our conceptions of life differed. I remember
how we differed about furniture' (II, iv, 5). The wedding itself is
put in the larger perspective of the condition of England.

Under the stress of tradition we were all of us trying in the fer-
menting chaos of London to carry out the marriage ceremonies of a

Bladesover tenant or one of the chubby middling sort of people in some dependent country town. (II, iv, 4)

So far, we have seen how Wells depicts England in topographical and architectural terms as an organism undergoing a process of change. For him, as for Masterman, 'arises the question of the future of a society, evidently moving in a direction which no one can forsee, towards experience of far-reaching change'.[20] As radicals, both men saw the necessity of change, but the change they saw in progress was not of a rational or fruitful kind. Wells saw it as a process of disease and decay. 'Again and again in this book,' says George at the end of *Tono-Bungay*, 'I have written of England as a feudal scheme overtaken by fatty degeneration and stupendous accidents of hypertrophy' (IV, iii, 2).* It is this governing idea of change as disease and decay which, I think, connects the 'quap' episode to the total design of *Tono-Bungay*, and provides an answer to those critics who have seen it as an irrelevant intrusion.†

In his *Anatomy of Criticism*, Northrop Frye makes the following reference to *Tono-Bungay*:

> The destroyer which appears at the end of H. G. Wells's *Tono-Bungay* is notable as coming from a low mimetic writer not much given to introducing hieratic symbols.[21]

---

* Cf. the deterioration of Ponderevo's physique as his wealth and power increase. George notices how, compared to his appearance at Wimblehurst, his head seems to have shrunk and his belly expanded, though 'he evidently wasn't aware of the *degenerative* nature of his changes' (*my italics*) (II, ii, 2). George himself becomes ashamed of 'the slackness of body and soul that had come to me with the business life' (III, iii, 1) and goes into rigorous training.

† E.g. 'It is brilliantly done, but it is plainly an afterthought' (Walter Allen, *The English Novel*, p. 317). 'Wells, for all his energy, often flags towards the end of a book—not, I feel sure, because his imagination was exhausted, but merely because he wanted to get on with something else and was impatient with the work in hand. Towards the end of *Tono-Bungay* he had this desire for a change, but satisfied it by incorporating the new material in the same book' (Norman Nicholson, *H. G. Wells* (1950), p. 65. No external evidence is cited). The only critic who, to my knowledge, has recognized the thematic connection between the 'quap' episode and the rest of the novel, is Gordon N. Ray, 'H. G. Wells Tries to Be a Novelist', *Edwardians and Late Victorians*, English Institute Essays, 1959, edited by Richard Ellmann (New York, 1960), p. 147.

A certain amount of elucidation of Fry's terminology may be advisable. He divides the literary modes into five classes: mythic, romantic, high mimetic (epic and tragedy), low mimetic (comedy and realistic fiction), and ironic. He regards this system as a cycle corresponding to the historical development of literature, according to which modern literature is dominated by the low mimetic and ironic modes. Since the system *is* a cycle, however, the ironic mode tends to return to the mythic—Joyce being the most obvious example.[22] Frye characterizes Wells as a low mimetic writer, whose mode is defined thus:

> If superior neither to other men nor to his environment, the hero is one of us: We respond to a sense of his common humanity, and demand from the poet the same canons of probability that we find in our own experience. This gives us the hero of the *low mimetic* mode, of most comedy and realistic fiction.[23]

If we take England, rather than George Ponderevo, to be the hero of *Tono-Bungay*, however, that novel fits very neatly into Frye's definition of the ironic mode:

> If inferior in power or intelligence to ourselves, so that we have the sense of looking down on a scene of bondage, frustration, or absurdity, the hero belongs to the ironic mode. This is still true when the reader feels that he is or might be in the same situation, as the situation is being judged by the norms of a greater freedom.[24]

Given Frye's notion of the contiguity of the ironic and the mythic modes on the literary-historical cycle, it now seems more likely that Wells should resort to hieratic symbols—that is, symbols whose meanings have accreted in the mythical, romantic and high mimetic modes. Frye himself remarks that science fiction is 'a mode of romance with a strong inherent tendency to myth';[25] and Bernard Bergonzi, using Frye's conceptual framework, has made a fascinating analysis of demonic and paradisal symbolism in *The Time Machine*.[26] I suggest that the 'quap' in *Tono-Bungay* is another example of this dimension in Wells's writing.

The quap is first described to George and his uncle by an adventurer, Gordon-Naysmith, who discovered it on the coast of West Africa, as

> the most radio-active stuff in the world. That's quap! It's a festering mass of earths and heavy metals, polonium, radium, ythorium,

carium, and new things too. There's a stuff called Xk—provisionally. There they are all mucked up together in sort of rotting sand. What it is, how it got made, I don't know. It's like as if some young creator had been playing about there. There it lies in two heaps, one small, one great, and the world for miles about it is blasted and scorched and dead. (III, i, 4)

The concept of a morbid kind of life, spreading decay and death, is immediately established, and is confirmed by George's subsequent paraphrase: 'he gave a sense of heat and a perpetual reek of vegetable decay . . . among charred dead weeds stands the abandoned station—abandoned because every man who stayed two months in that station stayed to die, eaten up mysteriously like a leper—with its dismantled sheds and its decaying pier of wormrotten and oblique piles and planks . . .' (III, i, 4).

Not until Ponderevo is faced with bankruptcy, and the development of a new type of filament has made the mineral content of the quap fantastically valuable, does George decide to take a ship to Africa and (illegally) confiscate the quap. The expedition is cursed with ill luck from the beginning. George and his men get sick. Finally, the quap, which has been obtained at such great cost, rots the hull of the ship in which it is carried back to England, and it sinks. The last desperate attempt to rescue the declining fortunes of Ponderevo has failed.

Seen as an action, the episode has obvious analogies with the archetypal story of the quest for a treasure which brings death to the questors, of which Chaucer's *Pardoner's Tale* is a well-known example. Particularly interesting in this respect is the psychological effect of the expedition on George and his crew. It makes them sullen, ill-tempered, and quarrelsome, and finally impels George to the motiveless murder of an African native (III, iv, 6).

But throughout the quap episode, physical deterioration is emphasized as much as moral deterioration. George and the crew 'were poisoned, I firmly believe, by quap' (III, iv, 3). Sores break out on the crew's hands when they handle the quap (III, iv, 5). At night there hangs over the quap-heaps 'a phosphorescence such as one sees at times on rotting wood' (III, iv, 3). This insistence upon disease and decay echoes at several points the metaphorical language in which Wells describes the disintegration of the English social organism. The connection is made explicit in the following passage:

If I am right it is something far more significant from the scientific point of view than those incidental constituents of various rare metals, pitchblende, rutile, and the like, upon which the revolutionary discoveries of the last decade are based. Those are just little molecular centres of disintegration, of that mysterious decay and rotting of those elements, elements once regarded as the most stable things in nature. But there is something—the only word that comes near it is *cancerous*—and that is not very near, about the whole of quap, something that creeps and lives as a disease lives by destroying; an elemental stirring and disarrangement, incalculably maleficent and strange.

This is no imaginative comparison of mine. To my mind radio-activity is a real disease of matter. Moreover, it is a contagious disease. It spreads. You bring these debased and crumbling atoms near others and those too presently catch the trick of swinging themselves out of coherent existence. *It is in matter exactly what the decay of our old culture is in society, a loss of traditions and distinctions and assured reactions (my italics).* When I think of these inexplicable dissolvent centres that have come into being in our globe . . . I am haunted by a grotesque fancy of the ultimate eating away and dry-rotting and dispersal of all our world. So that while man still struggles and dreams his very substance will change and crumble from beneath him. I mention this here as a queer persistent fancy. Suppose that is, indeed, to be the end of our planet; no splendid climax and finale, no towering accumulation of achievements but just—atomic decay! I add that to the ideas of the suffocating comet, the dark body out of space, the burning out of the sun, the distorted orbit, as a new and far more possible end—as Science can see ends to this strange by-play of matter that we call human life. (III, iv, 5)

This is another passage whose thematic importance is conveyed by its verbal excitement, and, like other such passages in *Tono-Bungay*, it is not much concerned with individual character and action. It is clotted with words connotative or denotative of disease and decay: *disease* (3), *decay* (3), *disintegration, disarrangement, rotting, dry-rotting, cancerous, contagious, destroying, debased, maleficent, crumble, crumbling, dissolvent, eating away, dispersal.* This profusion is not, however, tautological. The elaborate description of the quap strikes echoes at various points with other parts of the descriptive 'frame' of the novel. *Disease, contagious,* and the italicized *cancerous* link up with other pathological metaphors in the novel, particularly in the description of London. *Dry-rotting,* crumble, crumbling, eating away, and disintegration are terms which might be applied to material structures, such as buildings. One recalls George's description of England as 'this rotten old warren' (III, iii, 7). In this passage, as throughout the novel, change is associated with decay.

The immediate justification for the plethora of epithets is that the narrator is struggling to give definition to a half-apprehended something: 'There is something . . . cancerous . . . something that creeps and lives as a disease. . . .' Throughout the novel George speaks in the same tone of a man trying urgently to define something new, unrecognized, threatening. Compare the passage on London again: 'The effect . . . is to me of something disproportionately large, something morbidly expanded. . . .'

These verbal interrelationships with the total fabric of the novel enforce and confirm the explicit connection George makes between the quap and the condition of England. It is difficult therefore to sustain the charge that the episode is an irrelevance. Seeking wealth to revive the failing Ponderevo fortune, George discovers an enormously valuable but death-dealing treasure. Coming from a decadent and disintegrating 'civilized' society he encounters in the primitive jungle a frightening tangible agent of decay and disintegration. And in words which remind us irresistibly of the pessimistic myths of Wells's science fiction, the threat of the quap is expanded to embrace the destiny of the entire race.

For all its vividness and power, the quap symbol is not allowed to dominate *Tono-Bungay*. The frame of architectural and topographical description remains the principal vehicle for the themes of the novel. It is the only constant element in a novel which is otherwise deliberately chaotic in structure, and it fittingly dominates the very last chapter: 'Night and the Open Sea', in which George describes a cruise down the Thames in the X2, a destroyer he has designed.

> It is curious how at times one's impressions will all fuse and run together into a sort of unity and become continuous with things that have hitherto been utterly alien and remote. That rush down the river became mysteriously connected with this book. As I passed down the Thames I seemed in a new and parallel manner to be passing all England in review. I saw it then as I had wanted my readers to see it. (IV, iii, 2)

The pages which follow need to be read continuously; I can only extract a few passages in which the motifs of the novel are most conspicuously recalled.

Wells sees the Thames as cutting an historical cross-section through England, in which the past is fossilized in the scenery and architecture of the banks.

> One begins in Craven Reach and it is as if one were in the heart of old England. Behind us are Kew and Hampton Court with their memories of Kings and Cardinals and one runs at first between Fulham's episcopal garden parties and Hurlingham's playground for the sporting instinct of our race. The whole effect is English. There is space, there are old trees and all the best qualities of the homeland in that upper reach. Putney, too, looks Anglican on a dwindling scale. And then for a stretch the newer developments slop over, one misses Bladesover and there come first squalid stretches of mean homes right and left and then the dingy industrialism of the south side, and on the north bank the polite long front of nice houses, artistic, literary, administrative people's residences, that stretches from Cheyne Walk nearly to Westminster and hides a wilderness of slums. (IV, ii, 2)

Once more the symbolic confrontation of north and south banks is introduced, the north bank feebly keeping up the old pretence, the south bank unashamed of its modern barbarism. After St Paul's:

> the traditional and ostensible England falls from you altogether . . . the trim scheme of the old order is altogether dwarfed and swallowed up. . . . Again and again in this book I have written of England as a feudal scheme overtaken by fatty degeneration and stupendous accidents of hypertrophy. For the last time I must strike that note as the memory of the dear, neat little sunlit ancient Tower of London lying away in a gap among the warehouses comes back to me, that little accumulation of buildings so provincially pleasant and dignified, overshadowed by the vulgarest, most typical exploit of modern England, the sham Gothic casings to the ironwork of the Tower Bridge. That Tower Bridge is the very balance and confirmation of Westminster's dull pinnacles and tower. That sham Gothic bridge; in the very gates of our mother of change, the Sea! (IV, iii, 2)

No passage could better illustrate Wells's literary strategy in *Tono-Bungay*: to present England as an organism undergoing a process of change and decay, both the organism and the process being depicted in terms of architectural and topographical description. The irony of the situation is that England is unaware of its condition, or ignores it. In the Houses of Parliament a debased oligarchy goes through the motions of its 'incurable tradition of commercialized Bladesovery' (note the pathological epithet), its futile attempts to pretend that nothing has changed being aptly symbolized by another pseudo-Gothic building, Tower Bridge, placed 'in the very gates of our mother of change'.

> For the third part of the panorama of London is beyond all law, order, and precedence, it is the seaport and the sea. One goes down the widening reaches through a monstrous variety of shipping, great steamers, great sailing-ships, trailing the flags of all the world, a monstrous confusion of lighters, witches' conference of brown-sailed barges, wallowing tugs, a tumultuous crowding and jostling of cranes and spars, and wharves and stores, and assertive inscriptions. Huge vistas of dock open right and left of one, and here and there beyond and amidst it all are church towers, little patches of indescribably old-fashioned and worn-out houses, riverside pubs and the like, vestiges of townships that were long since torn to fragments and submerged in these new growths. And amidst it all no plan appears, no intention, no comprehensive desire. That is the very key of it all. Each day one feels that the pressure of commerce grew, grew insensibly monstrous, and first this man made a wharf and that erected a crane, and then this company set to work and then that, and so they jostled together to make this unassimilable enormity of traffic. Through it we dodged and drove, eager for the high seas. (IV, iii, 2)

This is a brilliantly vivid description, the congestion of diction and syntax imitating the congestion of the scene. But again one observes the consistency of the tone with other heightened descriptions in the novel. The twice-repeated *monstrous* evokes the same kind of fear as the image of London as a huge corpse swollen with cancer, or as the account of the sinister properties of quap. There is the same insistence on the lack of *plan* or *intention* as in the earlier description of London. There is the familiar association of growth with destruction ('torn to fragments or submerged in these new growths'). There is the familiar trick of attributing life to things rather than to people. There is the characteristic search for a *key* to the spectacle of anarchy.

Why is George so eager for the high seas? It is evidently not because of a desire to escape from Change, since the sea is the Mother of change. Rather it is a gesture of acceptance of change. George rushes to embrace the destructive element, figuring in his voyage the inevitable decline and extinction of his country, and finding a kind of freedom in this pessimistic vision:

> Out to the open [sea] we go, to windy freedom and trackless ways. Light after light goes down. England and the Kingdom, Britain and the Empire, the old prides and the old devotions, glide abeam, astern, sink down upon the horizon, pass—pass. The river passes, England passes . . . (IV, iii, 2)

It is a mood akin to that of *The Waste Land.*

> What is the city over the mountains
> Cracks and reforms and bursts in the violet air
> Falling towers
> Jerusalem Athens Alexandria
> Vienna London
> Unreal[27]

Whereas the pessimism of Eliot's poem is qualified by the counsels of oriental mysticism, the pessimism of *Tono-Bungay* is qualified by what might be described as scientific mysticism: 'The note that sounds clear in my mind when I think of anything beyond the purely personal aspects of my story,' says George, invoking for the last time the key-words of his descriptive frame, 'is a note of crumbling and confusion, of change and seemingly aimless swelling, of a bubbling up and medley of futile loves and sorrows'.

> But through the confusion sounds another note. Through the confusion something drives, something that is at once human achievement and the most inhuman of all existing things. . . . I have figured it in my last section by the symbol of my destroyer, stark and swift, irrelevant to most human interests. Sometimes I call this reality Science, sometimes I call it Truth. But it is something we draw by pain and effort out of the heart of life, that we disentangle and make clear. (IV, iii, 3)

The striking of this final note has been much criticized. Mark Schorer, for instance, has this to say:

> The significant failure is in that end, and in the way that it defeats not only the entire social analysis of the bulk of the novel, but Wells's own ends as a thinker. For at last George finds a purpose

in science. 'I decided that in power and knowledge lay the salva-
tion of my life, the secret that would fill my need; that to these
things I would give myself.'

But science, power and knowledge, are summed up at last in a
destroyer. As far as one can tell Wells intends no irony, although he may here have come upon the essence of the major
irony in modern history. The novel ends in a kind of meditative
rhapsody which denies every value that the book has been aiming
toward. For of all the kinds of social waste which Wells has been
describing, this is the most inclusive, the final waste.[28]

But is it true that Wells intends no irony? Certainly, in so far as
the destroyer is an achievement of engineering, it represents a
kind of scientific equivalent of that impersonal fulfilment and
unity of being which romantic and post-romantic poets have
embodied in images of organic life or of perfectly achieved art.
But Wells is fully aware of the irony of making this achievement
a destroyer. 'It is all one spectacle of forces running to waste,'
says George, recapitulating his story, 'of people who use and do
not replace, the story of a country hectic with a wasting aimless
fever of trade and money-making and pleasure-seeking. And now
I build destroyers!' (IV, iii, 1). The very name of the destroyer,
'X2', recalls the name of the unidentified ingredient in quap,
'Xk'. By choosing a destroyer as his symbol, Wells indicates that
in a social order given over to decay and death, even the impersonal achievements of science will be ironically double-edged;
that they will hasten and confirm, rather than alleviate, the incurable condition of England. How then, does the introduction
of the destroyer defeat Wells's social analysis in *Tono-Bungay*,
which has been all along ironic and pessimistic? As to Wells's
'ends as a thinker', *Tono-Bungay* is not the only one of his imaginative works which disturbingly questions the meliorism of his
public self.

VII

The Modern, The Contemporary, and the Importance of being Amis

As far as English literature is concerned, the important modern novelists were James, Conrad, Joyce, Lawrence, Forster, and Virginia Woolf. They are still the important modern novelists, although all but Mr Forster are dead, and most of them had written their best work by 1924. 'Modern' has, in fact, become a qualitative rather than a chronological term; and to any one with an elementary knowledge of recent literary history it is obvious that, in Britain, 'the contemporary novel is no longer "modern" '[1] —whether one takes 'contemporary' to include the work of authors such as Graham Greene or Evelyn Waugh, who established their reputations before the war (as does the critic I quote), or restricts the term to those writers who have emerged in the last decade.

This distinction between the modern novel and the contemporary novel is a commonplace of current criticism; but it has been given a new dimension by Stephen Spender in his recent book, *The Struggle of the Modern* (1963), in which he emancipates 'contemporary' as well as 'modern' from a chronological significance. He observes that all through twentieth-century literature there have been two kinds of writers. On the one hand there are those who engage in a direct, prosaic way with their social and political circumstances, and who, if they protest against these circumstances, do so with some degree of revolutionary optimism in the possibility of amelioration, an amelioration that literature

243

can help to bring about. These Spender calls 'contemporaries', and he includes among them such writers as Shaw, Wells, and Bennett. Orwell too, though Spender does not, I think, mention him, would fit very well into this category.

On the other hand there are those who distrust or detest their circumstances, to the extent of abandoning the hope of acting on them in a practical way. Instead, such writers seek a radical transformation of conventional forms of communication, through which to express poetically an inner crisis of sensibility, a crisis which often manifests itself in the search for a tradition which has been lost or broken. These are 'moderns': T. S. Eliot, James Joyce, and Virginia Woolf, for example. Spender draws attention to various significant literary quarrels and controversies which illuminate the differences between these two groups: the quarrel between Wells and James; Virginia Woolf's attack on Bennett, and Lawrence's on Galsworthy. Lawrence, of course, as Spender acknowledges,[2] does not fit neatly into the 'modern' category. Like all such broad classifications, Spender's distinction between the 'modern' and the 'contemporary' is open to qualification; but I think it is a useful one.

It is clear that, today, the English novel is dominated by 'contemporaries', in Spender's sense. While the 'modern' tradition is carried on in America, France and Germany, in Britain only William Golding, Iris Murdoch, and Lawrence Durrell, of the novelists who have produced any considerable body of work, can be intelligibly placed in this perspective, and then with important reservations.

It is possible to take two views of this situation. Anyone who has had a literary education, who has experienced the work of the great moderns instructed by such education, will tend to feel dissatisfied with 'contemporary' work, with its thinness of texture, its lack of complexity, its simplifications and evasions, its indifference to significant form. Spender quotes a spokesman for the other side, Miss Pamela Hansford Johnson:

> The full retreat began in the years between 1922 and 1925, the years that saw *Mrs Dalloway* and *Ulysses*. It was the retreat into perimetal experiment in verbal and oral techniques: and it pretty well dominated the English novel for the next thirty years. . . . What shrivelled away was any contact between man and society. 'Bloomsday' is Bloom's alone, and no one else's. Mrs Dalloway, if

she is anything at all, is merely herself, walking in her own dream of a private world. Everything dropped away from the novel but Manner: all that counted was how the thing was done, and never the thing itself . . . the followers of Virginia Woolf and James Joyce began to lead the novel into sterility. And nobody saw anything wrong in that inexorable process. Why not? Because life was growing too hard for writers to face, and quiet lay in impotency alone.[3]

This passage focuses in a very revealing way the characteristic assumptions which divide the contemporary from the modern. It recapitulates some of the arguments used by Wells against James, and it reverses the attack of Virginia Woolf on Bennett: the assumptions behind Miss Hansford Johnson s remarks are just those which, in Virginia Woolf's view, exerted such a deadening influence on Bennett's work.

The centre of this continuing controversy is the meaning of the word 'life'. Life, to the contemporary, is what common sense tells us it is, what people *do*: go to school, fall in love, make political choices, get married, have careers, succeed or fail—in Miss Hansford Johnson's words, 'man and society'. To the modern, Life is something elusive, baffling, multiple, subjective—in Virginia Woolf's famous words, 'a luminous halo, a semi-transparent envelope surrounding us from the beginning of consciousness to the end'.[4] The contemporary tends to have a fairly simple faith in the competence of ordinary prose discourse to represent 'life'; the modern feels the need to employ an elaborate linguistic craft to fix and identify the uniqueness of every individual experience.

The analysis of language is in fact the most precise way of indicating the difference between modern and contemporary writing—and of suggesting the loss involved in shifting from the former to the latter. Let us compare two passages, one from James Joyce's *A Portrait of the Artist as a Young Man* (1916), and the other from John Braine's *Room at the Top* (1957).

A girl stood before him in midstream, alone and still, gazing out to sea. She seemed like one whom magic had changed into the likeness of a strange and beautiful seabird. Her long slender bare legs were delicate as a crane's and pure save where an emerald trail of seaweed had fashioned itself as a sign upon the flesh. Her thighs, fuller and softhued as ivory, were bared almost to the hips, where the white fringes of her drawers were like feathering of soft white down. Her slateblue skirts were kilted boldly about her waist and dovetailed behind her. Her bosom was as a bird's, soft and slight, slight and soft as the breast of some darkplumaged dove. But her long fair hair was girlish: and girlish, and touched with the wonder of mortal beauty, her face.[5]

Parked by a solicitor's office opposite the cafe was a green Aston-Martin tourer, low-slung, with cycle-type mudguards. It had the tough, functional smartness of the good British sports car; it's a quality which is difficult to convey without using the terms of the advertising copywriter—made by craftsmen, thoroughbred, and so on—I can only say that it was a beautiful piece of engineering and leave it at that. Pre-war it would have cost as much as three baby saloons; it wasn't the sort of vehicle for business or for family outings, but quite simply a rich man's toy.

As I was admiring it a young man and a girl came out of the solicitor's office. The young man was turning the ignition key when the girl said something to him and after a moment's argument he put up the windscreen. The girl smoothed his hair for him; I found the gesture disturbing in an odd way—it was again as if a barrier had been removed, but this time by an act of reason.

The ownership of the Aston-Martin automatically placed the young man in a social class far above mine; but that ownership was simply a question of money. The girl, with her even suntan and her fair hair cut short in a style too simple to be anything but expensive, was as far beyond my reach as the car. But her ownership, too, was simply a question of money, of the price of the diamond ring on her left hand. This seems all too obvious; but it was the kind of truth which until that moment I'd only grasped theoretically.

The Aston-Martin started with a deep, healthy roar. As it passed the cafe in the direction of St. Clair Road I noticed the young man's olive linen shirt and bright silk neckerchief. The collar of the shirt was tucked inside the jacket; he wore the rather theatrical ensemble with a matter-of-fact nonchalance. Everything about him was easy and loose but not tired or sloppy. He had an undistinguished face with a narrow forehead and mousy hair cut short with no oil on it. It was a rich man's face, smooth with assurance and good living.[6]

Both passages describe a crucial moment of awareness in the life of a young man. For Stephen Dedalus, the young girl is a means of release from the spiritual apathy he finds himself in after the sexual and religious crises of adolescence. The vision of the young girl, arousing neither desire nor disgust, is a symbol of the liberating, recreating power of art, to which he can now dedicate himself with confidence. The language in which the vision is described is intricately wrought, with meticulous attention to sound and cadence, as well as to imagery and diction. The moment is sublime, and the language is correspondingly heightened above the level of ordinary prose by 'poetic' devices of repetition and inversion. Running through the passage is imagery of birds ('sea-bird', 'crane', 'feathering', 'down', 'dove-tailed', 'dark-plumaged', 'dove'), which is a thematic feature of the whole novel, linked with the myth of Daedalus and Icarus, and the daring, transcending power of art which this myth embodies. The language, here, is in the best sense 'artificial', and the vision is in the literary sense 'romantic'. Yet no falsification or distortion is involved. The girl who wears, for Stephen, such a magical aura, remains a solid figure of flesh and blood. She also wears 'drawers': the mundane word is accommodated in the passage without drawing any kind of ribald response. To sum up: Joyce has contrived to select and arrange his words beautifully *and* truthfully.

The passage from *Room at the Top* is longer, but much looser and thinner in texture. The words do not give and receive life and meaning to and from each other. The only metaphors in the passage are the dead metaphors of cliché, like 'rich man's toy' and 'mousy hair'. It must be said, of course, that the author is limited to the kind of vocabulary that can plausibly be put into the mouth of his not particularly sensitive or articulate narrator. But failure in the fundamental literary task of realization in language cannot be justified by an appeal to literary decorum. The narrator's admission that he is using the language of the advertising copy-writer is a revealing one, and he resorts, later, to the same jargon: 'The Aston-Martin started with a deep, healthy roar.'

The interest of the passage is mainly of a factual or journalistic kind: in many readers it will evoke a mild 'thrill of recognition' (it certainly did in my own case, when I first read it), because of its acute observation of physical details which act in our society as an index to class and status. Young men of means in England today *do* dress like that; young men of the narrator's class, on the other hand, put oil on their hair, wear the collars of their open-necked shirts *outside* their jackets, and so on. But perhaps one should use the past tense, for the passage has already dated. And as the significance of such details fades still more, the lack of verbal realization in the passage will become still more evident. For even if some learned scholar of the future devotes a footnote to explaining the significance of a vintage Aston-Martin as a status symbol in the early 1950's, there is little in the text which will assist the reader to see and feel the car in his imagination. The reader must himself have observed an Aston-Martin of the appropriate period in order to compensate for the vagueness of the writer's description.

There are, of course, significant differences between the experiences rendered in these two extracts, as well as between the ways in which they are rendered. Joyce is writing about a rather special young man having a rather special experience. Stephen Dedalus is the artist, whose activity enriches and intensifies experience both for himself and for others, and the passage is itself art in action. Braine's Joe Lampton, as his name aggressively asserts, is a very ordinary young man, having a very ordinary experience: envy. It is easy to identify with him—perhaps too easy. We are invited to indulge ourselves vicariously in a gratifying, but essentially demoralizing emotion. The narrator goes on to recognize and reject his envy, but there is nothing in the *language* which places, defines, and evaluates the emotion, as there would have been, I think, if Joyce had treated the same episode.

I hasten to add that I choose to compare John Braine with Joyce because Braine is a reasonably representative contemporary novelist, and not because he is the best challenger our period can muster. The latter motive would not, however, have seemed quite so bizarre six or seven years ago as it does now; and this reflection leads one to consider the very different problems presented to criticism by the modern and the contemporary writer respectively.

The modern disturbs us with the novelty of his vision and his technique; and since most critics and readers are basically conservative, he tends to be despised or neglected in his youth and maturity, and revered in his old age or when he is dead. The contemporary, on the other hand, is usually much more immediately accessible to the general public. He may attack them, but he does so in terms they understand, in the language they use, appealing to experiences they share. The danger with the contemporary—and it is as much a danger for himself as for the critic—is that, seduced by the superficial thrill of recognition, or by the coincidence of the writer's values with our own, we may overestimate him.

On the other hand it is idle to suppose that we can completely detach a 'contemporary' work from its manifold and intricate connections with the culture and society it describes—particularly if that culture and society is our own. The importance of being Amis, for instance, is in a sense greater than the sum of his works, individually considered as autotelic works of art. His novels, stories, poems, reviews, even *obiter dicta* reported in the newspapers, have focused in a very precise way a number of attitudes which a great many middle-class intellectuals of the post-war period find useful for the purposes of self-definition. If I may cite myself as an example, I suppose that, as a Roman Catholic, I could scarcely be more distant from Amis's view of the eternal verities. And yet I constantly experience a strange community of feeling with him, and find that he speaks to me in a way that the great classic novelists do not, in an idiom, a tone of voice, to which I respond with immediate understanding and pleasure and without any conscious exertion of the kind required by critical reading.

Not long ago I was discussing with a friend the unlikelihood of my being able to buy a bigger house. 'I haven't got much capital,' I explained. 'In fact, capital's a rather silly word for what I've got.' This second sentence, I realized even while my friend was laughing, was a characteristic Amis locution. His books had taught me that trick of turning a humorous irony simultaneously upon my own pretensions and the pretensions of language itself—in this case the pretensions of commercial language to fit a particular financial situation, my situation.

And here, I think, there is some encouragement for the literary critic. For it suggests that Amis's use of language may be as inextricably part of his importance as Henry James's was of his, or Joyce's was of his. That James and Joyce are vastly *more* important writers need not disturb us. They use language more ambitiously and with more consistent success; Amis less ambitiously and with less consistent success; Braine less and less still. The important thing is that they can all be measured on the same scale—the creative use of language. For ultimately language is the only tangible evidence we have for those vast, vague, unreliable qualities which we bandy about in literary criticism: 'truth to life', 'moral seriousness', 'psychological insight', 'social awareness'.

The question presents itself: if James's and Joyce's uses of language produce higher works of literary art than Amis's, why doesn't he follow their example? It is a good question, and I shall suggest later that Amis is well aware of its force. The obvious answer—'It's too difficult'—is only partly true. I shall touch on other possible answers later. At this point I wish to emphasize that Miss Hansford Johnson's dissociation of 'the way a thing is done' from 'the thing itself' is a critical fallacy; that ultimately we can no more dissociate form from content in the work of a 'contemporary' than we can in the case of a 'modern', temptingly easy though it may appear to do so; that ultimately we are driven back to the critical examination of the verbal structures, large and small, of which a work of literature is composed. It seems to me that Amis is the most interesting and rewarding of our contemporaries just because he accepts this theory of literature, although he remains keenly aware of the circumstances which divide him from those writers—the great moderns—who seem to have put it most whole-heartedly into practice. If this is the case it may be useful to consider *Lucky Jim*, for instance, as a literary artefact rather than as a sociological document, a vehicle of protest or the dossier of a new culture-hero.

Lucky Jim is a comic novel, and Amis is an admirer of Henry Fielding, the first great English comic novelist. It might be profitable therefore to look at Fielding's definition of the function of this form. It deals, he says, in the preface to *Joseph Andrews*, with the Ridiculous, and the only source of the true Ridiculous is affectation, which has two aspects: vanity and hypocrisy. Like most comic literature Fielding's comedy is based on contrast, on incongruity: between, for instance, people's actions and their motives. Fielding shows this contrast by commenting on particular situations from his omniscient elevation over the story. The omniscient method, however, is very difficult to employ today, when there are few agreed moral assumptions, and where many people (including Amis) cannot accept the idea of an omniscient God. Although Amis works with contrasts, the consciousness which registers them is not the novelist's, but Jim Dixon's. The mind which sees the incongruity of appearance and reality, of what the Welches and Margaret hypocritically or vainly think themselves to be—sensitive, cultured intellectuals—and what they really are—boring, selfish zombies—this mind is Jim's, and only at a second remove the novelist's. If this were the whole story—if Jim were merely a register of other people's false appearances, Jim might be merely a boorish prig, as many of his literary offspring are; but the saving grace of Amis's novel is that Jim himself is involved in the comedy, he is himself a hypocrite. Temperament and circumstances impel him to present a false appearance to the world: he pretends to be a keen young scholar and university teacher, when in fact he detests his subject and despises his colleagues; he pretends to be sympathetically attracted to Margaret when in fact he finds her plain and tedious. What makes us value Jim above the other shams in the novel is the fact that at least he admits he is a sham, chiefly to himself; and that his deceptions—as in the case of Margaret—can reflect a kind of moral decency as well as a kind of moral cowardice.

The main source of comedy in the novel is therefore the contrast between Jim's outer world and his inner world. While he tries—not very successfully—to show the outer world the image of an industrious, respectable well-mannered young man, his mind seethes with caustic sarcasm directed against himself and others, with fantasies of violence done to enemies, of triumph for himself. So that the characteristic appearance of a page of Amis is an exchange of pedestrian dialogue broken by long paragraphs of densely-woven comic and satirical commentary emanating from the hero's consciousness. The first chapter of *Lucky Jim* exhibits this pattern. Jim and his Head of Department, Professor Welch, are strolling through the university grounds, and Welch is describing an amateur concert:

> 'There was the most marvellous mix-up in the piece they did just before the interval. The young fellow playing the viola had the misfortune to turn over two pages at once, and the resulting confusion . . . my word. . . .'

Quickly deciding on his own word, Dixon said it to himself and then tried to flail his features into some kind of response to humour. Mentally, however, he was making a different face and promising himself he'd make it actually when next alone. He'd draw his lower lip in under his top teeth and by degrees retract his chin as far as possible, all this while dilating his eyes and nostrils. By these means he would, he was confident, cause a deep dangerous flush to suffuse his face.

Welch was talking yet again about his concert. How had he become Professor of History, even at a place like this? By published work? No. By extra good teaching? No in italics. Then how? As usual, Dixon shelved this question, telling himself that what mattered was that this man had decisive power over his future, at any rate until the next four or five weeks were up. Until then he must try to make Welch like him, and one way of doing that was, he supposed, to be present and conscious while Welch talked about concerts. But did Welch notice who else was there while he talked, and if he noticed did he remember, and if he remembered would it affect such thoughts as he had already? Then, abruptly, with no warning, the second of Dixon's two predicaments flapped up into consciousness. Shuddering in his efforts to repress a yawn of nervousness, he asked in his flat northern voice: 'How's Margaret these days?'

The other's clay-like features changed indefinably as his attention, like a squadron of slow old battleships, began wheeling to face this new phenomenon, and in a moment or two he was able to say: 'Margaret.'

'Yes; I've not seen her for a week or two.' Or three, Dixon added uneasily to himself. (I)

This passage lays down the basic contrast between Jim's inner and outer worlds, and shows Jim aware of the hypocrisy involved in preserving the discrepancy. It also involves him in uncertainty about other people's inner lives, which may well be as secret as his own, an uncertainty reflected in the anxious multiple questions which characterize Jim's thought: 'But did Welch notice who else was there while he talked', etc. Welch and Jim fail to connect, not only with each other, but with themselves. Jim has to 'flail' himself into an appropriate response, 'shudders' in the effort to suppress an inappropriate reflex. Welch's responses are characterized by images of inefficient locomotion—battleships in the quotation above, and shortly afterwards, when his mind has wandered from the subject of Margaret, a motor car: 'After no more than a minor swerve the misfiring vehicle of his conversation had been hauled back on to its usual course' (I). (Welch's execrable driving of his awful car is of course an important attribute of his character, and plays a vital part in the plot—his failure to get Christine to her train in time at the end of the novel unites her with Jim.) The rest of this paragraph gives a good illustration of Jim's fantasy-life of violence:

> Dixon gave up, stiffening his legs as they reached, at last, the steps of the main building. He pretended to himself that he'd pick up his professor round the waist, squeeze the furry grey-blue waistcoat against him to expel the breath, run heavily with him up the steps, along the corridor to the Staff Cloakroom, and plunge the too-small feet in their capless shoes into a lavatory basin, pulling the plug once, twice and again, stuffing the mouth with toilet-paper. (I)

Of interest in this passage is the use of the definite article rather than the possessive pronoun—'*the* furry grey-blue waistcoat', '*the* breath', '*the* too-small feet', '*the* mouth'. This might be interpreted merely as a means of avoiding grammatical confusion with the possessive pronoun, which refers to Jim, in '*his* professor'; but this could have been avoided equally well by substituting 'Welch' for 'his professor'. The phrasing of the passage has in fact a positively expressive function. 'His professor' draws attention to the power-relation existing between Welch and Jim, which the latter seeks to reverse in fantasy. The definite articles have the effect of de-personalizing Welch, so that the violence of Jim's fantasy is comically acceptable; while at the same time they call attention to and render ridiculous and objectionable the particular physical features of Welch's appearance.

One of the characteristic devices by which the inner and outer worlds are linked in the novel is, as the first extract illustrates, the way in which Jim picks up a phrase, usually a cliché—his own or another person's—and mentally subjects it to sceptical scrutiny: ' "... my word" ... Quickly deciding on his own word ...' ' "I've not seen her for a week or two." Or three, Dixon added uneasily to himself.' One of the most amusing variations on this device is Jim's response to Welch's question about the title of his learned article, where, in a manner that I have already suggested is characteristic of Amis, he turns a withering scorn simultaneously upon his own pretensions and upon the pretensions of scholarly language (and therefore upon the scholars who use it):

> It wasn't the double-exposure effect of the last half-minute's talk that had dumbfounded him, for such incidents formed the staple material of Welch colloquies; it was the prospect of reciting the title of the article he'd written. It was a perfect title, in that it crystallised the article's niggling mindlessness, its funereal parade of yawn-enforcing facts, the pseudo-light it threw upon non-problems. Dixon had read, or begun to read, dozens like it, but his own seemed worse than most in its air of being convinced of its own usefulness and significance. 'In considering this strangely neglected topic,' it began. This what neglected topic? This strangely what topic? This strangely neglected what? His thinking all this with-out having defiled and set fire to the typescript only made him appear to himself as more of a hypocrite and fool. 'Let's see,' he echoed Welch in a pretended effort of memory: 'oh yes; *The Economic Influence of the Developments in Shipbuilding Techniques,* 1450 *to* 1485. After all that's what it's . . .' (I)

This conversation takes place in Welch's car, and the continuation illustrates how Amis exploits stylistic incongruity for comic purposes in a very traditional way (it goes back to Fielding and mock-heroic). Here the precise ordering of events, and the cool, measured tone, contrast with the potentially disastrous nature of the situation:

> Unable to finish his sentence, he looked to his left again to find a man's face staring into his own from about nine inches away. The face, which filled with alarm as he gazed, belonged to the driver of a van which Welch had elected to pass on a sharp bend between two stone walls. A huge bus now swung into view from further round the bend. Welch slowed slightly, thus ensuring that they would still be next to the van when the bus reached them, and said with decision: 'Well, that ought to do it nicely, I should say.' (I)

Jim is well aware of the way his inner life compensates for the unsatisfactory nature of his outer life. 'The one indispensable answer to an environment bristling with people and things one thought were bad was to go on finding out new ways in which one could think they were bad' (XIII). His face-pulling, rude gesturing, and practical joking are only an extension of this strategy—an attempt on Jim's part to give some physical expression to his inner life of protest. After finishing his hated, hypocritical lecture on 'Merrie England', for instance:

> With a long, jabbering belch, Dixon got up from the chair where he'd been writing this and did his ape imitation all round the room. With one arm bent at the elbow so that the fingers brushed the armpit, the other crooked in the air so that the inside of the forearm lay across the top of his head, he wove with bent knees and hunched, rocking shoulders across to the bed, upon which he jumped up and down a few times, gibbering to himself. A knock at his door was followed so quickly by the entry of Bertrand that he only had time to stop gibbering and straighten his body. (XX)

For most of the action this kind of behaviour remains secret and furtive, and much comedy derives from Jim's attempts to keep it secret. But as long as he does so, he is involved in evasion, compromise, hypocrisy. The issues of the novel can only be resolved when Jim wills his inner life to coincide with his outer life. The crisis comes when he fights Bertrand and knocks him down:

> After some seconds, Bertrand began moving about on the floor, but made no attempt to get up. It was clear that Dixon had won this round and, it then seemed, the whole Bertrand match. He put his glasses on again, feeling good; Bertrand caught his eye with a look of embarrassed recognition. The bloody old towser-faced boot-faced totem-pole on a crap-reservation, Dixon thought. 'You bloody old towser-faced boot-faced totem-pole on a crap reservation,' he said. (XX)

At last thought and speech, the inner and the outer worlds coincide. From this point everything starts to go right for Jim. He loses his job, but gets a better one; he loses his girl (Margaret) but gets a nicer one. Jim ceases to be a guilty hypocrite and reaps his reward. We can accept this solution because the comic mode of the novel permits the kind of simplifications that make it possible: that people are as simply nasty as Bertrand, for instance, or that people like Bertrand will fall down when you hit them, or that their falling down will solve problems.

Amis's determination to discard such simplifications in subsequent novels has placed an increasing strain on his literary resources. The language of *That Uncertain Feeling* is unmistakably Amis's, but it has a new sobriety of purpose:

> Feeling a tremendous rakehell, and not liking myself much for it, and feeling rather a good chap for not liking myself much for

it, and not liking myself at all for feeling rather a good chap, I got indoors, vigorously rubbing lipstick off my mouth with my handkerchief. (VII)

Like Jim Dixon, John Lewis is trying to reconcile his inner life with his outer life, but in an opposite direction. Whereas Jim struggled to make his outer life realize his inner life of protest and romantic self-fulfilment, John Lewis seeks to discipline his outer life by the moral principles of his inner self. 'It wasn't so much doing what you wanted to do that was important, I ruminated, as wanting to do what you did' (VII). Amis doesn't seem to have reckoned with the new technical problems posed by such a radical shift of viewpoint; and those parts of *That Uncertain Feeling* which are most obviously continuous with *Lucky Jim*—such as Lewis's impersonations of a plumber and a Welsh peasant woman—though amusing in themselves, seem least integrated with the total movement of the book. The dilemma of the hero is worked out in terms (his adultery, his repentance, his renunciation of the 'fixed' library job, and his flight to the colliery town of his childhood, away from the wicked sophisticated set of Aberdarcy) which make the comic elements in the novel seem mere embellishments, as well as appearing too simply moralistic in themselves. By this latter remark I mean that the assertion of the value of poor but honest provincial domesticity cannot survive the habit of rigorous, sceptical scrutiny generated by Amis's use of language. He has armed us to reveal his own deviations into wishful thinking.

Amis is in fact involved in a kind of philosophic problem concerning ethics; and his language, which makes subtle discriminations in simple and superficially clumsy prose, often reminds one of modern philosophical discourse. Amis's epistemology, as it manifests itself in his novels, is profoundly anti-metaphysical, determinedly positivist, nearly solipsist. 'Nice things [are] nicer than nasty things'; and only the individual can decide what is nice and what is nasty for him. The axiom comes from *Lucky Jim* (XIV), but John Lewis endorses it in the cultural and social spheres—preferring *Reveille* to English Literature, for instance, and the new privileged classes to the old privileged classes ('at least this crowd had enough bad taste to drink brandy before "dinner" ')—though he rejects it in the moral sphere. But if nice things are nicer than nasty things, and there are no sanctions external to oneself, why not indulge in everything nice, 'do what one wants to do' and let 'wanting to do what one does' follow naturally?

This is the argument of Patrick Standish, the hero of *Take A Girl Like You.* If *Lucky Jim* sends one back to Fielding, the later novel reminds one of Richardson. It is essentially a modern *Clarissa.* Richardson's novel, it will be remembered, opposes the puritan values of the angelic heroine to the libertinism of the satanic rake, Lovelace, who abducts her and, after a long-drawn-out struggle, rapes her while she is drugged. Amis's Clarissa is Jenny Bunn, who leaves her decent, traditional Northern background to take a job in the decadent pink-gin-and-Jaguar world of Southern England. There, Patrick Standish, the Lovelace of the story, lays prolonged siege to her virginity, and eventually seduces her when she is disarmed by drink. Not only are the plot-lines similar, but both novels feature long debates between the protagonists on the subject of sexual morality, and both are remarkable for their final ambivalence—as if an openness to experience prevented both authors from coming down conclusively on the side they wanted to come down on: Clarissa and renunciation in Richardson's case, Patrick and hedonism in Amis's.

Patrick's strategy is to try and convince Jenny that her belief in pre-marital chastity is an outmoded concept from which the moral and social content has long been hollowed out.

> 'It's because you've had the kind of upbringing—very excellent in its way, I'm not saying anything against it—but it's the kind with the old idea of girls being virgins when they get married behind it. Well, that was perfectly sensible in the days when there wasn't any birth control and they thought they could tell when a girl wasn't a virgin. Nowadays they know they can't and so everything's changed. You're not running any risk at all. But you've had that kind of upbringing and that's why you feel like this. Do you see? It's just your training.'
>
> 'Maybe it is, but that doesn't make any odds to me. I just don't care why I think what I do, it doesn't change anything. What about why you think what you do? There must be reasons for that too.'
>
> 'The difference is that I haven't got my ideas from anyone else, I've thought them out for myself.'
>
> 'So have lots of other people who don't think the same as you.

Wherever you get your ideas from it doesn't make them any better.'

'At least mine work. Because they fit in with the way life's lived, which is more than yours do.'

'That remains to be seen. And fitting in's not the only thing.' (IV)

Jenny can hold her own in this kind of debate about the epistemology of ethics, but she feels the force of Patrick's arguments because she generally shares Patrick's empirical discriminations between the nice and the nasty in life, and because her own faith in marriage as a solution to the sexual problem is disturbed by such portents as the ugly confessions of the drunken sailor beneath her window, the married lives of her friends, and the repulsive appearance of the mothers whose children she teaches. Patrick's position too, however—and this is both the strength and the weakness of the novel—is undermined by experience. His dedication to the physical life is troubled by obsessional fears of impotence, old age, and death, filtered through the characteristic mockery of Amis's slangy but intricate rendering of consciousness, in which the language restlessly coils back upon itself to qualify what has just been asserted, so that the protagonist, instead of progressing confidently, is driven further into doubt:

> All that type of stuff, dying and so on, was a long way off, not such a long way off as it had once been, admitted, and no doubt the time when it wouldn't be such a long way off as all that wasn't such a long way off as all that, but still. Still what? Well in the meantime, this cardiac business of his was obviously psychogenic, or—what the hell was that other—genic one?—neurogenic, ... (XXIII)

This particular obsession of Patrick's reaches its climax in the macabre interview with Lord Edgerstoune, who draws an elaborate analogy between the sexual instinct and a battery which eventually runs out. Throughout *Take A Girl Like You* the comedy has a bitter, destructive quality, dissipating Patrick's commitment to the physical life. On the weekend debauch in London, the strip-clubs fail ludicrously to yield their expected gratifications, and the night spent with the demi-mondaine results in humiliation and guilt.

The issues of the novel, like the issues of *Clarissa*, hinge on the seduction of the heroine. In the handling of it one can see Amis twisting and turning in the impasse he has created for himself. The seduction itself, in all its furtive squalor, misery, and remorse, is brilliantly done—so brilliantly that it alienates Patrick from the reader. And yet his argument that it had to happen is in a sense true, because no alternative set of values is established in the novel which would make Jenny's preservation of her virginity meaningful. On the other hand the attempt at the very end to make the *loss* of her virginity meaningful is disastrous:

> She knew more or less what their future would be like, and how different it would be from what she had hoped, but she felt now that there had been something selfish in that hope, that a lot of the time she had been pursuing not what was right but what she wanted. And she could hardly pretend that what she had got was not worth having at all. She must learn to take the rough with the smooth, just like everybody else. (XXVII)

One misses, in the language of this passage, the reflexive, self-scrutinizing element which usually guarantees the sincerity of Amis's characters. If there was something 'selfish' in Jenny's former hopes, is there anything selfless in her present position? Is she any nearer to pursuing what is right? Is it, in fact, possible, in the world of the novel, to 'want' what is 'right'? It seems that it is impossible, in which case Jenny's attempts to cheer herself up seem sentimental and evasive. As if aware of these considerations, Amis closes the novel on a note of helpless regret:

> 'Well, those old Bible-class ideas have certainly taken a knock-ing, haven't they?'
> 'They were bound to, you know, darling, with a girl like you. It was inevitable.'
> 'Oh yes, I expect it was. But I can't help feeling it's rather a pity.' (XXVII)

It solves nothing of course, and when comedy raises issues which it cannot resolve, or cannot resolve without strain, it leaves a sour aftertaste, a lingering echo of discords. Such is the effect left on the reader by *Take A Girl Like You*.

Most great classical literature was attached to a metaphysical system of some kind; and the chief problem for writers from the Romantics to the present day has been to find some substitute for a defunct metaphysical orthodoxy. Their solutions are well known: Wordsworth's Nature, Shelley's Neo-platonism, Eliot's Tradition, Yeats's System, Lawrence's Dark gods. But in a sense all these solutions are working hypotheses which do not demand categorical assent from the reader. Transcending these hypotheses in almost every case is a belief in art itself as a substitute for metaphysics, a belief which reached its apex in the great moderns. Such a belief permits a para-metaphysical use of language—the recovery, through such devices as symbolism, irony, ambiguity, and paradox, of areas of experience ruled out by positivism; and such a belief has been associated with the adoption of a certain life-style—the cosmopolitan, the exile, or the Bohemian. Just how much Amis dislikes this kind of life-style and this kind of literary style is clear from his portrait of Gareth Probert, the Dylan Thomas-type playwright, and his verse play, in *That Uncertain Feeling*:

> . . . there were various linguistic clues, and I felt myself on safe ground in inferring that the whole business was rather on the symbolical side. Words like 'death' and 'life' and 'love' and 'man' cropped up in every few lines, but were never attached to anything concrete or specific. 'Death', for example, wasn't my death or your death, or his death or her death or our death or their death or my Aunt Fanny's death, but just death, and in the same way 'love' wasn't my, etc., love and wasn't love of one person for another or love of God or love of blackcurrant purée either, but just love. There were also bits from the Bible turned back to front ('In the word was the beginning' and so on), and bits of daring jargon ("No hawkers, circulars, or saints', 'Dai Christ'). Dear, dear, the thing was symbolical all right. (IX)

Certainly the modern mode can produce this kind of nonsense. But if Wittgenstein's dictum, 'The limits of my language are the limits of my world', is true, Amis has imposed very restrictive limits upon the world of his books by his rejection of the modern mode. These limits are scarcely felt within the simplified comedy of *Lucky Jim*, but they press hard on the attempt in later novels to incorporate more of the multiplicity of experience. His language, turned back at the metaphysical frontier, returns to sabotage the positivist, common-sense epistemology at the centre of his work, producing that sour, spoiling, comedy which creates such dissonances in *Take A Girl Like You*. The idea of death in that novel, for instance, inhibits the comic impulse towards freedom and happiness, but at the same time is itself deprived of meaning and dignity.

I have treated *Take A Girl Like You* and *That Uncertain Feeling* rather summarily, in order to discuss at some length Amis's third novel *I Like It Here*. On the whole it has been the least regarded, and certainly the most unfavourably criticized of Amis's works. Yet it seems to me that *I Like It Here* is a most interesting example of a special genre, which perhaps begins with *Tristram Shandy*, and which is particularly common in our era. I mean the kind of novel which is not so much turned outwards upon the world as inward upon literary art and upon the literary artist himself. I am thinking of such novels as Evelyn Waugh's *The Ordeal of Gilbert Pinfold* and Nabokov's *Pale Fire*. It is characteristic of such novels that the central figure is himself a writer, often with an auto-biographical reference, that there is a lot of parody, many literary jokes, and much discussion of literary questions, and that in this way the author is able to get a surprising distance on his own literary identity.

Garnet Bowen, the central character of *I Like It Here* is a professional writer, and a kind of projection of the most hostile public image of Amis himself, i.e. a man who earns an enviable amount of money from writing, without producing anything of real merit, and without having a very elevated conception of the writer's calling.

> Until a couple of years ago Bowen had been supposed to be a novelist who was keeping himself and his family going on the proceeds of journalism, wireless talks and a bit of lecturing. In the last six months or so he had started being supposed to be a dramatist who was keeping himself and his family going by the same means. He had never really supposed himself to be much more than a journalist, wireless talker and occasional lecturer. (I)

The attitudes of philistinism and vulgar ribaldry which showed signs of becoming unconscious mannerisms in *That Uncertain Feeling*, are here pushed to the extreme of conscious self-parody.

> 'Very much the same thing happened in Elgar's career,' Bowen blurted out before he could stop himself. He tried to cheapen it with 'So a fellow was telling me, anyway,' but only succeeded in making himself sound modest. A moral failure on this scale came

about through attending too closely to what people were saying. Those perishing vodka martinis at the International Musicians' Club that time must have weakened his protective shell without him noticing. He had thought that the film-producer chap who was buying them all had merely been boring him. And now here was this gross betrayal into non-ironical cultural discussion. (XIII)

Prevented by his wife from using the word 'bum', Bowen uses it mentally throughout the novel as a kind of collective noun for things he doesn't like:

> Currency bum, Bowen thought to himself when she had gone. Allowance for self, wife, three children and car bum. Arrangements for drafts on foreign banks bum. Steamer tickets bum. Return vouchers bum. Car documents bum. Redirection of correspondence *by landlord* bum. Permission from Secretary of Extra-Mural Studies to absent self from end-of-session Tutors' and Lecturers' Discussion and Planning Meeting bum. Passport bum. Passport photograph bum. Visa bum. (II)

On embarking for Portugal, he opens a telegram from his mother-in-law: 'ALL MY LOVE GOE SWITH YOU MY FARLINGS SEND ALL NEWS AND KEEP PHOTOGRAPHICAL BUM TO SHOW ON RETURN BON VOYAGE + MOTHER. There is a God, Bowen thought' (III).

All through the novel there is this kind of delight in strange locutions, odd pronounciations, verbal errors and unconscious puns. It is indeed a recurrent feature of Amis's work,* and the one which brings him closest to the techniques of 'modern' fiction. Foreigners 'speak funny', not only in the sense that they make mistakes, but that these mistakes have a kind of comic truth—as in the overseas students' pronunciations of English authors and titles: Grim Grin, Ifflen Voff, Zumzit Mum and Shem Shoice, not to mention *Sickies of Sickingdom* by Edge-Crown. 'Shem Shoice' is invoked very appropriately here.

The special interest of *I Like It Here* is that it is deeply con-

---

* Cf. the occasion in *That Uncertain Feeling* when John Lewis is accosted by two Lascars:

> One . . . seemed to ask me: 'Where is pain and bitter laugh?'
> This was just the question for me, but before I could strike my breast and cry 'In here, friend' the other little man had said: 'My cousin say, we are new in these town and we wish to know where is piano and bit of life, please?' (XI)

cerned with the contemporaries-versus-moderns issue. The discussion of it centres round the Wulfstan Strether mystery. 'Wulfstan Strether' is the pen-name of a writer of considerable reputation who has kept his true identity from the world, and from his publishers, who assumed that since his last book, in 1946, he had died or given up writing. Now a new book has come from a man in Portugal claiming to be Strether, and the publishers, with whom Bowen hopes to get a job, are not sure whether it is genuine or not. Bowen is asked to make investigations during his trip to Portugal. He is also given the proof of the new book, called *One Word More*.

Strether is, of course, the name of the hero in Henry James's international novel *The Ambassadors*,* and the passage from *One Word More* is a very creditable parody of bad James, or of an inferior novelist in the James tradition, say Charles Morgan:

> *It was with a sense of having by now earned the right to attempt penetration of the hard confident sheen that had, since the first morning of his stay, overlaid in her grey-green eyes the smoky tumult he had glimpsed there that spring evening (the strange light all velvet and honey)—it was with such a sense that, presented now with her vigilant yet dreamy profile (it wasn't much good wasting time at* this *stage on speculations about the significance of that comma-shaped mole on the nostril-wing) as they stood at the open-flung window—before which in the flinty afternoon sun a bourgainvillaea waved—Frescobaldi brought to utterance: 'Do you come here often?'*
> *'What a strange question,'—lightly.*
> *Well, he was not to be put off. 'You're waiting—'he teased. (IX)*

And so on. Amis-Bowen's objections to this kind of international, aesthetic fiction—they are essentially the same as his objections to Gareth Probert's play—come at the end of the parody, which concludes:

> *But she followed him, her hand lighting upon his arm. She had understood. She, somehow, had seen it too.*

---

* 'Wulfstan' is probably meant to suggest some element of mid-European foreignness—Strether has Conrad as well as James on his bookshelves. But it is not perhaps irrelevant to recall, as well, Bishop Wulfstan, author of the Anglo-Saxon *Sermo Lupi*, which might have been included in that 'course of lectures on some piece of orang-outan's toilet requisite from the dawn of England's literary heritage' which Bowen recalls from his days at the university. (VIII)

You go out of your way to tell us how, Bowen inwardly recommended, as once to Frank Sinatra in the long ago.* He wanted to put the man who had written that in the stocks and stand in front of him with a peck, or better a bushel, of ripe tomatoes and throw one at him for each time he failed to justify any phrase in the Frescobaldi–Yelisaveta scene on grounds of clarity, commonsense, emotional decency and general morality. (IX)

Literary criticism cannot solve the problem of the authenticity of *One Word More* for Bowen. Although he knows the appropriate techniques ('he could turn an honest dollar by getting in first with something he might provisionally entitle "Full Fathom Five: an examination of light and water imagery in the later work of Wulfstan Strether" '), he is so unsympathetic to the 'modern' mode that he cannot distinguish between bad Strether and forged Strether. When Bowen meets the man, who is provisionally called 'Buckmaster' until his identity is settled, he gets no nearer to a decision, though he begins to suspect that the man is an imposter. Buckmaster-Strether converses as if reciting *T.L.S.* leaders of thirty years ago.

> Could a man who had really written all those novels really be bounded by James and Conrad and Edith Wharton and Meredith, could he really not have noticed anything that had happened since? (XIII)

Bowen makes up his mind when Buckmaster-Strether takes him to visit Henry Fielding's grave:

> Bowen thought about Fielding. Perhaps it was worth dying in your forties if two hundred years later you were the only non-contemporary novelist who could be read with unaffected and whole-hearted interest, the only one who never had to be apologized for or excused on grounds of changing taste. And how enviable to live in the world of his novels, where duty was plain, evil arose out of malevolence and a starving wayfarer could be invited indoors without hesitation and without fear. Did that make for a simplified world? Perhaps, but that hardly mattered beside the

---

* This refers to an earlier scene in which Bowen abruptly turns off the radio: 'Sinatra sang. "When you did that to me I knew somehow th—" You tell us how, a part of Bowen's mind recommended.' (I) The Amis-hero is at least consistent in the exercise of his critical faculty. Cf. John Lewis shaking his head over the 'maladroit change of image' in the caption to a tabloid's cover-girl. *That Uncertain Feeling.* (VIII)

existence of a moral seriousness that could be made apparent without evangelical puffing and blowing. (XV)

Buckmaster pays an efficient tribute to Fielding, and then, as Bowen had feared, opens 'the floodgates of English Men of Letters eloquence':

'But we are surely not to say,' it came rolling out, 'that the utterances of comedy, whatever their purity or power, can move us as we are moved by the authentic voice of tragedy. That alone can speak to us of the loneliness and the dignity of man. And this, my friend, means that much as I reverence this master of the picaresque, I am unable to consider him my equal. In the field of the novel he is indeed the collossus of the eighteenth century, but I cannot feel that posterity will place him beside . . . will care to place him beside the collossus of the twentieth.'

A monosyllable of demented laughter broke from Bowen before he had time to arrange a coughing fit. Too good to be true, eh? And so much too good to be true that Buckmaster must inevitably be able to see it like that as well. Bowen stopped coughing and his eyes went glassy. That was it. Of course. . . . He knew now what Buckmaster was. The evidence might not have convinced others, but it did him. (XV)

Later, Bowen explains to his publisher why he decided Strether must be genuine:

'. . . given that sort of intelligence he wouldn't have dared to put himself on show as the kind of prancing, posturing phoney who'd say he was better than Fielding. Nothing to be gained by it. And too much danger of affronting my conception of how great writers behave. He'd have been perfectly safe in sticking to humility, reverence and what-have-you. But he didn't. So that meant he couldn't have been putting on an act.'

'I think I follow you. But don't you in fact expect great writers to be prancing phoneys or whatever you said?'

'Of course I do, as far as people of the great-writer period are concerned, that is . . . roughly between *Roderick Hudson* and about 1930, death of Lawrence and the next bunch all just starting off— Greene, Waugh, Isherwood, Powell. Or perhaps 1939. But you couldn't expect Buckmaster to know I saw it like that. He'd grown up in that period himself, poor old devil. It couldn't possibly strike him in that way.' (XVI)

These passages neatly draw together the threads of the literary debate that runs through the novel. Amis–Bowen's ideal literature is not the tragic, but the comic, not the cosmopolitan post-romantic artistic self-consciousness of the modern 'great-writer period', but the sane, morally serious, healthy engagement with life of a Henry Fielding. This might seem a provincial and self-satisfied view if it were not ironically qualified in a number of ways. Fielding's is a 'simplified world' and Bowen's is far from simple. And though he is bound to regard moderns, such as Strether, as phonies, he recognizes their integrity within their own system of values, and recognizes too that he is himself a phoney. There are many passages in the novel in which Bowen subjects his own writing to scathing sarcasm. And there is an extremely interesting scene in which he ruefully acknowledges the attraction of the modern mode, and its inacessibility for himself.

A Portuguese boatman tells him a story about a Finnish ship which is moored in the bay. Apparently its crew, some years before, mutinied and killed the captain. They were subsequently captured and tried. The captain's father came out from Finland to take possession of the ship, but because of its design—unsuited to sardine fishing—he could not sell it. Nor could he raise the money to return to Finland. Thus he is condemned to a life of exile, living alone on the ship and working in the fish market.

> A powerful, useless thrill ran through Bowen. Here was a marvellous story for someone, but not, unfortunately, for him. Only a rather worse or much older writer than himself could tackle it satisfactorily. (XII)

Bowen feels the artist's instinctive relish in the possibilities of this 'germ', as James would have called it. But it is not for him. An older writer could have done it; but anyone who tries to do it now would be a worse writer than himself, because, it is implied, he would be working in an obsolete tradition, the 'modern' tradition. 'W. Somerset Maugham (on grounds of age, not the lack of merit) was the kind of chap.' This is a complicated private joke: it was the Somerset Maugham Award which enabled Amis to travel to Portugal and therefore to write *I Like It Here*.

The irony of this situation must have appealed to Amis: that he, a young 'contemporary', a reputed Angry Young Man, should have been given an award endowed by a writer of the modern 'great-writer period', one moreover who had publicly called the Angry Young Men 'scum'[7]; and that a condition of the award should be that it must be spent on the activity most characteristic of the modern great writers, and least congenial to the young contemporaries: travel. *I Like It Here* is a gently comic explanation of why travel will not serve the literary purposes it is supposed to serve, of broadening the mind and opening new areas of experience. At the end of the book Bowen tears up his abortive play and resolves to write something 'about a man who was forced by circumstances to do the very thing he most disliked the thought of doing and found out afterwards that he was exactly the same man as he was before'. That book is of course *I Like It Here*.

To return to the earlier passage, after the reference to Maugham, Bowen considers a Maugham-like or perhaps Conrad-like opening to the Finnish ship story.

> 'I have a notion that men are seldom what they seem.' Or 'Lars Ericssen'—something like that, anyway—'was the skipper of a small Finnish cargo vessel. He was a big bronzed man who never looked you directly in the eye. One hot summer off Tangier. . . .' Hmm. A rather worse or much older writer. Well, just say a writer, instead of a man who was supposed to be a writer. That would get it. (XII)

I Like It Here is not so much about the importance of being Amis as about the difficulty of being Amis—the difficulty of being committed to aesthetic, philosophical, and moral principles which seem more reliable but drabber than the principles on which most great 'modern' art was based. There must be few practising writers in England today who do not feel the pressure of this situation. Amis's acute awareness of the situation, his sardonic sense of the literary tradition and of the limitations of his own stance towards it, and above all his success in finding a language which articulates very exactly the temper of his generation, make him, I think, a writer of genuine literary 'importance'.

References

PART ONE

I

Introductory

[1] Mark Schorer, 'Technique as Discovery', *Critiques and Essays on Modern Fiction 1920–1951*, ed. J. W. Aldridge (New York, 1952), pp. 67–8. This article first appeared in *The Hudson Review*, I (1948).

[2] Philip Rahv, 'Fiction and the Criticism of Fiction', *Kenyon Review*, XVIII (1953), p. 277.

[3] *Ibid.*, p. 279.

[4] J. C. Ransom, 'The Understanding of Fiction', *Kenyon Review*, XII (1950), p. 197.

[5] Rahv, *op. cit.*, p. 280.

[6] *Ibid.*, p. 297.

[7] Cf. the present writer's 'The Critical Moment 1964', *Critical Quarterly*, VI (1964), pp. 266–74, for a discussion of this trend.

Modern Criticism and Literary Language

[1] M. H. Abrams, *The Mirror and the Lamp* (Oxford, 1953); Frank Kermode, *Romantic Image* (1957).

[2] I. A. Richards, *Principles of Literary Criticism* (2nd edition, 1926), p. 267.

[3] Northrop Frye, *Anatomy of Criticism* (Princeton, 1957), pp. 73–4.

[4] 'But as far as these four critics [Blackmur, Empson, Brooks, Ransom] are concerned, their development of a rigorous method has consisted mainly in the presenting of a single term and a more or less systematic expansion of its explanatory uses.' William Righter, *Logic and Criticism* (1963), p. 115.

[5] Richards, *op. cit.*, p. 273.

Poetry and Prose

[1] W. H. Auden, *The Dyer's Hand, and other essays* (1963), p. 23.

[2] Wordsworth, Preface to *Lyrical Ballads* (1805). *The Lyrical Ballads 1798–1805*, ed. George Sampson (1959 edition), p. 18.

References

[3] Wordsworth, *op. cit.*, pp. 30-1.

[4] Shelley, 'A Defence of Poetry', *Peacock's Four Ages of Poetry, Shelley's Defence of Poetry, Browning's Essay on Shelley*, ed. H. F. Brett-Smith (The Percy Reprints No. 3) (Oxford, 1921), p. 30.

[5] Coleridge, *Biographia Literaria*. Coleridge, *Select Poetry and Prose*, ed. Stephen Potter (1950), p. 251.

[6] *Ibid.*, p. 252.

[7] *Table Talk*, *op. cit.*, pp. 512-13.

[8] Paul Valéry, 'Remarks on Poetry', *The Art of Poetry*, Trans. Denise Folliott (1958), p. 206.

[9] *Ibid.*, p. 210.

[10] Laurence Lerner, *The Truest Poetry* (1960), pp. 220-1.

[11] *Ibid.*, p. 129.

[12] Allen Tate, 'Miss Emily and the Bibliographer', *On the Limits of Poetry* (New York, 1948), p. 53.

F. W. Bateson: Ideas and Logic

[1] *English Poetry and the English Language* (Oxford, 1934), p. 24.

[2] *Ibid.*, p. 16.

[3] *Ibid.*, pp. 19-20.

[4] *Ibid.*, p. 20 (*Persuasion*, Chapter IV).

[5] *Ibid.*, p. 20.

[6] See especially 'Verbal Style: Logical and Counterlogical', *The Verbal Icon: studies in the meaning of poetry* by W. K. Wimsatt with Monroe C. Beardsley (Noonday edition, New York, 1962), pp. 201-17.

[7] Bateson, *op. cit.*, p. 16.

[8] I. A. Richards, *Interpretation in Teaching* (New York, 1938), p. 136.

Christopher Caudwell: The Current of Mock Reality

[1] Caudwell, *Illusion and Reality: a Study of the Sources of Poetry* (1937), p. 272.

[2] *Ibid.*, pp. 225-6.

[3] *Ibid.*, p. 135.

[4] Wimsatt and Beardsley, *The Verbal Icon*, pp. 37-8.

[5] Lerner, *The Truest Poetry*, p. 129.

[6] R. A. Sayce, 'Literature and Language', *Essays in Criticism*, VII (1957), p. 120.

[7] Caudwell, *op. cit.*, p. 174.

The Argument from Translation

[1] Shelley, *op. cit.*, p. 29.

[2] Arnold Kettle, *An Introduction to the English Novel*, Vol. I (Grey Arrow Paperback edition, 1962), p. 39.

[3] Robert Liddell, *A Treatise on the Novel* (1947), p. 24.

[4] Q. D. Leavis, *Fiction and the Reading Public* (1932), pp. 212-13.

[5] *Ibid.*, p. 213.

References

Proust and Scott Moncrieff Compared

[1] Marcel Proust, *Du Côté de Chez Swann*, 42nd impression (Paris, 1919), p. 18.

[2] Marcel Proust, *Swann's Way*, translated by C. K. Scott Moncrieff (Penguin edition, 1957), p. 20.

Translation: Poetry and Prose

[1] J. B. Carroll, *The Study of Language* (Cambridge, Mass., 1953), p. 10. Quoted by Randolph Quirk, 'English Language and the Structural Approach', *The Teaching of English: Studies in Communication, 3*, ed. Randolph Quirk and A. H. Smith (1953), p. 22.

[2] Quirk, *op. cit.*, pp. 34–9.

[3] Shelley, *op. cit.*, pp. 28–9.

[4] Auden, *op. cit.*, pp. 23–4.

The Argument from Bad Writing

[1] Marvin Mudrick, 'Character and Event in Fiction', *Yale Review*, L (1960), pp. 205–6.

[2] Ian Watt, *The Rise of the Novel* (Penguin edition, 1963), p. 31.

[3] Jocelyn Baines, *Joseph Conrad: a Critical Biography* (1960), p. 166.

The Modern Movement in Fiction: a Digression

[1] Miriam Allott, *Novelists on the Novel* (1959), p. 314.

[2] *Ibid.*, p. 313.

[3] 'Turgenev and Tolstoy', *The House of Fiction*, Essays on the novel by Henry James, edited by Leon Edel (Mercury Books edition, 1962), p. 171.

[4] Joseph Conrad, Preface to *The Nigger of the 'Narcissus'* (1914 edition).

J. M. Cameron: These Words in This Order

[1] Cameron, 'Poetry and Dialectic', *The Night Battle* (1962), p. 122.

[2] Coleridge, *Biographia Literaria*, Chapter I.

[3] Coleridge, *Select Poetry and Prose*, edited Stephen Potter, p. 217.

[4] Cameron, *op. cit.*, p. 125.

[5] *Ibid.*, p. 129.

[6] *Ibid.*, p. 134.

[7] *Ibid.*, p. 133.

[8] *Ibid.*, pp. 136–7.

[9] *Ibid.*, p. 145.

[10] *Ibid.*, pp. 145–6.

[11] Cameron, 'The Justification of Political Attitudes', *op. cit.*, pp. 82–3.

References

Language and Fictional Illusion

[1] Cameron, *op. cit.*, p. 133.

[2] Roy Pascal, 'Tense and Novel', *Modern Language Review*, LVII (1962), pp. 1–11.

[3] *Ibid.*, pp. 2–3.

[4] *Ibid.*, p. 11.

[5] *Ibid.*, p. 7.

[6] Cameron, *op. cit.*, p. 139.

[7] See Watt, *op. cit.*, pp. 88–96, for a discussion of *Robinson Crusoe* as myth.

[8] A. D. McKillop, *Samuel Richardson: Printer and Novelist* (Chapel Hill, 1936), p. 124.

[9] Watt, *op. cit.*, p. 26.

[10] James Joyce, Letter to Mrs. William Murray, 2 Nov. 1921. *Letters of James Joyce*, ed. Stuart Gilbert (1957), p. 175.

F. W. Bateson and B. Shakevitch: Particularity

[1] Bateson and Shakevitch, 'Katherine Mansfield's *The Fly: A Critical Exercise*', *Essays in Criticism*, XII (Jan. 1962), pp. 39–53.

[2] *Essays in Criticism*, XII (July, 1962), pp. 335–51; (Oct. 1962), pp. 448–52.

[3] Bateson and Shakevitch, *op. cit.*, p. 46.

[4] *Ibid.*, p. 49.

[5] *Op. cit.*, XII (July, 1962), pp. 341–3.

[6] *Ibid.*, p. 347.

[7] *Ibid.*, p. 349.

[8] Watt, *op. cit.*, pp. 19–20.

[9] *Op. cit.*, XII (Oct. 1962), p. 449.

Conclusions to Section I

[1] I. A. Richards, *Interpretation in Teaching*, p. 7.

[2] *Style in Language*, ed. Thomas A. Seboek (New York, 1960), p. 416.

II

Concepts of Style

[1] Miriam Allott, *op. cit.*, p. 308.

[2] J. Middleton Murry, *The Problem of Style* (1922), p. 8.

[3] Abrams, *The Mirror and the Lamp* (Norton edition, New York, 1958), pp. 230–1.

[4] Murry, *op. cit.*, p. 8.

[5] Northrop Frye, *Anatomy of Criticism*, p. 268.

References

Stylistics

[1] The title essay in *Linguistics and Literary History: Essays in Stylistics* (Princeton, 1948).

[2] Spitzer, *op. cit.*, p. 11.

[3] Winifred Nowottny, *The Language Poets Use* (1962), pp. 9–10.

[4] Cf. Stephen Ullmann, *Style in the French Novel* (Cambridge, 1957), p. 27.

[5] Spitzer, *op. cit.*, p. 11.

[6] *Ibid.*, pp. 11–12.

[7] *Ibid.*, pp. 13–14.

[8] *Ibid.*, p. 27.

[9] *Ibid.*, p. 11.

[10] *Style in Language*, ed. Seboek, p. 418.

[11] Ullmann, *Style in the French Novel*, p. 9.

[12] *Ibid.*, p. 260.

[13] *Ibid.*, p. 23.

M. Riffaterre: Scientific Stylistics

[1] *Op. cit.*, p. 154.

[2] *Ibid.*, p. 155.

[3] *Ibid.*, p. 158.

[4] *Ibid.*, p. 160.

[5] *Ibid.*, p. 162.

[6] *Ibid.*, p. 172.

J. Warburg: Appropriate Choice

[1] *Op. cit.*, p. 52.

[2] *Ibid.*, p. 47.

[3] *Ibid.*, p. 50.

[4] T. S. Eliot, *The Waste Land*, lines 74–5.

[5] Warburg, *op. cit.*, p. 65.

[6] Quoted by W. H. Auden, *The Dyer's Hand*, p. 13.

[7] Wimsatt, *The Verbal Icon*, p. 217.

[8] Nowottny, *The Language Poets Use*, p. 143.

[9] Richard M. Ohmann, 'Prologomena to the Analysis of Prose Style', *Style in Prose Fiction*, English Institute Essays, 1958, ed. Harold C. Martin (New York, 1959), p. 9.

F. R. Leavis and the Moral Dimension of Fiction

[1] *Scrutiny*, IX (1941), pp. 306–22.

[2] F. R. Leavis, *Revaluation* (1936), pp. 42–61.

[3] F. R. Leavis, *The Great Tradition* (Penguin edition, 1962), p. 10.

[4] *Ibid.*, p. 16.

[5] *Ibid.*, p. 17.

[6] *Ibid.*, pp. 16–17.

[7] Q. D. Leavis, *Fiction and the Reading Public*, p. 212.

[8] *Ibid.*, pp. 212–14.

[9] *Ibid.*, p. 233.

[10] F. R. Leavis, *The Great Tradition*, p. 17.

[11] Wayne Booth, *The Rhetoric of Fiction* (Chicago, 1961), p. 137.

III

Conclusions: Principles

[1] Wimsatt, *The Verbal Icon*, p. 249.

[2] *Ibid.*, p. 248.

[3] *Ibid.*, p. 249.

[4] *Ibid.*, p. 5.

[5] Walter J. Ong S.J., *The Barbarian Within, and Other Fugitive Essays and Studies* (New York, 1962).

[6] Ong, *op. cit.*, p. 28.

[7] *Ibid.*, p. 20.

[8] *Ibid.*, p. 62.

[9] *Ibid.*, p. 37.

[10] C. H. Rickword, 'A Note on Fiction', *Forms of Modern Fiction*, ed. William Van O'Connor (Midland Book edition, Bloomington, 1959), p. 282. Reprinted from Rickword's *Towards Standards of Criticism* (1933).

[11] *Critics and Criticism*, ed. R. S. Crane (Chicago, 1952), pp. 616–47.

[12] Crane *op. cit.*, pp. 620–1.

[13] *Ibid.*, p. 622.

[14] R. S. Crane, *The Language of Criticism and the Structure of Poetry* (Toronto, 1953), p. 70. (Crane paraphrasing Aristotle.)

[15] Crane, 'The Concept of Plot and the Plot of *Tom Jones*', *op. cit.*, p. 631.

[16] Marvin Mudrick, 'Character and Event in Fiction', *Yale Review*, L (1960), p. 209.

[17] Henry James, 'The Art of Fiction', *The Future of the Novel*, ed. Leon Edel, (Vintage Books edition, New York, 1956), p. 21.

Conclusions: Methods

[1] Percy Lubbock, *The Craft of Fiction* (Travellers Library edition, 1926), pp. 1–3.

[2] *Style in Language*, ed. Seboek (1960), p. 419.

[3] Kenneth Burke, *The Philosophy of Literary Form* (Vintage Books edition, New York, 1957), pp. 56–66.

[4] *Ibid.*, p. 75.

References

Repetition

[1] Joseph Conrad, *Under Western Eyes* (1911), I, iii.

[2] Mrs Gaskell, *The Life of Charlotte Brontë* (Everyman edition, 1960), pp. 214–15. Also quoted by Jeremy Warburg, *op. cit.*, p. 56.

[3] Charlotte Brontë, Letter to G. H. Lewes, 18 Jan. 1848, Mrs Gaskell, *op. cit.*, pp. 239–40.

[4] See Raymond Williams, *Reading and Criticism* (1950), pp. 75–86, for a useful analysis of *Heart of Darkness* along these lines.

[5] David Daiches, *Virginia Woolf* (1945), pp. 64–5 and 72. The illustration, like the two following, is from *Mrs Dalloway*.

[6] Daiches, *op. cit.*, p. 71.

[7] *Ibid.*, p. 72.

[8] Righter, *Logic and Criticism*, p. 22.

PART TWO

The Vocabulary of 'Mansfield Park'

[1] Lionel Trilling, 'Jane Austen and *Mansfield Park*', *The Pelican Guide to English Literature, 5: From Blake to Byron* (1957), pp. 113–14.

[2] *Ibid.*, p. 116.

[3] G. B. Stern, Introduction to Collins edition of *Mansfield Park* (1953) pp. 19–20. (The source of Maugham's remark is not stated.)

[4] Kingsley Amis, *Lucky Jim* (1954), Chapter XIV.

[5] William Austen-Leigh and Richard Arthur Austen-Leigh, *Jane Austen: Her Life and Letters; a Family Record*, (1913), p. 306.

[6] W. Somerset Maugham, *Ten Novels and their Authors* (1954), p. 63.

[7] Trilling, *op. cit.*, p. 121.

[8] Trilling, *The Liberal Imagination: Essays on Literature and Society* (Mercury Books edition, 1961), pp. 206–7.

[9] G. B. Stern, *op. cit.*, p. 13.

[10] Walter Allen, *The English Novel* (Penguin edition, 1958), p. 114.

[11] Trilling, 'Jane Austen and *Mansfield Park*', *op. cit.*, p. 128.

Fire and Eyre

[1] Richard Chase, 'The Brontës, or Myth Domesticated', *Forms of Modern Fiction*, ed. William Van O'Connor (Midland Book edition, Bloomington, 1959), pp. 102–19.

[2] *Ibid.*, p. 110.

[3] *Ibid.*, pp. 111–12.

[4] See Walter J. Ong's essay, 'The Myth of Myth', *The Barbarian Within* (New York, 1962), pp. 131–45, for some cautionary words on the concept of 'myth' in literary criticism.

References

[5] Chase, *op. cit.*, p. 119.

[6] David Cecil, *Early Victorian Novelists* (Penguin edition, 1948), p. 105.

[7] Walter Allen, *The English Novel* (Penguin edition, 1958), p. 190.

[8] E. M. W. Tillyard, *The Elizabethan World Picture* (1943).

[9] *Ibid.*, p. 57.

[10] Mrs Gaskell, *Life of Charlotte Brontë* (Everyman edition, 1960), p. 384.

[11] Emily Brontë, *Wuthering Heights* (Penguin edition, 1946), Chapter XXXII.

[12] 'But what had befallen the night? The moon was not yet set, and we were all in shadow: I could scarcely see my master's face, near as I was. And what ailed the chestnut tree? it writhed and groaned; while wind roared in the laurel walk, and came sweeping over us.' (XXIII)
Compare Coleridge's use of interrogatives to create an atmosphere of mystery and the supernatural:

> 'Is the night chilly and dark?
> The night is chilly, but not dark.'
>
> 'The night is chill, the forest bare;
> Is it the wind that moaneth bleak?'
>
> 'And what can ail the mastiff bitch?'

The action of the first part of *Christabel*, of course, takes place in moonlight.

[13] See Cecil, *op. cit.*, p. 114, and Allen, *op. cit.*, p. 189. One thinks particularly of the characterization of Gerald Crich in *Women in Love*. 'St Mawr' is notable for its insistent fire-imagery, used to convey the marvellous yet frightening power and energy of the horse.

[14] Robert B. Heilman, 'Charlotte Brontë, Reason and the Moon', *Nineteenth Century Fiction*, XIV (1960), pp. 283–302.

[15] *Ibid.*, pp. 288–9.

[16] *Ibid.*, p. 292.

[17] Kathleen Tillotson, *Novels of the Eighteen Forties* (Oxford paperback edition, 1961), p. 269 ff.

[18] Quoted by Tillotson, *op. cit.*, pp. 272–3.

The Rhetoric of 'Hard Times'

[1] Humphrey House, *The Dickens World* (Oxford Paperback edition, 1960), p. 203.

[2] F. R. Leavis, *The Great Tradition* (Penguin edition, 1962), p. 249.

[3] John Holloway, 'Hard Times, a History and a Criticism', *Dickens and the Twentieth Century*, ed. John Gross and Gabriel Pearson (1962), pp. 159–74. Since I wrote this chapter David Hirsch has published another dissenting opinion, 'Hard Times and F. R. Leavis', *Criticism*, IV (Winter, 1964), pp. 1–16 —an effective but rather negative contribution to the debate.

[4] See House, *op. cit.*, pp. 103–11, and Raymond Williams, *Culture and Society 1780–1950* (Penguin edition, 1961), pp. 104–8.

[5] Holloway, *op. cit.*, p. 174.

[6] E.g.: 'He [Mr Gradgrind] then returned with promptitude to the national cinder-heap, and resumed his sifting for the odds and ends he wanted, and his throwing of the dust into the eyes of other people who wanted other odds and ends—in fact, resumed his parliamentary duties.' (II, xi).

[7] 'From one point of view Buckle's book can be seen as an attempt to erect the doctrine of *laissez-faire* into a philosophy of history, and to defend civilized society as a state of benevolent and genial anarchy.' House, *op. cit.*, pp. 173–4, commenting on H. T. Buckle's *History of Civilization* (1857–61), quoted with approval by Dickens in 1869.

[8] See House, *op. cit.*, p. 166.

[9] See note 13, below.

[10] Mary McCarthy, 'Characters in Fiction', *The Partisan Review Anthology*, (1962), pp. 260–1.

[11] Chapter ii of Book I is called 'Murdering the Innocents'.

[12] Randolph Quirk, 'Some Observations on the Language of Dickens', *Review of English Literature,* II (1961), pp. 20–1.

[13] House (*op. cit.*, pp. 206–8) says that Dickens deliberately went to Preston to observe the cotton strike there early in 1854, in order to gather material for *Hard Times*, and notes that his report in *Household Words* ('On Strike', 11 Feb. 1854) shows a somewhat surprised respect for the orderly and efficient conduct of the strikers. K. J. Fielding, in his *Charles Dickens: a critical introduction* (1958) argues (pp. 134–5) that 'the conditions described in *Hard Times* are much closer to the engineering strike of 1852 than to the dispute at Preston' and quotes a contemporary letter of Dickens:

> As to the Engineers . . . I believe the difficulty in the way of compromise, from the very beginning, is not so much with the masters as with the men. Honorable, generous and free-spirited themselves, they have fallen into an unlucky way of trusting their affairs to contentious men, who work them up into a state of conglomeration and irritation, and are the greatest pests that their own employers can encounter upon earth.

This is certainly the attitude Dickens adopts in *Hard Times*. But on a more fundamental level he also distrusted the trade unions as a threat to the liberty of the individual. He weakens his own case, however, by making Stephen refuse to join the union because of a mysterious and apparently meaningless promise he has made to Rachel (II. vi.). See Raymond Williams (*op. cit.*, pp. 99–119) for a discussion of the distrust of organized labour by Victorian novelists who sympathised with the oppressed working classes.

[14] Holloway, *op. cit.*, p. 171.

[15] Dorothy Van Ghent, 'The Dickens World: a View from Todgers's', *The Dickens Critics*, ed. George H. Ford and Lauriat Lane Jr. (Ithaca, 1961), p. 214.

[16] Chapters I, xi; I, xii; II, i; III, v.

[17] *Peacock's Four Ages of Poetry, Shelley's Defence of Poetry, Browning's Essay on Shelley*, ed. H. F. B. Brett-Smith (Oxford, 1921), p. 52.

[18] Dickens's commitment to 'Fancy' is not restricted to *Hard Times*, as P. A. W. Collins shows in his very thorough study of Dickens's use of the

References

word: 'Queen Mab's Chariot among the Steam Engines: Dickens and Fancy', *English Studies*, XLII (1961), pp. 78–90.

[19] Coleridge, *Biographia Literaria*, chap. XIII.

Tess, Nature, and the Voices of Hardy

[1] Vernon Lee, *The Handling of Words and other studies in literary psychology* (1923), pp. 222–41. Vernon Lee's method does not of course anticipate I. A. Richard's procedure in *Practical Criticism* (1929) exactly. His is primarily pedagogic in purpose; hers, critical. He deals with complete short poems, the context from which they are extracted being historical knowledge of the poem's origins; she deals with extracts from novels which are identified, though they are not discussed as wholes. The similarity resides mainly in their mutal reliance on the close analysis of limited pieces by reference to certain constant assumptions about good literary language.

[2] Lee, *op. cit.*, p. 224.

[3] *Ibid.*, p. 233.

[4] *Ibid.*, pp. 227–8.

[5] *Ibid.*, p. 234.

[6] *Ibid.*, pp. 240–1.

[7] Douglas Brown, *Thomas Hardy* (1961), p. 103.

[8] Ian Gregor and Brian Nicholas, *The Moral and the Story* (1962), pp. 143–4.

[9] *Ibid.*, p. 137.

[10] *Ibid.*, p. 144.

[11] John Holloway, *The Victorian Sage; studies in argument* (1953), p. 245.

[12] *Ibid.*, p. 263.

[13] The omitted words are 'had been left uncultivated for some years, and ... emitting offensive smells ... thus she drew quite near to Clare, still unobserved of him'.

[14] *Ibid.*, pp. 262–3.

[15] Robert Liddell, *A Treatise on the Novel* (1947), p. 118.

[16] Dorothy Van Ghent, *The English Novel: Form and Function* (Harper Torchbooks edition, New York, 1961), p. 201.

[17] Holloway, *op. cit.*, p. 263.

Strether by the River

[1] Crow, *op. cit.*, p. 189.

[2] Watt, *op. cit.*, p. 262.

[3] Leavis, *The Great Tradition* (Penguin edition, 1962), p. 178.

[4] Christof Wegelin, 'The Lesson of Social Beauty', an extract from the author's *The Image of Europe in Henry James* (1958), reprinted in Norton edition of *The Ambassadors*, pp. 442–58.

[5] Wegelin, *op. cit.*, p. 457.

[6] Watt, *op. cit.*, p. 262.

[7] Cf. Watt, *op. cit.*, pp. 263–8, on the tempering of 'irony' by 'humour' in the presentation of Strether.

[8] James, Preface to *The Ambassadors*, Norton edition, p. 9.

[9] Krook, *op. cit.*, reprinted in *Interpretations of American Literature* (New York, 1959), ed. Charles Feidelson and Paul Brodtkorb, p. 263.

[10] Short, 'The Sentence Structure of Henry James', *loc. cit.*, p. 72.

[11] Watt, *op. cit.*, p. 255.

[12] Watt, *op. cit.*, pp. 255–6.

[13] Watt, *op. cit.*, p. 257.

[14] Alexander Holder-Barell, *op. cit.*, pp. 118–19, and John Paterson, *op. cit.*, abridged and reprinted in the Norton Edition of *The Ambassadors*, pp. 462–63. Cf. also Robert L. Gale, *op. cit.*, pp. 5, 33, 34.

[15] As Paterson (*op. cit.*) shows, this is only one of many similar allusions to heroic or adventurous action in the figurative language of the novel.

[16] Holder-Barell, *op. cit.*, p. 119.

[17] Short, 'Henry James's World of Images', *loc. cit.*, p. 951.

'Tono-Bungay' and the Condition of England

[1] *Henry James and H. G. Wells: A Record of their Friendship, their Debate on the Art of Fiction, and their Quarrel*, edited with an introduction by Leon Edel and Gordon N. Ray (1958).

[2] Mark Schorer, 'Technique as Discovery', *Critiques and Essays on Modern Fiction 1920–1951*, ed. John W. Aldridge (New York, 1952), p. 72.

[3] James and Wells, *op. cit.*, p. 267.

[4] Preface to *The Ambassadors*, *The Art of the Novel*, ed. R. P. Blackmur (New York, 1935), p. 321.

[5] Schorer, *op. cit.*, p. 71 ff.

[6] Norman Nicholson, *H. G. Wells* (1950), p. 98.

[7] Vincent Brome, *H. G. Wells: a Biography* (1951), p. 108.

[8] Arnold Kettle, *An Introduction to the English Novel*, Vol. II (Grey Arrow paperback edition, 1962), p. 94.

[9] *Ibid.*, p. 95.

[10] Wells, *Experiment in Autobiography* (1934), p. 493.

[11] Disraeli, *Coningsby*, Book II, Chapter 1.

[12] *Past and Present* (Everyman edition, 1912), p. 1.

[13] C. F. G. Masterman, *The Condition of England*, ed. J. T. Boulton (1960), p. xiv.

[14] *Ibid.*, p. 181.

[15] Wells, *op. cit.*, p. 494.

[16] Robert Conquest, 'Science Fiction and Literature', *Critical Quarterly*, V (1963), p. 358.

[17] *Ibid.*, p. 356.

[18] Kettle, *op. cit.*, p. 98.

[19] Masterman, *op. cit.*, p. 35.

[20] *Ibid.*, p. 18.

[21] Northrop Frye, *Anatomy of Criticism: Four essays* (Princeton, 1957), p. 155.

[22] *Ibid.*, p. 42.

²³ *Ibid.*, p. 34.
²⁴ *Ibid.*, p. 34.
²⁵ *Ibid.*, p. 49.
²⁶ Bernard Bergonzi, *The Early H. G. Wells, A Study of the Scientific Romances* (Manchester, 1961), pp. 52–3.
²⁷ 'The Waste Land' ll. 371–6.
²⁸ Schorer, *op. cit.*, p. 73.

The Modern, the Contemporary, and the Importance of being Amis

¹ Frederick R. Karl, *A Reader's Guide to the Contemporary English Novel* (1963), p. 4.
² Stephen Spender, *The Struggle of the Modern* (1963), pp. 104–5.
³ Pamela Hansford Johnson, 'Literature', *The Baldwin Age* ed. John Raymond (1960), p. 182. Quoted by Spender, *op. cit.*, pp. 81–2.
⁴ Virginia Woolf, 'Modern Fiction', *The Common Reader* (Penguin edition, 1938), p. 149.
⁵ James Joyce, *A Portrait of the Artist as a Young Man* (Travellers' Library edition, 1942), p. 195.
⁶ John Braine, *Room at the Top* (Penguin edition, 1959), p. 28.
⁷ Karl, *op. cit.*, p. 231.

Index of Authors

This index includes authors referred to by name or title in the text and notes. References within quotations are excluded. Bold type indicates substantial discussion.